*The Reinvention of Mexico in
Contemporary Spanish Travel Writing*

The Reinvention of Mexico in Contemporary Spanish Travel Writing

JANE HANLEY

Vanderbilt University Press
Nashville, Tennessee

Copyright 2021 Vanderbilt University Press
All rights reserved
First printing 2021

Library of Congress Cataloging-in-Publication Data

Names: Hanley, Jane, 1981– author.
Title: The reinvention of Mexico in contemporary Spanish travel writing / Jane Hanley.
Description: Nashville : Vanderbilt University Press, [2021] | Includes bibliographical references and index.
Identifiers: LCCN 2021016945 (print) | LCCN 2021016946 (ebook) | ISBN 9780826502117 (Paperback) | ISBN 9780826502124 (Hardcover) | ISBN 9780826502131 (ePub) | ISBN 9780826502148 (PDF)
Subjects: LCSH: Spanish prose literature—21st century—History and criticism. | Travelers' writings, Spanish—Mexico—History and criticism. | Travel in literature. | Mexico—In literature. | LCGFT: Literary criticism.
Classification: LCC PQ6134.T73 H36 2021 (print) | LCC PQ6134.T73 (ebook) | DDC 860.9/3272—dc23
LC record available at https://lccn.loc.gov/2021016945
LC ebook record available at https://lccn.loc.gov/2021016946

CONTENTS

Acknowledgments   ix

INTRODUCTION   1
1. The Idea of Mexico: Historical and Touristic Narratives   23
2. Memory, Text, and Expectation   73
3. Violence, Instability, and Danger   113
4. Describing Selves in Worlds   153
   CONCLUSION: On Writing a Twenty-First-Century
   Hispanic Transatlantic   187

Notes   199
References   217
Index   229

ACKNOWLEDGMENTS

My thanks to all at Vanderbilt University Press who have helped bring this manuscript to press and reach its audience—Zack, Jenna, Cindy, Brittany, and Joell—and the excellent editorial acumen that has made this book much more readable.

The initial stages of this research were undertaken with funding through the Macquarie University Innovative Universities European Union Centre, and subsequent research trips were supported by Macquarie University grants and periods of research leave. I have relied on Macquarie's specialist librarians, as well as resources and materials available through the Biblioteca Nacional de España, the British Library, and material accessed during visits to Spain (Universidad Autónoma de Madrid, and many hours spent in the Madrid's Librería Iberoamericana and Librería Desnivel) and Mexico with funding support from Macquarie University, and in-kind support from ITESM and Universidad Marista de Mérida.

Chapter 2 is derived in part from a chapter published in *Conflict, Memory Transfers and the Reshaping of Europe*, and excerpts are published with the permission of Cambridge Scholars Publishing.

Chapter 3 is derived in part from an article published in *Journal of Borderlands Studies* 34, no. 1 (March 27, 2017), ©Association for Borderlands Studies, doi.org/10.1080/08865655.2017.1300779.

I have also received invaluable feedback and support from colleagues at Macquarie University and at other institutions. I especially extend my thanks to Estela Valverde, my most enduring mentor, without whom I would never have embarked on a research career. I am also grateful for feedback received on versions of this project over the years from Thea Pitman, Gabriela Coronado, Sarah Leggott, Martina Möllering, Ulrike Garde, Katie Poidomani, participants in the Sydney University Research Community for Latin America, and members of the Association of Iberian and Latin American Studies of Australasia. Components of this research have been presented at diverse conferences, and I am grateful for all the questions, recommendations, and comments received. I thank the anonymous reviewers of elements of this work for their intellectual labors at different times throughout the project, and for paying me the compliment of taking my work seriously enough to help me improve it. I thank most particularly those readers who gave their time to assess this manuscript in its entirety and proffered suggestions with generosity of spirit and intellectual acuity. I owe them a great debt, though all remaining failings are entirely my own.

Finally, thanks to Christian and Darcy, always.

INTRODUCTION

When we write our experiences, the words take on a life of their own, separate from the actions they describe; just as travel supposes an interaction with places and an intervention in physical space, the writing of travel interacts and intervenes in the space of ideas about place. This book explores the discursive space of contemporary transatlantic mobility and the idea of Mexico in Spain. How is transatlantic travel changing, and what are the possibilities for Spanish-Mexican encounters today? How do contemporary Spanish travel writers narrate their travels to Mexico? How do the stories they tell speak to other stories—histories of violence and present inequalities, and the changing sense of belonging to and being in places?[1] Ideas about places in general, and this place in particular, incorporate imagined histories, as well as signs of how power shapes the popular imaginary.[2] Some of the travel writers I discuss actively engage with the politics of past and present inequality and the power of words, whereas others take a descriptive approach. I trace the implications of their thematic interests and stylistic choices for narrative's ability to represent the encounter with the other and the author's own sense of identity. It is not possible to escape entirely the pitfalls of representing the other, and storytelling is always a form of shorthand. Making sense of experience is reductive, but the process nevertheless offers chances to bring to the surface and thus reinterpret stories that have settled into our subconscious, making us critique and reflect on them anew.

The works discussed are travel narratives by Spaniards about Mexico published around the turn of the millennium. This period is of interest because it coincided with the consolidation of an affluent traveling middle class in democratic Spain. It was also marked by changes in the relations between Spain and Latin America, as well as changes in historical discourses and ways of reading history in Spain that emerged as the country grappled with its passage from an ideologically scarred and traumatic twentieth century into an uncertain twenty-first. The nature of nation tangles with the experience of identity and culture as lived—and written—by contemporary Spaniards. The evolving image of Mexico in Spain and Spain's unstable relationship with historical narrative reveal the more general instabilities in our sense of place wrought by late capitalist globality (and its colonial antecedents). Focusing on Mexico in particular, rather than engaging with the full range of Spanish travel writing about Latin America, facilitates greater depth of analysis regarding the local specificity of travel destinations and the production of travel narrative as an exchange between traveler and host and place of origin and place of destination, as well as a more targeted unweaving of the illusory coherence of the notion of the national as a container for cultural identity. In addition, Mexico has several qualities that allow for valuable insight into the contemporary dynamics of mobility and their relationship to power: first, its location on the borders of the United States and cultural construction as a defining other during periods of defense of parlous Anglo-American hegemony; second, its vast population, at home and abroad, embodying and reforming unstable definitions of speaking and living in the Spanish language (and on the language's edges) in ways that destabilize Spain's historical self-representation in relation to language and culture; and third, its specific historical relationship to Spain itself and Spanish historical mythmaking, in the relatively recent past through the reception of post–Civil War Republican exiles and more remotely as partial geographical successor of New Spain, the Viceroyalty with its origins near the dawn of Spain's American imperial project and its peak period associated with the construction of Spain's strongest historical myths—as well as its subsequent decline.

That particular period birthed a world-spanning economic system with the consequences for power and exploitation of people and resources that implies: "The Americas were not incorporated into an already existing capitalist world-economy. There could not have been a capitalist world-economy without the Americas" (Quijano and Wallerstein 1992, 549). Thus, the Caribbean and Mesoamerica are symbolically significant sites for interrogating the contemporary cultural inheritances of that system. Finally, Mexico is one significant object (among others) of contemporary Spanish economic and soft power endeavors, including in tourism development, which demonstrate aspects of twenty-first century global power and the economic inheritances of global capitalism.

What is travel writing as an object of inquiry? The definition of the genre has been a source of much debate.[3] The kinds of books I tackle here draw on diverse literary traditions, and an over prescriptive definition would impose arbitrary limits and artificially homogenize a genre that is of most interest precisely for its diversity. Its heterogeneity makes it unruly, since the texts as described may have nothing in common save travel as an "essential condition of production," as Rubiés (2000, 6) notes. For the sake of this book having an end, however, I must limit the works discussed beyond the simple fact of travel. Tzvetan Todorov (1991, 104) locates the genre along the spectrum between texts emphasizing the subject, and hence the autobiographical character of the narrative, and those focusing on the object observed, and hence assuming the authority of impersonal description. Many texts, of course, are neither wholly one thing nor the other, ambiguity that is important in analyzing their discursive functions. To limit and organize the texts under analysis, I group works thematically along this spectrum, excluding those that exhibit only one extreme or the other; that is, works that may be interpreted as pure memoir and those written in a wholly impersonal register.

Conceptions of travel writing in Spanish emerged through a distinct literary tradition, with precursors in medieval pilgrimage and epistolary traditions that in the modern era developed further through the *crónica*. Travel writing's direct implication in colonial power also emerged earlier than in other western European literatures, from the sixteenth century rather than principally in the nineteenth and twentieth centuries as is more relevant to anglophone and francophone literature. Critical work on travel writing in the Spanish-speaking world tends to be a dialogue between the tradition of travel writing *about* Spain, which is a substantial area of study that has been nourished further by the emergence of travel writing as a major field of research internationally; the tradition of travel writing *by* Spaniards, which links to the tradition of travel writing *about* Latin America; and the emerging research area of travel writing *by* Latin American travelers. To compare, British travel writing emerges as a para-literary form, whereas German travel narrative nonfiction links to an intellectual literature focusing more on philosophy and scientific observation than on anything resembling ethnography. Many of the methods of inquiry and indeed the basic questions applied to the study of travel writing in other traditions may nevertheless offer valuable models for Spanish-language works, as long as the specific characteristics of such narratives and the styles upon which they draw are also taken into account.

Beyond the potential interest of a comparison of genre features in different traditions and as a source for tourism history, what can we learn from travel writing? As a form of testimonial nonfiction, travel narratives perform historical consciousness and embodied ethics of encounter, making these accessible to outside reading. It is quite common for narratives of encounter with place to engage with traces of historical events, the discernible presence of the past, such as imperial sites and architecture, or, to take one example particularly relevant to the Spain-Mexico transatlantic, stories of post–Civil War migration. How different writers deal with these traces speaks to their different possible accommodations with cultural identity and concepts of place, including both the idea of Spain and the idea of Mexico.

The engagement with histories of place and how such histories inform our sense of place is one of my primary interests in investigating contemporary Spanish writing about Mexico. The historical imagination as it is inscribed in travel writing and encounters with peoples and places suggests connections between, for example, past acts of violence and of resistance, and discursive interventions in ideas of self and other. This requires an explanation of the ways travel writers are also engaging in dialogue with written and other traditions of representation of place. As Julio Peñate Rivero (2004, 17) reminds us, "travelers travel with their eyes on the books they have read, anticipating the confirmation of these through their experiences, or even adapting their experiences to their previous reading."[4] And it is not only books that create expectations and fantasies of place, but all the memories, hopes, and referential processes that enter our imaginations to create an architecture of expectation before we physically present ourselves somewhere.

Travel writing has been a decidedly self-referential genre. Travel writers have always engaged in exchanges with previous travel narratives as a fundamental element of their relationship to place. Travel stories also reflect changes in the ways people understand mobility, and the evolving concept of the journey and the nature of transatlantic interconnection can partly be traced through travel writing. Paul Virilio (2005) proposes an understanding of all present-day journeys as repetitions of past voyages, a condition that serves to compound the recursiveness of travel writing. New texts engage with traditions, whether through active comment or determined silence—or even through ignorance—since writers contribute to an ongoing conversation about their subject whether they intend to or not. This idea of repetition and the exhaustion of newness leads directly to ideas I explore in this volume, such as the interplay between knowledge and experience in contemporary travel writing. The genre of travel writing functions as one historical record of experiences of acceleration and information surfeit, while simultaneously offering a window into what Brian Musgrove (1999, 33) describes as "the formations of western subjectivities out of the encounter with imagined others."

In investigating the meaning of mobility, I am contributing to transnational cultural studies to interpret texts in relation to global and local change. The travel narratives I discuss, therefore, are not expressions of Spanish culture as a categorizable, unified entity, but rather sites for understanding the ethics of encounter within the evolving Spanish-Mexican cross-cultural dynamic. Their analysis offers perspectives on the current social functions of definitions of home, self, difference, distance, and mobility. My research therefore incorporates elements of historiography, textual analysis, and an ethnographic approach to texts as socially determined objects. I used both comparative and contextualized readings to locate connections and divisions between diverse narratives of place.

Travel narratives are historically dynamic texts through which it is possible to explore the significance of the representation of Latin American otherness in the definition and experience of Spain (and Europe) as home. Individual texts reveal aspects of the constitution of a sense of place, through literary precursors and intertexts, through encounter, and ultimately through narration. Nor can the sense of place be disconnected from the complex influence of economic factors on the representation of place. Such influences are ever more important as the global travel industry continues to grow, constituting a substantial percentage of world trade.[5] Places are increasingly scrutinized and remodeled as commodities.[6] Leisure travel has come to be a defining experience of middle class life in wealthy countries, with voluntary versus involuntary mobility one parameter that highlights systematic privilege and dispossession. Narrative modes of representation of place and intercultural encounter have become significant sources of knowledge of other cultures for the consumers of difference who drive the tourism industry. Although the publication of travel accounts into books remains an exceptional rather than common travel experience, this form of extended storytelling nevertheless offers deep insights into the practices and paradoxes of travel today.

Clearly, texts from one cultural tradition, in a single language, and about specific places cannot provide unqualified universal insights. We must consider the context of production and reception of the travel accounts. This contextualized analysis creates a more meaningful process for understanding the kinds of insights such texts *can* offer. These are, above all, insights into how the author's sense of their origin and destination clarify the terms of the travel encounter and how the resulting narrative represents divergent relationships to that origin and destination through the representation of the other. Spain has been a limit point for Europe ever since the idea of Europe began to emerge. It has been located both at the edge of empire and been a source of European imperial expansion itself. While the process of identifying the familiar in opposition to the foreign or other is universal, in contemporary European encounters with postcolonial others we can see also the power of language to delimit. Travel writing is immersed in the struggle over representation. The genre has a deeply problematic historical relationship with Eurocentrism and the idea of the exotic. This relationship is complicated in Spain by its own history and present as object of the exoticizing gaze of the travel writer.

The relationship between European identity and the construction of otherness has been extensively analyzed over recent decades, probably most influentially in Edward Said's *Orientalism* (1978). Critiques like Mignolo's (2000) pick up on the absence in this account of a European self-conception of sixteenth-century westward expansionism and the narratives of territoriality and difference that it supposed. The European arrival in America is popularly imagined as a paradigm shift for Europeans. Repercussions in the imagined space between Spain and Mexico and how that space continues to evolve today are less easily defined. Mignolo (2000, 94) argues that the legacy of empire continues to shape European-American relationships, including a westward projection of European civilization that still informs travelers' mobilizations of cultural continuity and *hispanidad*. Adding this longer trajectory, the idea of discourses of cultural difference in the formation of European subjectivity intertwining with real economic and political power remains fundamental to understanding European cultural production, though the specific uses of the other in Europe evolve over time to serve different political ends.[7] European travelers portray difference through both echoes and critiques of these diverse regimes of othering.

While the ends change, imperialist discourse tends to persist in post-imperial travel writing, as both Mary Louise Pratt (1992) and David Spurr (1993) describe.[8] Pratt's influential formulation incorporates a sense of the mutual determination of representation and otherness, which do not have their origins only in Europe: "While the imperial metropolis tends to understand itself as determining the periphery (in the emanating glow of the civilizing mission or the cash flow of development), it habitually blinds itself to the ways the periphery determines the metropolis—beginning, perhaps, with the latter's obsessive need to present and re-present its peripheries and its others continually to itself" (Pratt 1992, 6). Pratt's work is widely cited in research on Latin America, however despite the above multidirectionality, the main relevance of *Imperial Eyes* is fundamentally to the study of European thought and the evolution of Eurocentric discourses, rather than to the study of Latin America per se, something of which Pratt herself is aware. However, even with the revised edition's incorporation of Latin American fictional writing, *Imperial Eyes* does not center Latin American perspectives about Latin America on the same terms as European perspectives (Lindsay 2009, 9). Leonard Guelke and Jeanne Kay Guelke (2004) have also critiqued what they describe as Pratt's insufficient focus on the physicality and context of the encounters to which she refers, including further historical detail about the activities of Latin Americans. This analytical tendency in Pratt's extraordinary work can be balanced by geographical perspectives, like that brought to bear by Patricia Price (2004) on the desert or Daniel Arreola (1996) on consumption and the urban. Combining these perspectives allows us to understand different aspects of the conflicts underlying encounters in contemporary travel narrative, and European identity discourse's internal contradictions as well as enduring consequences in the world, in both material and imagined geographies. When considering the material aspects of mobility, we discover also how travel and writing have changed, with our transformed experience of distance, the commodification of leisure, and the mediation of technology in communicating these narratives. How has the globalization of information and marketing of culture combined with the sense that the world is now known or available?[9] The impact on narrative strategy, descriptive novelty, and truth-effects have manifold consequences for the ways we imagine place through travel.

The cultural consequences of European and Latin American encounters have also been explored in relation to both European and American identity narratives. Todorov's contentious *The Conquest of America* (1984) posits that the result of the Spanish Conquest was determined through signs, identifying improvisatory, individualistic elements of European culture and the European notion of linear time as key determinants of victory over Aztec rigidity, ritual, and prophetic circular time. While Todorov's assessment of the Aztec Empire does not give full weight to the major gaps in and radical difference of Aztec histories of the events, and the interventions of other Mesoamerican actors, it is an important intervention in the interpretation of this encounter, which has most often been analyzed through the material rather than symbolic advantages held by the Spaniards. Counterbalancing a Eurocentric interpretive framework, Latin American theorists and philosophers have explored the constitutive effects of the Conquest and colonization for Americans themselves. Octavio Paz, to give just one influential example, underscores the material consequences of these transnational encounters for Latin Americans, and for Mexicans specifically. Irma Cantú (2006) reimagines travel writing from a Mexican center through Paz's claims to a Mexican universalism and subversion of the othering tactics of existing discourses of travel. Paz has been critiqued (for example by Roger Bartra [1992]) for a certain essentialism and hyper-conflation of Mexicanness and historical trauma. Others (for example García Canclini [1995]) defend the elements of Paz's thought that offer insights into the global enmeshment of cultures while also suggesting resistances to and ruptures of the effects of globalization. Mignolo (2000, 102), drawing on Jorge Klor de Alva, notes the problems of talking about "colonialism" to describe Spanish America, given the divergence between the *mestizo* societies there and the imposition of a government class over a large population of different race dominant in British and French empire. Mignolo nevertheless argues that given overall European expansionism and global effects of Eurocentric power it is more dangerous to decouple the American process from the later colonialisms than not. This argument brings us back to the value of travel writing as a source for understanding changing constructions of culture in relation to place and mobility.

To understand such cultural changes, it is important to consider the material impact of travel on destination cultures. There are many case studies on tourism development and impact in Latin America and specifically Mexico, particularly addressing sustainability and local communities.[10] Although these forms of social, economic, and ethnographic research are different in both objective and approach to my own, they provide a useful reminder that the places and peoples that figure narratively as destinations and encountered others are the everyday environments and subjects of their own stories. This is a vital component in avoiding the perpetuation of place as an object of consumption entirely knowable in description by privileged outsiders. Discourses of development, including those linked to ecotourism, ethnotourism, and voluntourism replicate and often reinforce and naturalize global structural inequalities with roots in European empires (Hanley 2019). If we link this submerged dynamic of inequality to travel writing, contemporary works often incorporate individualized reflections on commodification, the search for authenticity, for experience, and for a closer relationship to the natural world, as well as speculations on what might constitute a viable future, for both the individual traveler and the society from which they hail. Among the even more problematic results of privileging novelty through subjective experience is badlands travel and off-the-beaten-track narrative—difference of experience as the source of authority.

Discursive contagion—the inheritance of colonialist hierarchies in our structures of thought—pervades critical language also. Similarly, concepts of the importance of mobility to trans-disciplinary areas of study themselves draw on the language and imagery of travel literature, and thus encounter difficulties in deconstructing it from an imagined outside position. As Tim Youngs (2004) reminds us, language migrates and contaminates, and it can too easily be removed from its referents and reestablished as empty metaphor. Metaphor, moreover, can actively obscure the presence of the things—trauma, inequality, displacement, and so forth—to which the language employed originally referred. The processes of representation and abstraction in academic writing, with its potential to gloss over or set at a distance embodied experiences of suffering and joy, echo the abstraction and self-absorption of the traveling subject and the concomitant tendency to treat that which is seen as belonging to the subject by virtue of witnessing, and to then reinforce that possession through narrative. Language is contagious, and to adequately understand the ethics of cross-cultural encounter and its representation in travel writing, it is first (and continually) necessary to interrogate the ethics of one's own writing practices. Even the over-determination of the boundaries of genre for the purposes of limiting the so-called object of study (a problematic conceptual foundation of research in and of itself) suggests the heritage of hierarchical classifications of knowledge. Pertti Alasuutari (2006, 238) exhorts reflection on the limits of interpretation: "We can only analyze how certain appealing discourses and related subject positions are constructed, and what consequences it all has to relations of power and politics. And, if not simultaneously, the next day we must be ready to scrutinize our own starting points in that analysis: what were the premises on which the argument was built and what was therefore left unnoticed?" Researcher reflexivity, however, is an incomplete solution for accounting for the scholar's own role in the reproduction of discourses. In the context of travel writing studies in particular, Claire Lindsay (2009, 113) echoes Judith Butler's critique of first-person narrative from *Precarious Life* (2004), which Lindsay elaborates in the context of travel writing as providing a framework for exploring decentered narrative perspectives on displacement and violence in travel writing that better articulate "our positions as global actors." The decentered narrative perspective is closer to what Mignolo, following Abdelkebir Khatibi, describes as "an other thinking." Lindsay was discussing the problem of defining travel writing through the traveler, reinforcing the possession or control by the narrating subject, but the same problem applies if academic style devolves to the subjectivity of the writer to the exclusion of other factors. It is therefore my hope that this book reads as the interested, loving, sometimes bemused observations of an attentive audience member to the performance of Spanish-Mexican encounters and the cultural and economic conditions that influence their shape.

Much has been written on changing travel practices and experiences of place in the context of broader social change. Many of these studies approach contemporary travel from the perspective of an anthropology of place and travel.[11] Overall, the research methods advocated as a result incorporate a critical practice that deals with time, place, and social institutions *together*, and underline the necessity of situating cultural meaning with, beside, and against other forms of knowledge rather than as a singular narrative that risks reenacting that which it purports to critique. I locate texts as elements of and contributions to broader discourses. This situates features of texts, producers, and consumers within larger-scale social mechanisms, and historicizes and contextualizes single instances of representation as elements toward reinforcement or revision of various socially constituted ideas of place and difference. I attempt to generate a multilayered analysis of travel narratives that explores their operations at the intersection of geographical, historical, phenomenological, textual, and political forces.

My analysis draws on a concept of culture manifested through actions rather than as something abstracted from human behavior. This supposes looking at the text not as literary object but as part of a larger social production that depends on discourses of power and strategies of resistance (Gray 2003, 14). In discussions of contemporary travel writing, I apply techniques of narrative analysis that, rather than focusing on the internal logic and aesthetic characteristics of the texts, highlight points of concordance and dissonance with broader tropes surrounding the places mentioned and modes of mobility deployed. Paula Saukko (2003, 6) notes the inseparability of cultural production from systemic effects of power. The validity of conclusions depends on explicit linkages between the topic investigated and its social and historical context. Drawing together text, culture, and history means analytical categories multiply. On this basis, for example, genre and genre-slippage and interrogating the usefulness of concepts of Spanishness and Mexicanness become important. I have thus endeavored to indicate the interconnectedness of discourses of place but to avoid overly generalized interpretation—to mark also textual difference and authorial resistance to existing narratives of place. The value of considering individual narratives is evident. Each contemporary travel encounter and each recounting of it intervenes in a continuous process of defining and redefining places. Textual analysis, therefore, can tease out some of the possible answers to the essential questions for thinking about such narratives:

> At the level of textual analysis, one can ask what are the dominant modes of representation in western travel writing? What is the range of these frames and what are the discursive categories that they draw on? Who benefits from such frames and who does not? Do certain kinds of tourism present different modes of representation or is a cultural homology evident in their representation? What are the changes that take place in travel representations with changing geo-political interests of western nation-states? (Fürsich and Kavoori 2001, 161)

The interdisciplinarity supposed by bringing together questions of communication, historical imagination, and sociopolitical and cultural change means it is not sufficient to look only at the texts themselves. They must emerge as objects embedded in broader processes of meaning production and circulation.

From this position, general analyses of the changing meaning of travel and tourism are useful for framing questions about the effects of globalization and current understandings of transit and mobility. However, to approach the textual narration of Mexico by Spaniards specifically it is necessary to investigate Spain and Mexico's unique relationship in the history of mobility. Existing work on Spanish travel writers focuses mostly on European, North African, and Western Asian destinations. Henry Kamen (2003, 504–5) goes so far as to suggest that Spain failed to develop a travel literature of the scope seen in other imperial centers at all, which he attributes to a kind of fundamental incuriosity about cultural difference and blindness to the potential benefits of cultural exchange, a claim that itself produces a totalizing vision of culture (as well as sidelining diverse writings framed by experiences of mobility). The lack of a continuous scholarly tradition looking at Spaniards as travel writers certainly does *not* mean there were none. Paul Bowker's 2009 investigation into the transnational imaginary between Spain and Latin America in the early twentieth century is an example of the kind of work being undertaken to link twentieth century Spanish travel writers to longer traditions within Spanish literature, and extensive research has been carried out on nineteenth century writers, including the late nineteenth century and the tumultuous transition into the twentieth and the myriad ways Spanish writers traveling at the time reflected both on home and away (e.g., Nunley [2007]; Jenkins Wood [2014]; Raducanu [2015]; and an emergent thread of scholarship on the representation of Asia in Spanish travel writing, such as in the work of Prado Fonts [2018]).[12] Often, however, works looking at travelers from Spain focus on narratives that may be more usefully situated within imperial history, the construction of Spanish nationhood in the late imperial era, and subsequently in the post-Independence era within a literature of migration and exile.

In Spain's relationship to Latin America there are histories that shape the possibilities for understanding travel narratives in meaningful context, including histories of exile as well as debates around problematic narratives of pan-Hispanic solidarity. Discourses of *hispanidad* are linked to Spanish soft power and the articulation of Spanish identity during late imperialism. Christopher Schmidt-Nowara (2004, 192) argues that "a retrenched colonialism, in its interface with nationalism" allowed for the maintenance of economic and cultural power for key actors in Spain, and that colonialism itself "was a major vector for imagining the nation and its history." The hierarchies internal to pan-Hispanism reinscribe an intrinsic marginalization to the metropolitan center that persists from explicit empire into informal imperialist forms. "As economic and military hegemony were impracticable, the cultural solution implicit in *hispanismo*—the cultural empire—was chosen as the way to acquire the necessary level of international prestige" (Schmidt-Nowara 2008,

33–34). The propagation of an idea of cultural continuity between Spain and Spanish-speaking America evolves out of a consolidation of submerged geographical-racial inequalities in direct relation to emergent narratives of universal rights in the nineteenth century. People were categorized fluidly according to political and economic need, to limit their rights. In order to preserve political and economic power "inhabitants of the metropolis . . . and inhabitants of the colonies and faraway possessions would carefully be distinguished from one another" (Fradera 2018, 3). Universalist rhetoric, as in contemporary pro-democratic/pro-capitalist narratives, papers over exploitative structures. Embedded in the rhetoric of pan-Hispanism we find that the memory of empire may be a stronger presence than current postcolonial ties. Tony Morgan (2000, 59) suggests that "the absence of any post-imperial organization similar to the British Commonwealth betrayed the frailty of relations between Spain and her former colonies," citing this as a factor in contemporary Spain's European orientation.

In some cases, these concerns overpower any possible analysis of travel writing as a cultural practice, or through the concept of culture at all, as has been so popular in anglophone scholarship.[13] When Lindsay analyzes Latin American writers themselves narrating Latin America, she highlights the quandaries of travel and representation in the late twentieth century: the reformulations wrought by the end of formal colonialism, shifting centers and peripheries, and the expanding tourism economy, each of which have particular features in Mexico. A purely textual approach is inadequate for meaningful consideration of travel writing in Latin America—or anywhere. However, it is also tricky to think about texts in the context of sociopolitical regions and national borders, creating divisions based on author origin that can artificially reinforce dichotomies of culture and difference. It isn't productive to imagine Spanish writers as somehow antithetical to Mexican writers; a nuanced interpretation must take on the disruptive politics of encounter and the passages between the production of myths of cultural unity and the uncertainties of lived transcultural spaces. I take texts from the Spanish direction of transatlantic travel and explore the patterns that trajectory tends to create in structures of historical thinking and conceptions of place, rather than attempting to study Spanish productions of experiences in Mexican space as a way to encapsulate contemporary Mexico, or indeed even contemporary Spain. The extent to which national categorizations are still useful is in their ongoing power in discourses of place and their contribution to the texture of travel writing as part of social processes of naming and defining.

The select contemporary Spanish travel narratives discussed in this book are individual cultural products that witness, narrate, and recreate encounters—encounters between individuals, between origin cultures and destination cultures, between traveler and place, and between travelers and their own expectations and sense of self. Though travel stories are one site for rethinking our understanding of the complex processes of encounter, they are not unmediated sources of knowledge either about places or even about contingent encounters. The moment is already always narrativized, first in memory, then oral retellings, then formalized accounts where the story becomes part of the ongoing discourse surrounding both teller and place. Furthermore, contemporary travel and encounter occur within the framework of heavily mediated knowledge of places, and therefore travel accounts draw on and intervene in existing ideas of place and difference. The texts with which I am concerned represent visions of otherness and of self within the Spanish-Mexican dynamic and the effects of mobility on the historical imagination. One critique of both Anglo-US narrative and central Mexican narratives about the border is that they emerge from centers of control over that region without being *of* the region. How much more remote the view of Mexico from Spain? It is not, therefore, my claim that travel writing gives us a privileged view of Mexican reality; rather, it gives us a useful view of how Mexico is viewed, and how Europe (and particularly Spain) as a point of origin mediates that view. Spain, in relation to Mexico, provokes additional reflection about continuities between formal and informal colonialism, past and present migration, and modernity and capitalism. It also highlights cultural geographies of voluntary and involuntary mobility through two border zones between extreme wealth and extreme poverty. Europe itself is experiencing new convulsions over mobility and borders, and intertwining Spanish Mediterranean examples can—and in the case of some key moments of travel narration analyzed here, do—provide a comparative counterpoint to the idea of Mexico as it circulates in the world today.

The first chapter serves to introduce and frame Spanish-Mexican encounters in the context of the idea of America generally and Mexico specifically in Europe, and in the context of the representation of history, culture, and the sense of place within travel narrative. The construction of place image is explored through contemporary Spain as a point of origin, incorporating a discussion of quite profound reconceptualizations of history and destabilization of historical narratives. These have had substantial impacts on ideas of Spanishness as well as the European outward gaze, especially since post-Franco debates about historical justice in Spain connect closely to reformulations of trauma, memory, and restitution in Latin American postdictatorship; political conflict; and contested democracy. Chapter 1 also discusses tourism discourse and the development of Mexico as a destination, the function of country branding and destination image in the context of global media and tourism, and tourism discourse and destination branding's local effects, in order to articulate the connection between the construction of Spain as origin and the discourses of difference—and similarity—that appear in the narration of travel to Mexico. Chapters 2, 3, and 4 go into depth about concrete conditions that today transform the genre of travel writing and the responses to those conditions within the work of selected Spanish writers, with their diverse methods of engagement with the ethics of encounter. The analysis is organized thematically, taking into consideration in Chapter 2 the role of the historical imagination in a postcolonial transatlantic and postdictatorship Spain, as well as the roles of intertextuality, memory, and authorial subject positions. Chapter 3 addresses globalized communications and new politics of mobility. Shifting conceptions of cultural belonging under globalization and both Europeanization and pan-Hispanic movements, for example, create an altered context for Spanish-Mexican encounter. So too the shift in communications media and distribution of content, which has the potential to change the way stories are told and to whom. Chapter 4 analyses the effects of strong first-person narration in tension with an ethnographic gaze, representation of indigenous peoples in contemporary travel writing in relation to historical thinking, the reimagining of contemporary Spain in relation to histories of violence and alterity in Mesoamerica, and encounters with place as nature and place as touristic spectacle.

Chapter 1 frames Spanish travel writing about Mexico via a discussion of the tradition of travel writing as a genre and the context of travel writing in contemporary Spain, and the sense of Spain as a point of origin in the late twentieth and early twenty-first centuries following the postdictatorship remaking of history. This is significant because it is changing the discourses about historical understanding in Spain right now, linking Spanish histories and experiences to broader international debates about culpability, memory, and national identity. Spain's current crisis of history in dealing with its recent past, as well as its historical crisis when dealing with the loss of empire, are crucial to understanding the significance of historical imagination in Spanish society. The second important theme of Chapter 1 is the way Mexico as a destination permits an instructive analysis of the heritage of violence, otherness, appropriation, and travel writing as a problematic semi-colonial tradition, one that foregrounds the ongoing stake European nations have in differentiated mobility and global structural inequality. Taking this in conjunction with the specific dynamics of Spanish-Mexican encounter is particularly fruitful, because Mesoamerica was one of Spain's early and most important sites of conquest and imperial expansion in the so-called New World, and it therefore triggers certain kinds of historical reflection and allusions for Spanish writers traveling there. Furthermore, Mexico has been absorbed into the economic flows of globalization and the global tourism industry in key ways, partly because of proximity to the US and Central and South America and its accessibility for marine trade. For the same reason, Mexico is arguably now more significant than

Spain in determining the global profile and role of Spanish as a language, at least in its projection outside the Spanish-speaking world, due to its ongoing experience of migration and transmigration and its large population. The extent to which Spaniards recognize or contest their nation's own eroded influence over the Spanish language globally also plays out in travel writing about Mexico, along with various other forms of engagement with conceptualizing "Old" world versus "New." This contest over language and its relationship to cultural identity is one of the many ways traditional concepts of center-periphery are inadequate to understanding power and cross-cultural exchange. Along with language, present-day Spain and peninsular Spanish culture produce numerous tensions with Latin America over the meaning of historical narratives and their role in the formation and contestation of cultural identities.

Chapter 2 moves into a direct engagement with the central question of the diverse modes in which contemporary narratives of encounter reflect the contingency and instability of the historical imagination and the way this process is enacted in the space between Spain and Mexico. The focus is on travel narratives that explore the interrelationship between past experiences and the traveler's frame of reference for dealing with the strange and the new. In the key examples of Eduardo Jordá's *Lugares que no cambian* (2004; Unchanging places) and Francisco Solano's *Bajo las nubes de México* (2001; Beneath Mexican clouds), this occurs both through the memories that travelers bring to bear, and the personal experiences that shape their preconceptions of themselves as traveling subjects and of their destinations, including those enacted through reading, through literature, and through the development of an intertextual field of reference prior to departure. Chapter 3 also addresses the way reflexivity about narration relates to the development of historical awareness and historical consciousness, and whether it supposes a reflexivity about the actual role of the traveler in place.

In Chapter 3, my discussion of Alfonso Armada and Corina Arranz's *El rumor de la frontera* (2006; The murmur of the border) allows me to engage with the role of the Mexican-US border in the contemporary imaginary in a more textured way than is possible in the general overview of discourses of Mexicanness in Chapter 2. Looking at this fraught geography through contemporary travel writing also creates a space for exploring the tensions in the differentiated experiences of mobility globally and the intersection of mobility and power. The limits of the representability of trauma and suffering come into play here. The history of travel writing has a troubled relationship with the idea of the exotic in opposition to European civilization, and this relationship is doubled in Spanish literature since Spain has traditionally been an object of this exoticizing gaze. To understand the function of the exotic in contemporary discourse, I also analyze the idea of danger. Danger is one way contemporary travel writers distinguish their narrative from the overload of possible sources, few of which have the capacity of appearing to reveal someplace *new*. Novelty is key. In analyzing Alfredo Semprún's *Viajes desaconsejables* (2007; Imprudent journeys) I am interested in the connections between the European subject's information glut and the way the imagined death of distance affects travelers' encounters with difference and narration of the other. How do contemporary travelers illustrate encounters with places that their readers already believe they know? In a past era of European travel, discovery was the object and the capacity of the traveler to report objective reality was not in doubt, but the authority of the narrator is now contested. Despite this contestation, the consumption of places is still facilitated through cross-cultural intermediaries assuming an authoritative voice, including journalist-cum-travel writers like Semprún.

Chapter 4 explores the historical and material conditions of cross-cultural transatlantic space and how these inform the modes of self-representation of a strongly constituted first person narration. Suso Mourelo, author of *Donde mueren los dioses* (2011; Where the gods die), is an example of a professional travel writer who establishes an authorial persona, having published travel narratives about several destinations and writing in the anecdotal style common in the genre. His book on Mexico is here compared to Fermín Heredero's less commercial *Chiapas: Cuaderno de viaje* (2009; Chiapas: Travel journal), simultaneously a more ethnographic and transparently intertextual work. This is a productive comparison because both use a first person narrative voice, detailed recounting of quotidian aspects of their trips, and chronological transparency, rather than the extensive digressions and temporal and geographical leaps that characterized some of the works analyzed in other chapters. The other example in Chapter 4 is the explicit remobilization of Conquest-era narrative through contemporary subjectivity in Eloísa Gómez-Lucena's travel book *Del Atlántico al Pacífico: Tras los pasos de Cabeza de Vaca* (2018; From Atlantic to Pacific: In the footsteps of Cabeza de Vaca), and the ways taking a chronicle from the Conquest era as framing intertext influences the narrative construction of both Spain and Mexico.

The Spanish-Mexican transatlantic space performed by travel writers engages with two different historically inflected concepts of global location: Europe as a point of origin, and Mexico as a destination. The variations in how travelers engage with their environment and their hosts as well as the variations in how they narrate that encounter suggest different functions of power and privilege in the world today. Travel stories that focus more on the traveler's personal past and the literary and material history of Mexico support a historically contextualized perception of the individual nature of journeying but may obscure the structural conditions that broadly determine the terms on which different people travel. Others, oriented more toward the events and disruptions of the present day, indicate the testimonial possibilities of reflecting the diverse experience of mobility in a world ever more compressed, with millions of involuntarily displaced people, hundreds of millions of migrants responding to global-scale pressures that shift patterns of migration, border security and nationalist rhetoric, and a jump in the virtualization of place and communication. Where an outward orientation is paired with an unreflective assumption of authority to account for and recount difference, however, these narratives can still reinforce underlying hierarchies of global power even while evidently testifying to their consequences. My hope is this book identifies some of the productive possibilities as well as the limitations of a genre of writing profoundly implicated in the production of colonial and neo-colonial regimes of knowledge. These possibilities and limitations, in the Spanish-Mexican encounter, are articulated in the transatlantic passage between two places commonly, though differently, imagined as porous sites of unruly mobility as well as traditional depositaries of touristic desire.

CHAPTER 1

The Idea of Mexico

Historical and Touristic Narratives

Nothing enters us without displacing something: the new image wrestles with what was there, jellyfish-like, in the water, before, softly and without tragedy, spreading over it like algae. (Mistral 1978, 20)

The shape, feel, and texture of a place each provides a glimpse into the processes, structures, spaces, and histories that went into its making. (Adams, Hoelscher, and Till 2001, xiii)

European history and contemporary travel narrative's response to travel writing tradition are important to understanding its possibilities as a form today, whether it overtly engages with these histories and traditions or whether they remain subtext. As important, however, are ideas of the traveler's destination, Mexico in the case of this study, and how those ideas intersect with, influence, and contradict the traveler's experience as described. As Gabriela Mistral's evocation of displacement suggests, a fundamental part of the transformative experience of travel is its action upon preexisting ideas and expectations of place and the evolution of the mobile subject immersed in a strange environment. The environment itself, constructed over time, is contending with those expectations while also acting on the body of the traveler. How has the idea of Mexico changed in Spanish eyes from the past object of discovery, conquest, rule, and loss? Having left the framework of colonial governance behind and abutting a massive neo-colonial power, what kind of destination does Mexico become, as Spain also incorporates itself into a new European political geography and new sensibility to mobilities? How do social changes and convulsions inside and around it, including escalations of violence, transform the idea of Mexico abroad? And how can we connect practices of tourism to spaces of enactment of the *sistema-mundo capitalista/patriarcal cristiano-céntrico/ occidental-céntrico moderno colonial* (capitalist/patriarchal Christian-centric/Western-centric modern colonial world system) that Ramón Grosfoguel (2012) identifies as an underlying condition visible through modes of mobility—as well as to broader dimensions of twenty-first century mobility and the potential spaces for overcoming that system? Several different factors operate on Mexico's destination image for the Spanish traveler. Among them are deliberate campaigns by the Mexican government and Mexican tourism operators, other kinds of publicity and media content both desirable and undesirable, the expectations of the traveler formed from their own desires and experiences, and the lingering impressions of past representations of Mexico in Spanish popular culture. In drawing these dimensions of place-image together, we can see relationships between the historicity of cultural and spatial hierarchies and the interlinked economic and conceptual practices of leisure mobility.

Contemporary travel encounters are tiny performances of the manifold possibilities of mobility between Spain and Mexico. Each encounter occurs first within the socioeconomic matrix of global tourism. In exploring this relationship, it is important to consider the material dynamics of contemporary travel practices between Spain and Mexico as well as the concept of Mexico and how it relates to travel writing as a text. This material aspect—the way every voluntary journey is part of a massive global industry with huge implications for host communities—is often elided in textual analyses of travel writing. Readers accept—at least provisionally—the travel writer's frequent self-differentiation from the figure of the tourist, and in some sense their ability to stand outside what they are describing and assume what Debbie Lisle (2006) has termed a cosmopolitan gaze. Which factors in contemporary Spanish culture inform the historical and cultural horizons of Spanish travelers? What shapes their itineraries and destinations? And how is Mexico positioned as a destination globally and in Spain in particular? What understandings of Mexico influence both producers and consumers of travel narrative? These are some of the limitations on the travel narrative, whether the travel writer chooses to or even can acknowledge them explicitly.

Spain as Origin and Mexico as Destination

Before entering into the reasons Mexico figures in the ways it does in the European imagination, it is important to understand broader European ideas of America in relation to changing European ideas of individual agency, the effects of violence, continuing regimes of exclusion, and indeed the concept of Europe itself and European subjectivity. Paul Ricoeur (in Kearney 1995, 33) suggests an approach to thinking about Europe and difference that offers one way through the impasse of Eurocentrism as the sole paradigm for Europe's historical self-regard without denying the assertions of superiority upon which so many elements of the elaboration of a common concept of Europeanness have been founded: "The kind of universality that Europe represents contains within itself a plurality of cultures, which have been merged and intertwined, and which provide a certain fragility, and ability to disclaim and interrogate itself." With specific reference to travel and travel writing themselves, Patrick Holland and Graham Huggan (1998, 22) have also remarked on metropolitan multiplicity, the resulting muddying of categorizations of origin, and the nonviability of a one-way gaze. The disruptions and ambiguities of cultural identity are one of the primary interests of travel writing, and the confrontations engendered by departure and immersion in the unfamiliar create a space from which enunciations of the fragilities and paradoxes of Europe, rather than a reinscription of its master narratives, become possible.

Spain is a curious point of origin for travel writers given its own historical liminality in European identity-building projects, which brings a certain instability of perspective. In modern Europe Spain consolidated a certain fame as a romantic, uncivilized place, fundamentally different from its neighbors to the north.[1] The tradition of European travel to Spain, from medieval pilgrimage to the twentieth century, reinforced an idea of exotic Spain that continues to flavor its image internationally. The country remains to this day a frequent object of the exoticizing gaze of travel writers, a reality that shapes the touristic understanding of Spain's own travelers. The external image of Spain is linked to the historiographical demarcation of Spanish empire from later imperial projects. The *leyenda negra* (Black Legend) paints it as brutal in its essence, and the characterization of the consequences of the Conquest has thus become linked to later struggles over the construction of a Spanish identity and navigation of the tensions between cosmopolitan and national projects. As María Celia Forneas Fernández (2004, 228) writes, "Understand that from 1492, the image of Spain was changed by the chronicles of the Indies, with their brutal image of Edenic goodness and immeasurable evil."[2]

Spain also contributes to changing modes of writing encounter through an evolving journalistic subgenre that feeds into travel writing—the *crónica*. The classic *crónica* has its origins in the stories of the Conquest, but as Pitman (2008, 33–34) suggests, the form was also influenced and rejuvenated by mid-nineteenth literary trends in France, notably the *chroniques* published in the Parisian press, which employed sketches of social customs and encouraged the shift of the *crónica* into a shorter, more journalistic form. In this example, we can see how writing itself tracks conditions of historical exchange, from the form of the *crónica* as communiqué of imperial expansion to the reformation of European (and American) literary forms through the Franco-centric nineteenth-century intellectual and artistic networks.

In the twentieth and twenty-first centuries, travel writing has necessarily evolved in every literary tradition, reflecting changed conditions of travel and changed conditions of reading. The centrality of tales of adventure and/or discovery has shifted, and travel writing has taken something of an autobiographical turn. More successful iterations of the evolving genre have been based on the invocation of "a number of late-capitalist cultural possibilities . . . commodification, specialization, and nostalgic parody" that may approximate "a world of estrangement" and "resist uniformity" (Holland and Huggan 1998, 197, 217). Thematic and stylistic changes came alongside a shift in the idea of the self and challenges toward previous concepts of knowledge. The personal journey of the traveler has, in travel accounts, displaced *places*—the focus of exploratory, empirical, and romantic narratives. Travel writing has been both a Eurocentric and a self-referential genre—travel writers have long engaged in exchanges with previous travel narratives as a fundamental element of their relationship to place. Their predecessors provide today's writers with inspiration for how and where to travel and establish an image for a place that followers then choose to endorse or contest. Travel writing, unlike ethnography, is primarily a popular genre and as such has not been compelled to confront its own antecedents and premises. However, the tensions intrinsic to the genre's history still leak through in what Musgrove (1999, 44) terms the "unravelling, conflict and uncertainty in the traveling subject." Despite John Phillips's (1999, 64) claim that the "stable cultural frame" employed by the traveler to make sense of new experiences creates "an aesthetic control over strange landscapes as a kind of corollary to the colonizer's economic plunder," Phillips also acknowledges that "travel narrative concerns situations in which the stability of the self is often challenged." Control is incomplete, and readers can glimpse that partiality and fractured subject position. Travel writing teeters between the power granted through narration and the inability of the narrator to wholly absorb or represent what is strange. Travel narratives inarguably draw on stereotypes and reenact socioeconomic inequalities, but may also, and simultaneously, provoke critical responses. Substrata of unassimilability and unease can inflect even the most ontologically confident narrative voice.

The Spanish tradition of travel literature has both its own sacred texts and a few genuinely popular contemporary authors. There persists a freer (or at least less covert) comingling of fictional and factual accounts and divergent genre boundaries.³ Late twentieth-century (democratic-era) writers are quite diverse. Work broadly comprehensible as travel writing has come from many sources, including novelists, poets, anthropologists, historians, adventure travelers, and journalists. Author-travelers as diverse as Ana Briongos, Mónica Sánchez Lázaro, Miguel Barroso, Ígor Reyes-Ortiz, Ana Tortajada, Lorenzo Silva, Julio Llamazares, Miguel Ángel Díaz, Miguel Sánchez-Ostiz, José Ovejero, Iñaki Preciado Idoeta, Jesús Turbado, Paco Nadal, Luis Pancorbo, César Pérez de Tudela, and Carme Villabona at times wrote travel accounts among a range of other literary labors. Journalists like Enrique Meneses, Iván Puig i Tost, Maruja Torres, and Alfredo Semprún have published various chronicles and collections that include travel stories or developed written accounts of specific experiences or trips explicitly for book publication. There are numerous other examples of writers, both professional and occasional, who published at least one book that may be considered travel narrative. While there are many notable women travel writers, men still dominate the genre. Due to structural and personal barriers facing women, men simply publish more books—in Spain, twice as many (Riaño 2019). Travel itself remains easier for men for the same reasons. This has impacted the selection of texts available to study. Within this wide array of Spanish travel writing activity, there feature a few writers whose contemporary reputations, regardless of initial professional trajectory, have been built principally on travel narrative, most famously in the case of Javier Reverte. Subsequent chapters refer to some writers mentioned above and consider how travel writing relates to other literary forms through analysis of contemporary texts.⁴ This brief review of some contemporary travel authors is not supposed to position it as a genre uniformly available to aspiring writers, but rather foreground the ways travel writing is intrinsically conditioned by the circumstances of travel.

In the late nineteenth and twentieth century, conditions for Spanish travelers changed, as did the terms of Spain's relationships with many key destinations for Spanish travelers such as Spanish-speaking America, Western Europe, and Northern Africa. The relics of Spanish empire fell away, European borders were redrawn by war, most Spaniards on the move were temporarily or permanently migrating for economic and political reasons (e.g., the multiple waves of migration to Cuba), and global communications technology and air travel began to transform the significance of distance. Spain thus also offers an example of the trajectory of European travel writing and the politics of representation through the postcolonial period of globalization. The focus on Spain in transnational/transatlantic contexts contributes to understanding the evolving function of the national within global history and seeing Spain's present global dimensions as entangled with its historical networks.[5] Nineteenth- and early twentieth-century nation-building was not a rupture with empire but a transition, which therefore partly shaped the conceptualization of the global by reclothing imperialist cultural undercurrents in internationalist (and in Spain in particular, intra-nationalist) dress. Travel writing shows us textured examples of the way contemporary mobility, and our modes of interpreting cultural and geographical difference, are linked to the past both materially and conceptually.

Within Spain, contemporary relationships to history and, consequently, to Mexico's historically determined relationship to Spain, depend upon the specific conditions of Spanish experiences in the twentieth century. The Civil War and dictatorship established the conditions for much of Spain's twentieth century, radically altering not only the perceptions of those who experienced them but the opportunities of those who lived their lives in the late dictatorship and early democracy. Practical consequences included the loss of many of Spain's literary elite and the decimation of its budding general education and literacy systems, which marked a rupture in Spanish artistic and literary production. The Republican exile in Mexico in particular, as Héctor Perea (1996) makes clear, also assumed mythic status as a supreme act of solidarity that supposedly transformed both countries while resolving some of the tensions that had lingered between the two states and their peoples—

though he is quick to explain that this myth and the intellectual transformation suggested are an oversimplification of the complexities of waves of Mexican-Spanish mobility in the preceding decades. The mythmaking around the reception of Spanish exiles also covers over the complexity of the actual relationship such individuals had with their new home, which, despite an expectation of ideological alignment with the Mexican state (at least initially), also blended this political framework with the effects of "the laws of gratitude, and their—not always conscious—vestiges of Euro- and Hispanocentrism" (Faber 2003, 223). Sebastiaan Faber (2002, 205) also notes the ways the ideological and intellectual projects of the exiled Republicans shifted over time, including a partial co-option into the nation-building projects of the Mexican PRI. Mexico may seem more distant from Spain than some other Latin American destinations, with lower current migratory exchange and less general personal experience.[6] However, the points articulated above speak to its symbolic and practical significance in the twentieth century. Mexico also offers clear sites of alterity and American identity construction through indigenist and *mestizo* narratives (which were most unsettling to those generations of Spaniards—including many today—with an investment in cultural continuity and fraternity between Spain and the Spanish-speaking parts of the Americas), as well as through the geographically informed material realities of life between the US and Central America.

To return to the historical evolution of Spain as origin culture or homeland, practical consequences shaping Spanish life through the twentieth century included poverty for vast segments of the population, and the closure of Spain to much inbound travel and foreign influence. Furthermore, educational and population losses and the political climate of the time acted against the maintenance of a stable scientific community, one that could have sustained communities of thought around an intellectually motivated outward gaze. While Spain may once have been oriented toward the sea, given its strategic holdings at the mouth of the Mediterranean and history of ocean-going expansion, it has also undergone several periods of centrist concentration of power and centrist administrative structure. In past centuries this was based on monarchic control, but in the twentieth century it was perpetuated and aggravated under Franco. Public discourse for much of the twentieth century was not centrifugal but centripetal and did not perpetuate a coastal or voyaging national identity. All these factors influenced both the ability of most Spaniards to travel to any distant destination, including Mexico, and their exposure to and facility for writing about strange places. On a conceptual level, the Civil War and Francoism marked a culture of silence and revision of Spanish identity in sharply nationalist terms, with repercussions for Spanish modes of thinking history and thinking nation through the democratic transition and beyond (Aguilar Fernández 1996). Silence and closure are two of the damaging effects of the extreme exercise of state power over the population in a radically unequal contest, and the trauma of this experience effectively creates different resonances between contemporary Spain and those Latin American nations that have suffered similarly (or more) abusive governments. The influence of this social background on Spanish travelers' relationship to power, ethnicity, religion, and, in particular, historical thinking, appears throughout their writing on Mexico. We see it in the perception of political authority, the description of material traces of the colonial era, the evocation of cultural and linguistic continuities between Spain and Mexico, and even in direct references to the Spanish Civil War and Franco dictatorship. We see one of the most peculiar examples of how political memory in Spain unexpectedly shapes diverse modes of interpretation of even remote travel experience in the final pages of Eloisa Gómez-Lucena's travelogue *Del Atlántico al Pacífico*. Though the book as a whole narrates quotidian detail of the author's perambulations in search of both physical commemorations and cultural echoes of the presence of Álvar Núñez Cabeza de Vaca, the final section is what may otherwise seem an irrelevant extended contemplation of twentieth-century Spanish history, linked only by the possible relevance of archival resources held by the estate of the Duquesa de Medina Sidonia, the famous Duquesa Roja, a significant figure in anti-Francoist public debate. This leads to the writing of a species of informal interview-based profile of the Duchess, including elements of first person testimony and providing a concluding note that frames *Del Atlántico al Pacífico*'s constant expressions of repugnance at any kind of dogmatic or showy patriotism by bringing them into a direct narrative line with anti-Francoism.

Of course, direct dictatorial control came to an end in the 1970s and had lost some cultural influence much earlier. The aftermath inevitably fogged aspects of both discourse and action in late twentieth-century Spain. Another major factor was gaining ever-increasing importance at this time, however: the European Economic Community and the European Union project. Europeanization was already of immense importance when a significant event rolled around that saw Spain assessing its identity, its history, and its future direction, and that also brought Europeanizing tendencies into direct conversation with the relationship to America: 1992, the so-called Year of Spain, was a strong example of how historical thinking links to contemporary culture and lived inequalities. As a moment when Spain was both taking stock of the past for the quincentenary of Columbus' arrival in the Caribbean and projecting itself outward with the Seville Expo and the Barcelona Olympic Games, 1992 triggered a wave of self-analysis as well as political activity, and also provided rich material for examining millennial conceptions of what it meant to be Spanish. Both Morgan (2000) and Angie Chabram-Dernersesian (1996) cite polls from 1992 where a majority of respondents were at least accepting about Spain's colonial past, with many expressing outright positive feelings. On balance, Spain's events of 1992 seemed more celebratory than not, though in many Latin American nations there were large protests against the way colonization was being characterized in such positive discourses. In an analysis of Spanish-language media in 1992, Chabram-Dernersesian (219) characterizes these discourses as a revised "Colón-ialista" narrative: "[It] consciously seeks to distance itself from the old-style colonial discourse normally associated with the Golden Age of Spanish politics: the Empire. In its revised forms, the Colón-ialista narrative tempers its patriotic fervor, mediates its Spanish nationalism with a Euro-Latin American representation, and aggressively seeks to "modernize" itself in the contemporary world by ridding itself of anachronistic expressions and historic recriminations." Morgan (61) suggests that a strong thread of the emergent narrative was the increased emphasis on Spain's Arabic rather than colonial past, while Chabram-Dernersesian sees in it an affirmation of Spain's cultural and linguistic wealth. Both suggest that 1992 narratives signaled an attempt to reposition Spain internationally, though Chabram-Dernersesian identifies it as a general desire for greater prominence, where Morgan teases out elements that suggest Spain was Europeanizing at the expense of ties with Latin America, such as the establishment in 1992 of the Ley de Extranjería imposing new immigration restrictions on Latin American countries. Return migration, which has been such a driving force for confronting postcolonial realities in all the old colonial powers, is increasingly restricted in Spain. This is an example of the way global mobility reshapes internal conceptions of national identity and cultural difference, as has been seen once again more recently as Latin American migrants have become a more desirable group in comparison with African migrants and asylum seekers attempting to enter Europe through Spain.

Migration remains a site for much chauvinism, with the economic relegation of many Latin American migrants to the lower classes and the presence of the diverse Latin American Spanish on the streets of Spain's cities used as tools for reinforcing the supremacy of Iberian Hispanic culture. As an affirmation of the importance of Spain and her language on the international stage, 1992 narratives thus disconnected the strength of *castellano* from the colonizing process, negated Spanish regions and internal diversity, and reiterated a peculiarly Eurocentric definition of cultural wealth and importance. Latin America, therefore, may have served Spain in that moment as a way of shoring up Spain's historical significance within the European context and the significance of one of her languages on the world stage rather than as a meaningful current partner. The economic implications of Europeanization trump the cultural fraternities of a pan-Hispanist view of Spanish-speaking America. Indeed, European economic neoimperialism underpins many aspects of the soft power activities associated with the construction of transatlantic ties through the 1990s and beyond, echoing underlying passive imperialism described in Spain's post-1898 regenerationist movements (García Pérez 2000).[7]

Since 1992, Spain's movement into Europe has evolved, with all European nations developing complex relationships with the idea of Europe and the extent of penetration of a European identity into national and local cultures, as well as European trade policy and economic influence. This has sometimes served to reinforce ideas of cultural difference; as some European nations converge economically, many different European peoples have elevated cultural specificity as a driver of regional and national allegiance. However, the increasing flows of capital associated with international culture industries, the growing streams of information between places, a surfeit of lifestyle options available to the world's wealthier people, and indeed the great movements of people taking place in the world today constantly test the resilience of this kind of cultural allegiance. And, as we can see Europe as well as elsewhere, one component of the definition of specificity and difference articulates a commercial need for place branding of the kind that supports the consumption of both experiences and products that fit an often ethnically and invariably historically inflected cultural image.

In tracking aspects of travel from Spain to Mexico, it is important to understand how Mexico's own destination image both in Spain and more generally has and continues to evolve through both deliberate and incidental image defining mechanisms. These mechanisms include news and current affairs, the representation of Mexico in popular culture including film and literature, and the phenomenon of generic pop culture Latinization of the Spanish-speaking world internationally. In tension with the projection and circulation of Mexicanness we must consider the specificity of Mexico itself. It is a place with its own transformative, resistant materiality, histories, and peoples who speak as well as speaking back. Mexico, a geographical and conceptual limit-space for the place-politics of the late twentieth and early twenty-first century's US-centric world order, is also in its own right a major arena for changing concepts of mobility within contemporary globalization. As a site of migrant traversal as well as tourist circulation, Mexico is exemplary for exploring intersections of power and movement and their impact on embodied selves. Mexico cannot be ignored in any examination of contemporary transnational mobilities in the context of the flows of people, drugs, crime, capital, and ideas, both from north to south and south to north. Travel narratives track several facets of images of place through cultural representation, intertextual reference, and both negative and positive popular ideas. Literary place-images circulate within and are altered by the financial and cultural economies of travel and tourism. It is also vital, therefore, to draw out the multiple and resistant possibilities of place within the seemingly totalizing power structures of global capitalism. As Adams, Hoelscher, and Till (2001, xx) write, "the very political-economic processes that would seem to homogenize place, in fact, increase its importance." Global tourist demand drives the production of local difference and the performance of the exotic and hence also has localizing consequences in tourism development (López Santillán and Marín Guardado 2010). Huggan (2009, 12) also describes how tourism as a massive industrial product of global capital can provide resources for cultural distinctiveness. Beyond the performance of culture, in the narration of cross-cultural experiences, particular routes and their stories have the capacity to highlight the contradictions and inequalities that globalization creates—one of the positive possibilities of some travel writing's ambivalent "global consciousness" (37). Parsing out the connections between such macro-processes and the intercessions of individual and group actors is one useful way to understand relationships between power, mobility, and representation. The routes and perceptions of isolated traveler-writers give processes of cultural differentiation in the tourism economy and the impact of place-image flesh and meaning. Given this book's focus on situating individual travelers from Spain in relation to broader historical narratives and political debates, it is necessary to briefly discuss the material and economic aspects of Spain as a point of travel departure at the end of the twentieth century, since these constitute the other dimension that constructs the routes and perceptions of the travel narratives analyzed. Thus alongside Spain as homeland (however ambivalent) we consider the idea of Mexico in the Spanish—and global—imagination as the overlapping conceptual field required for understanding the interventions of contemporary Spanish travel writers in representations of Mexico. In the analysis of contemporary travel narratives by Spanish writers in subsequent chapters, the mobilization of cultural concepts of Spanishness is compared to both experiences of Mexico and circulating notions of *lo mexicano*. To what extent do they actively or implicitly perpetuate historical inequalities? How does the sense of history displayed in the text incorporate also a sense of the impact of the traveler as such, rather than limiting itself to the place and journey's potential to change the traveler's individual sense of identity? Fluidity and contradiction in contemporary narrative signal the inheritance of first encounter and the destabilization of Eurocentric worldviews. To properly frame this analysis, the remainder of this chapter explores the positions in which Spain and Mexico find themselves in the global travel economy in a material sense and how this connects to both historical discourses about place and contemporary economies of representation.

Spain in the Travel Economy and Managing Mexico

Travel stories tell us as much, if not more, about the point of departure as the destination. To examine the transnational dynamics of Spain-Mexico voyages in contemporary Spanish travel writing, it is vital to think about Spain as origin and what travel means in Spain today. As described in the preceding chapter, Spain as a destination is significant in the tradition of European travel writing. Spain has acted as a site of exotic otherness, as the beginning of Africa, as wilderness, as battleground, as sun, sand, and sea. This creates potential awareness of what it means to be the object of the traveler's gaze. Even when not explicitly articulated, Spain's powerful invocation of itself as a product for tourism is inescapable in contemporary Spanish culture. Spanish travelers, more than many others, may claim some insight into the intersections and disjunctions between the idea of place—its international place-image or, in tourism studies parlance, its destination brand—and the experience of dwelling. However, as explored throughout this book, the extent to which individual writers then engage with their own role in the global travel economy and reflect on their actions in Mexico is variable.

Travelers who publish their stories have a great stake in the congruity between travel choices and public selves. Tourists choose destinations with images that align with their personal values and sense of self (Sirgy and Su 2000, 344). This does not necessarily imply that the destination is similar to home, but rather that the sense of adventure, security, luxury, or hardship is coherent with the traveler's idea of their journeying spirit. Spain's leisure travel traditions and Latin America's positioning in the Spanish tourism market both link to this production of a traveling self. For many years, domestic travel during long summers and for village festivals was a fixture of Spanish life, and major international travel was a meaningful option for relatively few Spaniards in comparison to other Western Europeans. However, increasing incomes and the rapid expansion of the middle class in the late twentieth century drove a boom in international air travel in Spain. Traveler-writers still tend to distinguish themselves from mass tourists through the mobilization of a cosmopolitan or distinctively interested gaze (with variable degrees of self-critique and reflection on the artificiality of this distinction and employment of irony).[8] That said, travel writing itself is, Steve Clark (1999a, 1) suggests, a "mixed and middlebrow" genre, and part of the readership for it derives from that very same expanded middle class who are the majority consumers of tourism.[9]

In the early 2000s, roughly contemporaneously to many of the travel stories under discussion, both short and long international trips rose steadily in popularity. Holidays outside of Spain became more common, and while much of this growth was driven by low cost air carriers and short breaks inside Europe, non-European destinations also saw significant growth, attributable to rising incomes, flexible leave, and decreased cost (Euromonitor "Tourism Flows Outbound – Spain" 2007). The increased market share of El Corte Inglés, a high-end retailer, also reflects the changed holiday aspirations of middle-class Spaniards. Mexico became one of the destinations with the fastest growth in popularity in Spain, along with Brazil, Argentina, the Dominican Republic, and Costa Rica. The 2007 Euromonitor report ("Tourism Flows Outbound – Spain," 3) suggests this concentration is partly due to the presence of Spanish hotel chains and airlines, but also because *"cultural and language similarities are stressed"* as well as ease of access and lower prices" (emphasis added).

The numbers of Spaniards traveling for holidays at some point in the year increased steadily (with dips related to terrorist incidents and economic downturns) from 1999, and by the late 2000s encompassed almost half the total population (Euromonitor "Travel and Tourism – Spain" 2007). On average, Spanish holiday takers were for the first time equally likely to be male or female, far more likely to be in the twenty-five to thirty-four age group with their higher disposable incomes and fewer children, and with a potentially more modern and flexible view of both frequency and destination of travel. Beach destinations remained popular, but countryside, mountain, and cultural destinations gained (Euromonitor "Travel Retail – Spain" 2007, 5). Traditional packages were also still popular, but alongside much faster growth in areas of adventure/trekking holidays and fly-drive packages with greater flexibility (Euromonitor "Travel Retail – Spain," 1). Many of these trends were not limited to Spain. They reflected ongoing stratification of travel interests according to class and subculture and the increasing worldwide importance of niche tourism, with greater cultural capital attached to independent travel. The way Spanish travelers thought about planning their travel and engaging with their destination before departure had also changed. While many bookings continued to be made through travel agents, the online sector saw the fastest growth, and most internet users at least looked for information about their destination and transport online before booking travel. The number of internet users in Spain had risen rapidly, more than doubling in a short time to include more than 80 percent of households, though it remained below the EU average. (Of course, this also indicates that there were—and are—still many millions of people in Spain who never used the internet, and it is essential to remember who is excluded when talking about both mobility and circulation of ideas.) The majority of overall internet sales in Spain were in the travel and tourism industry, and almost all travel outlets had an online presence (Euromonitor "Travel and Tourism – Spain"). This transformation in the way Spaniards specifically and contemporary travelers more generally engaged with distance and with distant places is an important aspect of the late twentieth- and early twenty-first-century context for representation of places and communication of experiences. Travel writers are part of this economy via the conditions of their individual journeys, the transparency of those conditions for their readers, the circulation of travel narrative as part of broader patterns of commodification of cultural difference, and their contributions to the popular images of places.

These trends in the role of travel in Spanish society coincided with changing dynamics of transatlantic Spain-Mexico relations, both economic and cultural. María Inmaculada Álvarez (2006, 8–9) notes that Spain has been a major investor in Latin American tourist infrastructure, particularly in the period under discussion, bearing out the significance of the above-mentioned Spanish-owned transnational corporations in the hospitality, banking, and retail sectors that collectively have a substantial impact on economic relations in the Spanish-speaking world. Such investments also elevate Spain's soft power. Alongside Spain's self-declared guardianship of *castellano* as a language and its expansive celebratory post-1992 Hispanism, such Spain-centered economic structures and capital relations are elements supporting tropes of Spanish superiority. These tropes are not linked only to imperial nostalgia but also, as already indicated, to cultural and economic Europeanization and to nation-buttressing soft power. They are further complicated by Latin American migrants' presence in Spain and the intimacy and long histories of transatlantic diasporic relations. Other factors also destabilize any reading positing an uncomplicated Spanish superiority in Spaniards' conceptions of Mexico, including the inscription of Spain into the pan-Hispanic global consumable of undifferentiated "Latin chic," as José Martí Olivella (2001) terms it, which partly reverses the polarity of perceived cultural convergence. Spain is often subsumed into Latin chic with no more power to define it as a global brand than any individual Latin American nation. Nor is Spanish superiority straightforward to maintain even without venturing beyond its own internal narrative, given the politics of Latin American subalternity and the complexities of strategic resistance, addressed in more detail later in this chapter.

What Paul Julian Smith (2003), in the context of film production, terms the "transatlantic traffic" of the shared space in which representation emerges out of collaboration and mobility between Europe and America is a further example of the necessity of interrogating transnational intersections to understand cultural inscriptions, not merely to use categories suggested by a neocolonial, and strictly nation-bound, center and periphery. John Beverley (1999, 150) argues for the limits of the nation as a categorization within globalization, a useful reminder of the problems inherent in recurring to the national in discussing culture, community, and belonging. Beverley does suggest, however, that the nation-state retains some importance as a mediator in the relationship between human subjects and the global. The point of origin, including its "national" qualities, is important in shaping the dynamics of Spanish outbound travel. Alongside being representatives and enactors of their own cultural identities, travelers become negotiators of and audiences for the cultural identities of others, and this negotiation and performance begins long before departure. John Urry (1990) has drawn out some of the functions of tourism as part of place-negotiation in a global order, incorporating a sense of power as relational and enacted through exchanges and performances. As critical tourism scholars suggest, the projection of destination branding is not merely economic; it has significant political and cultural consequences (Anthony 2005, 6; Fehimović and Ogden 2018; Aronczyk 2013). Some form of destination branding and preestablished place-image reaches all travelers, regardless of their purpose or concept of self. In travel writing it is possible to track the extent to which these contemplative travelers consume this product or use it to consider their own role and actions as its market—or, most likely, both. It is not easy, even for travelers who recognize that all spaces are subject to social ordering and that there is no "other" space, to understand and communicate the limitations of their own perspective. "Travel writers too often take comfort in recognizable spatial categories such as safety and danger. . . . They retreat back into a utopian ideal and set about re-ordering their destination accordingly" (Lisle 2006, 192). Nevertheless, travel narratives have the potential to disrupt preconceived cultural maps and binaries via the emergence of "fissures in the prevailing geographical imagination," whether intended by the writer or not (Lisle 2006, 202). Part of the purpose of drawing the tourism economy into the contextualization of contemporary traveler-writer routes and tales from Spain to Mexico is to ensure that where fissures open up in the texts discussed, their critical potential is connected explicitly to the material impacts of global capitalism.

If Mexico is one site for identifying the new meanings of mobility in the twenty-first century, it is important to identify how Mexico's place-image relates to pragmatic aspects of the economies of tourism and migration. As already suggested, destination marketing and countries as global brands are two significant dimensions of postglobalization travel economies. Travel narratives manifest some of the connections between historical discourses and contemporary senses of place that are subsumed in these brands. The *idea* of places in the twentieth and twenty-first centuries cannot be decoupled from the deliberate management of those ideas in relation to tourism as a national industry. This is something travel writing can help us see more clearly. Countries have a lot in common with corporations in the impact their image has on the viability of the product, which in this instance is tourism (Papadopolous and Heslop 2002). However, the significant difference is that country image is far less unified and far more influenced by different actors with very different agendas and needs. While the mass-market tourism image of place is usually strategically coordinated, a country's complexity and uncertainty of direction lead to "a dilution of the unitary interest that would be needed and resulting in the actors' adoption of more short-term and personal interests as the drivers of their decisions" (Papadopolous & Heslop, 307). Furthermore, active image management is hindered and subverted by existing tropes and perceptions about places, for example, the persistence of stereotypes, the difficulty of deliberately transforming them— and the impossibility of ignoring them (Jiménez-Martínez 2018). Although major events with wide international media dissemination can transform stereotypes rapidly, it is rarely in ways destination marketers might wish, certainly a reality in the case of Mexico. The general image of Mexico in Spain is reasonably positive. Based on survey data of a selection of Spaniards (Madrid only): "Mexico is perceived as a *friendly* country, somewhat *ecological*, with a degree of *political stability*, with a *future*, but *poor*. There is a balanced perception related to *security, development, similarity with Spain*, and *cultural development*" (Rodríguez Ducallín et al. 2006, 193, italics original).[10] There are continuities between this summary and the image communicated in travel narrative; however, what the texts studied in subsequent chapters allow is an interrogation of the historical, cultural, and individual factors that shape perception and experience.

Wally Olins (2002) carries the analysis of the function of preexisting place-image a step further, into the territory of most relevance here: the relationship between place-image, tourism branding, and cultural myths of national identity. One significant element is the illusion of immutability that surrounds concepts of nationhood. The idea of a nation and national unity is one of the foundations that permitted *inter*national systems of government to retain some relevance and efficacy within the macro-forces of global capitalism. For members of a community to cohere around a place and believe themselves to belong together, as Anderson (1991) most resonantly described, the symbols of their cultural commonality must seem plausible and grounded in some notion of historical truth. According to community perception, "corporations change, merge, divest, invest and rebrand and reinvent themselves but nations do not change, they are immutable"—or seem to be (Olins 2002, 242). Of course, the national community founded on a myth of cultural cohesion is not the only model for government or social organization, but the concept of nationally aligned cultural difference is a big part of what tourism is selling. The myth of an essential national character obscures the extent to which nations actively work to reshape these identities in response to changing needs and for different audiences, and the historical conditions under which national myths emerged.

Travelers to Mexico are transacting with an industry that is deeply implicated in social and economic change—some of it extremely exploitative—throughout Latin America. This linkage of recreation and suffering is fundamental to industrialized travel, and it is also visible in the struggles over destination image. Factors such as "rising income and wealth disparities," "environmental degradation," "criminal activity," and "the spread of infectious diseases" are reduced to image problems when conceiving of a place as an object of consumption (Strizzi and Meis 2001, 191). In the 1990s Mexico was the number one destination for international travel to (and within) Latin America, and Latin America itself has had a steadily rising share of the world tourist market in recent decades (183). In 2008, for example, Mexico played host to more than 13.5 million travelers, and in-country spending and travel needs undeniably support significant employment sectors and hospitality industries within the country ("Buenas cifras" 2008). The effects of these industries, of course, are not unreservedly positive. The so-called image problems provide one set of negative factors in the Mexico brand, and attempts are made to counter them through tourism promotion strategies offering alternative tropes of paradisiacal beaches, exotic cultures, or even simply cheap shopping. In *Exporting Paradise* (2001), Michael Clancy explores the actions of stakeholders and destination marketers in Mexico in the late twentieth century. While Spain, as mentioned previously, has been a big investor in Mexican tourism infrastructure, the major changes to Mexican tourism development have been state-led, including state-run hotel chains and state investment funds. Late twentieth-century tourism development depended on earlier foundations, including nineteenth-century transport infrastructure development, early archaeological projects during the Porfiriato, and postrevolutionary stabilization and modernization—as well as heightened emphasis on indigenous history within nationalist narratives of Mexican identity (Berger and Wood 2009, 6–7). Dennis Merrill (2009, xiii) claims that all the foundations for the subsequent direction of the industry, especially as it pertains to the US as the primary market for Mexican tourism promotion, were already in place in the 1940s, even though the true industrialization of Mexican tourism came later. Clancy (2001) summarizes some of the changes brought by the comprehensive state-directed tourism strategy of the mid-century, including interventions like large state investment in coastal resorts from the late 1960s: "No longer is the country primarily known for either border pleasures or 'lo Mexicano'; instead it has become a major sun and sea destination" (49). This period established Mexico as a provider of packages and resorts; however, the niche that Mexico, among many countries, is now trying to promote is heritage and cultural tourism: "state activities during the 1990s have focused on launching three ambitious projects aimed at capturing segments of the quickly changing global tourism market. The first two, known as 'Colonial Cities' and the 'Ruta Maya' (later renamed Mundo Maya) have in effect marked a return to promoting *lo Mexicano*. . . . Both projects target history-oriented tourists" (115). The Mundo Maya project, to describe some of the dimensions of one example that has significant resonances with the narrative construction of difference, is conceived as a regional/multinational so-called touristic multiproduct, which encompasses niches of "sun and sand, culture, ecotourism and adventure, diving, cruises, business and conventions" (SECTUR, 2014).[11] What is telling is the way this panoply of touristic activity, not at all specific to the Central American Mayan world, is assembled under an ethnically inflected brand that is usually communicated visually with some combination of ruins, verdant nature, or symbols of indigenous alterity. Development strategies are not limited to international projection but also affect domestic markets, something that is explicitly articulated in the strategic vision for the Mundo Maya. Lindsay (2009, 70) picks up a related internal differentiation in which the Distrito Federal is created as another foreign market for the packaged exoticism of Mexico's regions, positioning locations like the Mayan south even inside Mexico itself as a consumable periphery to adorn the metropolitan lifestyle of middle-class *chilangos* (residents of Mexico City).

Visitors to Mexico are increasingly likely to engage in cultural activities such as visiting museums and colonial cities (Euromonitor "Tourist Attractions – Mexico" 2007, 1). Though this still remains a minority of travelers overall, it is an important segment for the purposes of Spanish travel writers because it directly links their experience to their own nation's past and may also provoke comment on the construction of historical and cultural narratives—particularly notable in the case of the historian-traveler Eloisa Gómez-Lucena, whose whole travel book (discussed in Chapter 4) is partly historiographical and whose itinerary is decided by access to historical sites and museums. Mexico has actively attempted to diversify its tourist market. Mexico shows generally steadily rising numbers of visitors from Spain, recently around a quarter of a million per annum, the vast majority traveling for leisure (Euromonitor 2014 "Tourism Flows Outbound – Spain"). Spanish tourist receipts are significant for Mexico, and constitute one of the highest non-American sources of tourism income (Euromonitor 2014 "Tourism Flows Inbound – Mexico"). The previously mentioned changing travel habits of Spanish travelers, which I will discuss in more detail below, are an important driver of this rise, but Mexican tourism campaigns in Spain also play a significant role. While a huge majority of arrivals in Mexico originate in the United States, the Mexican government has funded major campaigns in other countries to increase visitor diversity. Seven percent of Mexico's international tourism promotion budget in 2007 was spent on European campaigns (Euromonitor "Tourism Flows Inbound – Mexico" 2007, 2). Euromonitor reports that while Mexican campaigns in Spain are part of a promotional trend in Spanish-speaking nations, in 2006 Mexico was the most notable tourism destination presented on Spanish television. Of course, in the same media landscape other messages, such as reports of instability and violence, significantly taint the purity of the state-designed brand message. Spanish travel to Mexico has not risen as quickly as North American travel to Mexico, though there was a trend of rising spending per Spanish visitor, confirming the value of Spain in the Mexican tourism industry. The proliferation of niche and subcultural tourist groups is also significant for Mexico, with different place-images developed for backpackers, for example, as opposed to business travelers. There are several major niche tourist markets for Mexico, including gay specialty travel and language study tourism, both impacting tourist infrastructure and increasing the emphasis on marketing aspects of culture over climate. Also significant for Spanish-Mexican transnational mobility in particular is family reunion travel, which is closely tied to factors vital to understanding the context of travel narratives including histories of exile and immigration and their influence on the creation of multigenerational intellectual and emotional links that transcend national borders.

The personal links and stories created by past travelers are just one example of the ways the image of place resists purely strategic, profit-oriented management. While a country's government does influence its destination image through positive marketing campaigns as well as internal regulation of travel infrastructure and services providers, it cannot often control how the country is represented in international media. Major political and natural events that are reported around the world revise existing images of countries. Some of the significant elements of the idea of place that are affected by media stories include perceptions of personal security, accessibility, natural beauty, price, and facilities. While the deliberate campaigns described above have an impact, a sudden event or a broadly disseminated media image or story can act more rapidly to alter the destination image, and high media literacy within the audience reduces the impact of overt advertising in comparison to the perceived truth of other forms of media. Some events, such as structural political changes, do reshape the experience of place itself as well as the idea of it, but other events play out more at the level of simulation than fact.

Popular ideas about national identity, though subject to deliberate action, also metamorphose rapidly with large-scale social change. In a figuration particularly relevant to thinking about decolonizing Latin America, "When political upheavals take place, colonial masters are overthrown or a new regime emerges . . . the nation reinvents itself" (Olins 2002, 245). New popular narratives cohere around histories, events, and symbols to legitimize new regimes of power. With reference to the idea of Mexico in Spain specifically, Mexican independence must be considered a fundamental moment redefining Mexico in the Spanish imagination through the nineteenth century. Pitman (2008, 151–52) characterizes this moment as less a rupture than the commencement of "its on-going relationship with Spain as more fraternal, or sisterly, than antagonistic." This fraternity contained many underlying complexities as indicated, though, given the soft power projects tangled up in Spanish discourse around pan-Hispanism.[12] Exchanges and movements of people between the two countries persisted through various periods of turmoil, including the Napoleonic wars, the Mexican Revolution, and the Spanish Civil War.[13] "Mexicans have contributed decisively to Spanish cultural life particularly during the last century, and vice versa"—though it is the latter that Spaniards more commonly recognize (Pitman 2008, 152). The redefinition and adjustment of Mexicanness in Spain is a constant process, influenced by fundamental social and political changes, by turmoil resulting in migrations such as those mentioned above, and by major national and international events that gain traction for different reasons as part of the Mexico place-image. Recently, these have included emphases on violent events, upswings in narco activity, and even natural disasters.

Examples of events that have shifted the idea of Mexico during recent decades include natural disasters like hurricanes. Wilma in 2005, for example, disrupted the carefully scripted representation of the Caribbean coastline that is such a major feature of Mexico's tourist brand. Similar disruptions of tourist destination branding have been tied to security issues associated with the acceleration of the narco-wars, which in 2010 saw resort destinations like Cancún and Puerto Vallarta targeted by bombs and an escalation in general of noncombatant collateral violence in the drug war. Other past events affecting the image of Mexico during the period of travel addressed in this book include Zapatista demonstrations and confrontations with police and unions, cases of environmental and urban planning failures (exemplified by 2005's gas pipeline explosions), and general economic downturns leading to increasing crime and civil unrest, including financially motivated kidnapping.

These factors have contributed to negative security perceptions around Mexico; however, it was only the North American travel freeze around the 2009 flu pandemic that ultimately resulted in a contraction of the Mexican tourist industry for the first time in a decade (Grant 2009). Mexico struggled to manage the association of the country with the H1N1 flu pandemic.[14] The timing of the tourism shrinkage alongside the global financial crisis had serious economic and social consequences for Mexico. This is further immediate evidence of the close interrelationship of travel and social justice, and the ways leisure travel for global elites is fundamentally tied to problematic dynamics of constraint/liberation and immobilization/mobility. The extent travelers engage with or ignore these aspects of Mexican daily life constitutes a major thread of the textual analysis of travel accounts in later chapters of this book. Negative image factors that produce a place as a site of danger and exposure to extreme experiences sometimes create an alternative exoticism, which is linked to the touristic commodification of criminal and exploitative activities, such as drugs, prostitution, and, at the extreme end of criminal tourism markets, pedophilia tourism. Vicky Baker (2008) describes the rise of cocaine tourism in Colombia in relation to drug-centric international perceptions of Colombian life, which is a telling example of this effect and serves as a comparison point for current shifts in Mexico's international image. The failure of government and law enforcement and the eruption of criminality in public life produces a different kind of tourist engagement, which does not always take positive or even particularly considered forms. Some of the major forces influencing the current shift in the global place-concept of Mexico, such as escalating narco violence and economic downturn, are not equally dramatic in all travel narratives discussed in the following chapters, since the texts selected extend over a couple of decades and have different organizing themes and destinations. Despite escalating violence and border crises there was a relatively steady expansion of tourism to Mexico in the 1990s and 2000s, and the extremes of civil conflict and the overt erasure of territorial control were more concentrated in the period since the 2000 election of Vicente Fox. The ways travel narratives engage with these themes serve, however, as signal reminders of the potential pace of changes in place-image and their impact on the actual experiences possible in those places as well as the material conditions for their inhabitants, and relate to the representation of violence and danger in travel writing.

Portrayals of current affairs may also be positive in their representations of travel to and from the country, as in the case of the eco-credentials garnered for Mexico via hosting the United Nations Climate Change Conference in Cancún in 2010, or through organized sporting events or Mexican sporting success. Travel itself is directly marketed through newspaper supplements and television travel shows, often reporting on subsidized fully funded junkets. Popular fiction showing transnational connections between Spain and Mexico add another layer of mystique to the representation of Spanish-Mexican mobility. Julien Mercille (2014, 119) argues that the representation of Mexico "as chaotic and lawless, implying that outside intervention is legitimate" in English-language US popular culture products reinforces US foreign policy approaches and hemispheric hegemony. The Anglo-American production of myths about Mexico is not the primary source for imagining Mexico in Spain itself, but given the influence of US cultural production in globalized popular culture it inevitably plays a part, alongside other cultural products.

Even within Spanish-language popular culture, international distribution patterns influence what kinds of stories are widely heard. International successes like Arturo Pérez-Reverte's novel *La reina del sur* and its subsequent adaptations are mainly for non-Mexican audiences and certainly reinforce drug stereotypes, but also evoke some of the different types of postglobalization flows of people, capital, and things, as well as suggesting something—though not in detail—about their consequences.[15] Feature films with significant international distribution and audience reception, both those by Spanish directors, such as Agustín Díaz Yanes's 2008 *Sólo quiero caminar*, and those by Mexican directors, like Alfonso Cuarón's 2001 *Y tu mamá también*, often tell stories based around networks between Spain and Mexico and feature Spanish characters or travel to and from Spain in significant ways. These are just two examples that portray different segments of society, the former repeating some of the most clichéd messages about crime, and the latter using rural Mexico as a backdrop to a transformative personal journey, but transnational interconnectedness is a frequent theme across a wide range of films representing Mexico. In addition to Mexican directors' increasing international prominence, there is a growing industry of film collaboration and joint funding and production between the two countries. Along with the Spanish-Latin American mobilities regularly portrayed within many films themselves, this transnational mobility has contributed to the evolution of "transatlantic traffic" in film, with similar transatlantic processes present though perhaps less visible in other culture industries as well.

Many portrayals of Mexico touch at least in passing on power relationships, wealth, and exploitation and how they are connected to globalization, frequently taking a foray into the Mexican-US border zone as an ultimate arena for comparing the relative lightness and weight of different forms of mobility as it is embodied in the twentieth century. Gritty, realist aesthetics of transnational mobility flavoring some portrayals mark a shift from slightly earlier breakthrough depictions of Mexico that reached a global audience, such as the folkloric historical-culinary fantasy *Como agua para chocolate* (1992). *El crimen del padre Amaro* (2002), a later success with tonal similarities (the intermittent romantic melodrama harks back to *Como agua*), bases its A plot on the pervasiveness of corruption underpinned by drug crime as an entry point to the hypocrisy of the church, instead of retaining the historical source novel's tighter comic satirical focus on sexuality, class, and religion. The cultural associations implied by picking up the narco plot in shifting the story from nineteenth-century Portugal to twentieth-century Mexico are obvious. These few (and far from comprehensive) examples of the kinds of popular cultural texts set in Mexico that garnered international success in the late twentieth and early twenty-first centuries speak to recurrent tropes in global imaginaries of Mexican place-image: eroticization, violence, lawlessness, drugs.[16] Fiction and nonfiction accounts of Mexico in other media and genres are not the focus of this book, but they do frame both the intertextual space of the travel narratives studied and the interpretive schema of potential readers.

Short of massive worldwide events like the flu pandemic, changes in national image tend to be incremental, except in the case of nations that have low international brand awareness to begin with (notably, Kazakhstan, according to Borat). Individual cultural products build on or move to contradict what has gone before, in much the same way travel narratives respond to existing traditions of representation of place, and travel writers intervene in popular ideas of place, even though their individual narratives reflect geotemporally specific experiences. Such responses to existing ideas are not limited to direct intertextual references, but also engage with other arenas of cultural projection that have helped to define the idea of place.

Transatlantic traffic of both people and ideas is, obviously, not a twenty-first century phenomenon. Exchange between Spain and Mexico has been continuous since the colonial era. In artistic and literary movements—and the physical movements of artists and writers—the space between the two nations is a generative constant, influencing transnational awareness via personal experiences of contact as well as the messages conveyed in the durable products of such cultural exchanges. One telling example of this kind of transnational cultural space can be traced through the natural tendency of music to travel as well as the processes of commodification of subcultural difference with which the commercialization of music is bound up (Álvarez 2006). Commodifying music produces cultural difference for consumption by others. In the example of music, there is clear evidence for the shift toward international or global senses of *latinidad* and *hispanidad* drawing mostly on Central and North American cultures and less and less on Spain (although Spanish actors may be willing to take advantage of *latino* tropes, particularly where they may be profitable via tourism and other culture-marketing industries). This carries consequences for Spain's self-image, as already mentioned at the beginning of this chapter, but is also significant for Spaniards' concept of Latin America. Both Spain and Mexico have been drawn into new forms of image-oriented pan-Hispanism via global Latin chic for anglophone and other markets.

Alongside this broader commodified *latinidad*, there are many other place-concept factors that are specific to Spain's relationship with Mexico in particular, such as the histories of Spanish-Mexican migration mentioned previously and particular moments of transnational connection between Spain and Mexico. While the different fields of representation mentioned above may influence teens' and adults' perceptions of contemporary Mexico as a destination, first impressions of Mexico for most young Spaniards are formed in educational institutions and in the home, through general histories and educational resources for children. In broaching this topic, we return to the theme of Spain's relationship to its own history and to its current place in the world. Educational systems and the histories they reproduce have a burden of coloniality flavoring the worldview presented to children. The early twentieth century rise of the political right in Spain, as in many other parts of Europe, drew on a nineteenth-century tradition of nationalist historical mythmaking. Nationalists under Franco continued this tradition by enshrining "an ultra-conservative reading of Spanish history—one that had, significantly, been challenged under the Republic" (Graham 2004, 29). This is the pivotal connection between debates over the meaning of the Civil War and Spain's national story in a broader sense; repressive Francoism depended on legitimizing the memory of Imperial glory. At least some element of the woundedness of Spain after the Civil War sprang from the imposition of a simplistic relationship to history—with the use of the term *imposition* here drawing on Carolyn Boyd's (1997) careful analysis of Francoist educational programs that concedes that no such attempt at ideological indoctrination through historical mythmaking is ever universally applied or consistently effective. Nevertheless, part of the challenge of a productive, inclusive post-Franco model of historical thinking has been the incorporation of a renovated challenge to these myths. Later discussion of individual travel writers' representations of their Spanish origin in their work will touch again on inherited ideas about history and power.

It is also worth noting here that a "European" education was traditionally also part of the formation of middle and upper class Latin Americans. Harvey (1992, 83) cites one example of a Latin American narrator who "formed a false picture of Europe from his father's description, and is disappointed on his arrival there because its reality is totally different from that which he had imagined." European westward projection to the Americas framed the residents of each continent's understanding of the other, regardless of the direction of the gaze. Latin American intellectual confidence and self-definition, initially shaped by national identity building around independence, were further transformed in the twentieth century by events like the Cuban Revolution and other instances of defiant Latin American self-assertion in the face of global opprobrium or resistance. The American continent, in such projects, symbolizes the future of humanity, free to realize itself—although, ironically, the utopian vision of America had long been established in Eurocentric projections of European desire and lack.

The Idea of Mexico: Text and Context

For Mexicans themselves, certain aspects of the colonial past became one source for the development of national narratives, including on the one hand repudiation of empire and on the other adoptions of practices and absorption of values generated in the colonial era and incorporated into concepts of Mexicanness. This section explores some of these tensions in Mexican uses of historical narrative in national identity, and Mexico's external projection to tourists and travelers and how that too is tied up with historical contingencies.

Thus, alongside destination marketing, popular culture, and news media, the idea of Mexico in Spain and associated expectations and desires requires returning to the ways a sense of place builds through stories, accreted over a long time, which can't be erased overnight but only incrementally retold, recontextualized, or brought to new audiences. Travel practices themselves and the processes of their narration are not only affected by economic conditions but also by cultural shifts. After the colonial era, Latin America understood *from* Latin America was one of the most powerful forces reshaping the idea of America in the context of globalism, power, and representation. "The most fundamental transformation of the intellectual space at the end of the twentieth century is taking place because of the configuration of critical subaltern thinking as both an oppositional practice in the public sphere and a theoretical and epistemological transformation of the academy" (Mignolo 2000, 95). This oppositionality itself becomes connected to the imagining of place, and attempts to reject existing dichotomies and assumed logics, especially in contrast to the colonial discursive systems that were more dominant in the past, are still complicated by the accreted weight of ideas of place and difference, and how these reinforce global inequality. Furthermore, the turn toward interculturality brought about by such critical modes of thought strengthened the visibility of the other, "a necessity to resignify cultures that had been excluded from history and from intercultural dialogues" (Chávez 2015, 168).[17] However, the very mechanisms of intercultural dialogue are constantly at risk of cooption in the service of "re-coloniality" or instrumentalization for so-called ethnic neoliberalism, as argued by Catherine Walsh (2009). Travel literature itself, to the extent that it struggles to escape from an impulse to definition and categorization—either negative *or* positive as we see below in the example of neo-colonial primitivism, reinforces the logics underpinning an unequal world system.

In a discussion of the Ángel Rama's *ciudad letrada* and the genealogy of literary production in Latin America, Beverley (1999, 8) asks whether "literature was functionally implicated in the formation of both colonial and postcolonial elites in Latin America." This intertwining of writing and the reproduction of social inequality puts in question whether there can be a literature of popular democratization. Literature is ideological, and literature that speaks to the idea of place also posits forms of geographically situated cultural identity—

whether in national foundation texts of Latin American self-definition or in Latin America seen from outside, such as in travel writing of any era. Whether these forms are naturalized or supposed to be historically contingent and collectively constructed reveals the kinds of ideological practices woven into the act of writing.

The other complication arises directly from locating Latin America's self-definition within the sphere of culture or society. Conflating Latin American ontologies with literature and representation repeats the persistent idealization of writing that has so pervaded Eurocentric historiography and social theory, and almost always in ways that exclude the unspeakable excess, "that which cannot be adequately inscribed in the literary text—that is, the *preliterary* and therefore unrepresentable" (Beverley 1999, 58). It is necessary to hold on to this idea of Latin America as a space of postcolonial difference that creates its own specific self-enunciations and ideas of the consequences of modernity and globalization, yet simultaneously understand that literature is an intrinsically problematic sphere for the performance of identity. This suggests the limits of the text as a representation of place and the limits of writing as a process of inscribing place-image within discursive systems of meaning that cannot be separated from global regimes of power. Travelers and writers encounter opacities that resist their interpretation, that create contradictions in the spaces between their framework for understanding Mexico, their process of narrativization, and the material conditions of their journey.

Carlos Monsiváis's essay "Travelers in Mexico" (1984) tracks changes in travelers' perceptions of Mexicanness in response to political and social upheaval, and the ways their symbolic uses for the place often support their home countries' more materially profitable uses.[18] Monsiváis cites different concepts of Mexico prevalent in travel narratives of different periods, some common to the travel writing of the time and some specific to Mexico. The former generalized tropes include the supposed authority of the nonpartisan outsider, and the traveler as representative and arbiter of civilization (57–58; 65). The latter particular to Mexico include the integration of humanity into the landscape; the objectification of Mexican people as suffering bodies without agency; and the attraction-repulsion of the primitive (50; 52). I argue that these are not unique to Mexico, but constitute forms of reinscription of neocolonial hierarchies and can be found in a wide range of contemporary travel writing. Neocolonialist primitivism—and the attraction to the supposedly unmediated relationship to the natural world—is the direct antecedent of fantasies of authenticity that underpin the antitourism current in postglobalization travel. Authenticity myths require freezing the other in a state of instinct, be it Edenic innocence or bestial violence, and permit the consumption of blood and cruelty as spectacles to alleviate existential ennui. In contemporary travel texts, this appears as "the scrutiny of 'the primitive' as an attempt to rediscover values supposedly lost in developed societies" (Unceta Satrústegui 2005, 196).[19] Monsiváis's (1984, 61) useful distinction is the one travelers make between the Mexicans with whom privileged travelers interact, and indigenous Mexican people, often reduced to signs without agency. This signification of indigeneity and difference is one dimension of what Sofía Reding (2009, 66–67) describes as travel writing's ongoing tendency to "negate the humanity of the Other believing this attitude supports the security of a system that in reality leads towards the abandonment of one's own humanity," reproducing the hierarchical logics of empire but now in defense of capital.[20]

Daniel Cooper Alarcón's *The Aztec Palimpsest: Mexico in the Modern Imagination* (1997) further updates travelers' uses of Mexico. Cooper Alarcón expands the frame of reference to interrogate the interconnectedness of *ideas* about place and their material consequences via political mobilization and tourism economies. Though *The Aztec Palimpsest* establishes the reinscription of coloniality in some external representations from nearer the end of the twentieth century, the contemporary source material is relatively little analyzed, though it is suggestive of the coloniality of global capitalism. As in José Rabasa's *Inventing America* (1993), though here more explicitly, the central idea of Cooper Alarcón's work is the palimpsest as a construct for understanding the way discourses around place work through and overlay existing images and texts, altering rather than replacing. Cooper Alarcón (1997, 93) suggests that the controlling image of Mexico in English-language discourse is that of the Infernal Paradise, a thematic commonality linking discourses enacted through "literary works, scholarship, historiography, journalism, cinema, photography, and tourism." His approach is influenced by both Said's interpretation of hegemonic groups' discursive manipulation of the other, and Pratt's analyses of the selective uses of culture for the limits of a unidirectional understanding of power. Michel de Certeau (1984) also offers support for the ambiguities of the cultural uses of otherness, which may have unexpected operations and effects despite or even because of the incorporation therein of colonial discourses. These antecedents provide a framework for Cooper Alarcón's resultant analysis of "history, cultural identity, ethnicity, literature and politics *in relationship to each other*" (xvi; original emphasis). *The Aztec Palimpsest* tracks some of the links in this discursive network, such as the reinscription of colonial discourses and recirculation of colonial motifs in nineteenth-century travel writing and the way postcolonial travel literature can still use the language of colonialism to play out European and Anglo-American cultural superiority and indirect power (42; 50). Along similar lines, Lindsay (2009, 1–2) notes Latin America's present vacillation, at least in the European imaginary, between roles as a distant tourism paradise and a continental human rights emergency. Cooper Alarcón's study of persistent tropes of Mexicanness carefully interweaves texts with material actions and consequences. Place-image has a huge impact on the way both visitors and inhabitants of the place can exist within it. Just one of the obvious channels for this impact is the way discursive constructions of place inevitably influence national elites, such as those with a major role in directing Mexican tourism policy. "Literature and other discourses produced outside the Third World determine what will be perceived by the tourist as culturally authentic, and with tourism appearing more and more as an economic panacea to developing nations, there is tremendous pressure to adapt their cultures to the discursive constructs created of them by the First World" (Cooper Alarcón, 176).

In this kind of process of economic adaptation to cultural tropes, we can see both the rearticulation of primitivism in neocolonial authenticity myths and the potential commodification of processes of interculturality mentioned above. In addition to Cooper Alarcón's insistence on the importance of Mexican as well as foreign actors, and the consequences for Mexicans of discourses of Mexicanness, useful from his work is the exploration of the simultaneous coexistence of multiple myths. This multiplicity functions not only at the level of discourse, and not only in tourist promotion to niche markets nor the textual interventions of novels, films, or travel writing itself, but also in the minds of individual travelers, who do not necessarily construct a single monolithic image but rather layer their experiences with their expectations to formulate a subjective—and contingent—narrative sense of place. Travel writing's (sometimes unrealized) potential to dwell in contradiction and observe without defining is one of its genuine intercultural possibilities.

The transatlantic space between Spain and Mexico must be considered in symbolic terms in addition to the consequences of migration, cultural collaboration, and tourism management. There are many elements of broader myths of Mexicanness that resonate in Spain much as they do elsewhere, such as indigenism and pre-Columbian history as foundations for claims about national character, but the uses of ethnic and racial difference are also complicated by the specific histories the countries share. Approaches to Mexico from Spain must also deal with Spanish historical culpability, whether that be through self-reflexive critique or through the evocation of common culture. This second possibility is a reinscription of the Occidentalism Mignolo argues is at the heart of Europe's westward expansion, in which the Americas were perceived as an offshoot or daughter of Europe rather than an oppositional other as was the case with Asia. Ángela Pérez Mejía (2004) also attributes the shaping of the idea of America in more recent centuries to the influence of empiricism in European thought, as the scientific projects that were attached to the expansionist projects of later colonialism reimagined the meaning of places via the classification of the natural world.[21] "The territory of America had become, along with Africa and Australia, the location *par excellence* of nature, and it was necessary to discuss this location in order to shape an idea of the cosmos" (15). The two conceptualizations, as cultural offshoot and as location of nature, continue to resonate in contemporary descriptions of Mexico. Historical sites like museums and the architecture of colonial towns, for Spanish travelers, are explicitly connected to their own national history. Environmental hermeneutics are more complex, bringing to bear the projection of abundance for exploitation that underpinned the colonial project and is reenacted in global capitalism, as well as the irreducibility of the world beyond human signification.

Gustav Siebenmann (2007) proposes several other factors influencing the image of Latin America that are particular to Spain and Spanish discourses around national identity, linguistic and ethnic community, and historical celebration and shame. These factors are framed in the context of social change and social stasis between the centenary events of 1892 and 1992, and hence how the idea of America was revised from the nineteenth century to the end of the twentieth. The key factors are economic and political migrations, the naming of transatlantic spaces, literary representations in Spain and the popular redefinitions of Latin America springing up around the Latin American Boom, and the centenaries themselves as symbolic markers of and catalysts for debate around Spanishness and Americanness. At the end of the nineteenth century, with the Spanish Empire in its death throes, Spanish representations of the Americas showed simultaneous resentment and insistent pro-Spanish triumphalism, as well as emergent discourses of postcolonial Spain-centric pan-Hispanism around Spain as *madre patria*, emphasizing Hispanic ethnocultural continuities and Iberian origins (Siebenmann 2007, 174–75, 179). Post-1898 pro-European social attitudes strengthen, and a vengeful/negative image of Latin America connected to the fates of Spanish emigrants in the period emerges; pro-Europe and anti-Latin American sentiments complicate the subsequent return of a discourse of genial brotherhood (176, 182, 193). By 1992, some of the anxiety had gone out of the idea of America, although the cooption of the centenary as part of a concerted year-long effort to project a particular modern Spanish identity was certainly cause for anxiety (among other critical reactions) in not only

Latin America but many parts of the world. Spain's progress does not erase ongoing Eurocentrism and the pernicious implications of persistent pan-Hispanism for Spanish-Latin American encounters, nor the extent to which Spanish-proposed concepts of fraternity elide material differences between Spain and Latin America. The gradual increase in usage of *América Latina* as a term over *Ibero-* or *Hispanoamérica* may, as John Chasteen (2001) suggests, carry some association with Latin America's and particularly Mexico's Francophilia. *Hispano-* and *Iberoamérica* on the other hand evoke greater linguistic and cultural continuity that assists with the constitution of a pan-Hispanic global present—especially one centered on Spain. According to José Gaos (in Abellán 2009, 151) all these terms assume the inclusion of the European metropolis alongside the colonies. Indeed, Siebenmann argues that tensions over naming, and the historical implications and controversial origins of the various terms, by virtue of being situated in Spain's relationship to Latin America rather than taking the lead from debates within Latin America itself, suggest implicit denial of America's right to self-denomination (180). Siebenmann largely attributes the change in usage to interpersonal contact, such as the presence of Latin American migrants in Spain, while acknowledging that migrants also triggered new prejudices and resentments, including new derogatory terms for Latin Americans such as *sudaca* and diminutive ones like *latinoché* (179, 193). This more recent interpersonal contact with the community, as well as hostility it engenders, is part of a longer history of mobility, one that has in contemporary Spain tended to favor a pro-Mexico vision of transatlantic migration in Spain. Though the number of Mexicans living in Span remains minimal in comparison to populations from other Latin American countries, so that historical contact retains greater weight compared to present contact, the perception of Mexicans is also impacted by personal experiences with Central and South American immigrants.

Spanish pro-Mexico sentiment is partially, as previously mentioned, an effect of Mexico's reception of Civil War refugees. This particular group of migrants is central to the emergence of the alternative concepts of belonging and displacement that reinforce pan-Hispanic fraternity, encapsulated in Gaos's term *transterrados* to describe the persons who experience a sense of familiarity in their new environment rather than absolute rupture and loss (Abellán 2009, 146). As Perea (1996, 21–22) is careful to point out, however, our understanding of the meaning of this event must be tempered by consideration of the many migrations in both directions before the 1930s, most notably the manner in which the idea of Mexico and Mexican-Spanish relations in Spain was altered by the active participation of Mexicans in Spain's intellectual and literary life in the decades before the Spanish Civil War. This augmented the profile of Mexican culture in Spain in the early twentieth century, but also embedded the specific concept of exile integration that was later so much to the benefit of Republicans in Mexico: "not to consider refugees as such nor maintain them on pensions, but to effectively assimilate them into the cultural life of the host nation, thus taking advantage of all their virtues.... The idea was to rescue the human qualities of the displaced, with all their professional and moral characteristics" (Perea 1996, 59).[22] Before even that most immediate moment of welcome and exchange, Perea traces a long history of Mexican and Spanish travelers, both transient and more permanent, who wrote with energy and passion about their host countries for engaged readers in both nations. This bidirectionality is also described by Faber (2002), well into the 1940s. As mentioned above, permanent migration is now relatively minor in comparison to flows from or to other countries; however, within a larger transatlantic intellectual community, the cultural and literary networks between Mexico and Spain remain very vibrant, with more weight for writers perhaps than for general recreational travelers. The Mexican-Spanish relationship can draw more on historical narrative and recreational or professional mobility than on cohabitation, such that cultural histories still play a major part in framing the experience of Spaniards in Mexico.

Alongside this cultural background on the idea of Mexico in Spain, understanding contemporary Spanish travel writing first requires understanding the role of travel writing in and about Latin America and the meaning of travel in literature. The essential background to analyzing travel writing is its fundamental taintedness with regards to power.[23] Geographies of cultural and economic difference bear the inheritance of historical power, and the politics of origin, mobility, and place shape both discursive and individual associations with the idea of travel. One element of Latin Americans' own relationships with travel arises from the traces of Eurocentrism—as well, of course, as the practical realities of global economic and political power—with which Latin American travelers must inevitably engage. Fernando Pérez Villalón (2004, 54) describes this dynamic: "The particularity of coming from non-central zones, of setting out from the periphery. The point of departure, thus, is a precariousness. The point of arrival may be another precariousness or a more stable zone, charged with history, known ahead of time for the aura of prestige conferred upon it by history, art and literature."[24]

This sense of the periphery, incomplete as such a conceptual geography must be, nevertheless retains some weight, which is greater as the traveler engages with precisely the hegemonic narratives most dependent on a center-periphery division, such as those around European history, art, and literature. Acknowledging the precariousness and contingency of the place of origin potentially also opens the Latin American traveler to some of the ambiguities and insecurities of self that constitute the most productive encounter with otherness and that may be less accessible from a European point of departure, at least when Europeanness is conflated with a sense of ontological security. It is telling that it was possible for a Latin American traveler, Luis Oyarzún (in Pérez Villalón 2004, 67), to write in the mid-twentieth century, "I have felt in Europe as a dominant characteristic the presence of history, which gives meaning and perspective to the present, as mediocre as this might be. As such a thing is totally unknown to us in America, it provokes in the American's soul the most violent and definitive experience."[25]

More telling still is Pérez Villalón himself, in 2004, accepting Oyarzún's understanding of history. This European historiography is steeped in the assumptions of modernity with its grand narrative of progress, and perpetuates, when the journey is performed in the other direction, the dangerous illusion of a history-less America. This same illusion is implied in the following statement by José Luis Abellán (2009, 37): "Effectively, for a European arriving in America, the sensation of liberation from a historical past is enormous."[26] In both statements the prejudice toward understanding history through its visible presence in the built environment—buildings, museums, and so on—and through national narratives—the story of the Spanish or European people—is carried to a pernicious conclusion. The persistent trope of a different American relationship to literature and a difference in sense of origin plays into the dynamics of transatlantic encounter from both directions. Even supposing an equivalency in the meaning of travel as both concept and practice in Latin America and other places is dangerous. Lindsay (2009, 51) traces the hybridity of travel writing and travel practices as they have been enacted in Latin America, merging politics, leisure, self-discovery, ethnography, and consumption. The forms of hybridity are specific, just as they are specific in Spain, and respond to a historically constituted cultural value of mobility and of the sense of origin.

Given the slipperiness of travel as a concept in any time and place, there are particular elements of the Latin American relationship to mobility that also inflect the way non-Latin Americans' narratives about America should be understood, since they too are partial producers of American places. One significant element is the impact that outside representations have had on the image of places, including the transatlantic histories and marketing and media already mentioned, as well as other forms of representation. The gaze of outsiders has significantly contributed to mythologies of Mexicanness, especially of key sites. There are two sides to this mythologization: its influence on the idea of the Americas for Europeans, and the effect of mythologization of places for the way Americans themselves engage with those places. Some of the instability around the idea of America comes from its origins in the usage of America as a paradigm shift in Europe and evolution of the same as discussed in the previous chapter. "'America' is the product of the European historical story that tried to assimilate the new territories at the expense of the Aboriginal populations, which, translated into more practical terms, configures America as an immense surface of resource-rich lands with abundant cheap labour" (Abellán 2009, 12).[27] The power dynamic in the centuries after the initial encounter between Spain and America remained extremely unbalanced, even after independence, early stage decolonization, and the resultant shift in global polarities. Furthermore, many of the structures and conceptualizations of the colonial era were such that following independence from Spain "an elite of 'Creoles' or 'natives' took power and reproduced the patterns implanted by colonial rulers" (Mignolo 2003, 101). The reinforcement of a colonialist vision of Latin America came by way of textual revisiting of colonial tropes, for example by nineteenth-century travelers in their nineteenth-century works on Latin America, and more pervasively through the British and French practices of informal empire in cultural, commercial, and—more surreptitiously—political spheres. Interventionism, persisting through the imperialist maneuvers of the United States that were then in their infancy and that subsequently mutated but never subsided, significantly impeded Latin America's establishment of a clear space for self-definition and self-representation.

Postindependence and then postrevolutionary Mexico produced powerful narratives of distinctive national identity, however these continued to interact in peculiar ways with the heritage of empire, and not only in the hierarchical and racial underpinnings of its social organization. For example, Mexican nationalist engagement with modernism reworks tropes of primitivism, close contact with nature, and the evocation of a fundamental psychological sorrow in *mestizo* and indigenous souls. Such exaltations of pre-Columbian heritage and new indigenism owe some debt to the formulations of Mexico built up by past arrivals to its shores. Even the language a Mexican philosopher like Alfonso Reyes uses to characterize the project before American nations is redolent with European constructions of America: "Our America must live as if it were always preparing itself to realize the dream that its discovery triggered in the thinkers of Europe: the dream of utopia, of the happy republic" (in Abellán 2009, 161).[28] America, in this model, is the future, but such an evocation of the future rests upon the acceptance of European history as a plausibly universal past. The overwhelming influence of the outside gaze in the narrativization of Latin America contributes to the reticence with which Latin American writers themselves write travel stories. The problematic connections between travel writing and global systems of inequality and domination inevitably drive the ambivalent relationship Mexican authors of travel chronicles have with the genre, simultaneously denying it and participating in it while incorporating an occasionally uneasy mesh of postmodern and postcolonial strategies (Pitman 2008). The degree to which Spanish travelers manifest similar unease demonstrates their capacity—and contemporary travel writing's capacity as a genre—to critically unsettle its own established cultural modalities in light of the real linkage between travel and domination.

All contemporary travel writing is an intertextual negotiation, responding explicitly or implicitly to existing images and ideas, and the mythologization of Latin American places has played a major role in the subsequent function of those places both materially and symbolically. As discussed with reference to the work of Cooper Alarcón, Mexican state and private tourism operators actively manipulate myths of Mexicanness, but these myths have also had a huge influence on literary traditions, including the emergence of Mexican national literatures. Sites described in travel writing, according to Lindsay (2009, 18), accrue "dense layers of textuality" that are reinforced by repetitions of the kind mentioned in nineteenth-century writing. As myths around specific identifiable sites within Mexico grow stronger, their imaginative representation outside Mexico begins to stand in for the whole nation, its sprawling geography and cultural diversity dissolved into the kind of imagistic brevity that is simpler to hold in one's mind. One of the strongest emergent myths of Mexico coming into the twenty-first century is narcoterror Mexico, a Mexico of violence and danger. It is not entirely new; part of the lure of the exotic has always been the edge of danger, and the postglobalization fantasy of authenticity, as already suggested, implies popping the safety bubble that cushions and numbs the privileged. The elevation of narcoterror stories to the forefront of the global consciousness of Mexico tends to reinscribe the power differential and sense of superiority always implied by danger and difference.[29] Suffering has always been a marker of the transformative journey, but it has now become part of traveler-consumer choice. Chapter 4's discussion of Semprún's *Viajes desaconsejables* further explores how the fetishizing of danger intersects with the production and consumption of certain kinds of contemporary travel narratives. Similarly, analysis of Armada and Arranz's *El rumor de la frontera* delineates some of the ways Mexico, via its multifaceted border zone, operates within a global discourse of violence, trouble, and the trafficking of drugs, sex, and other fantasies. Tourism development, often presented in official discourse in purely pro-growth economic terms, almost inevitably incorporates undesirable impacts, especially at the local levels and in poorer nations in which the profit capture is most extreme, with negligible employment opportunities and income available to residents nearby. It is common for communities to be displaced and domestic migrants brought in from other parts of the country, traditional local economies to be eroded or completely destroyed, and the associated informal and black economies that follow tourist dollars to rapidly gain power, especially over lives of increasing precarity. The displacement of previous modes of subsistence and the growth of informal as well as entirely illegal tourism-adjacent industries combine to draw vulnerable populations into drug and sex tourism, including pedophile tourism, while reducing the stability and connectedness of home communities increasingly plagued by violence and by alcohol and drug abuse themselves.[30] The disparity between all-inclusive touristic luxury and peripheral service and informal work is quite marked. However, other forms of tourism are not exempt from fostering exploitative and outright criminal activities either. Indeed, in certain cases poverty and crime themselves become the object of consumption, as they stand in for authenticity in an illusory opposition between resort and slum.

The exoticization of danger is just one semiotic field among many that come into play in destination image and, correspondingly, travel writing, wherein the external gaze works to solidify relations of inequality. Abellán (2009, 245–46) locates the origin of contemporary European hunger for the exotic and different as a source of creative energy during the decadence of interwar European civilization. Drawing on Enrique Dussel, however, he also suggests that it provoked a more serious accounting for global inequality and questions of power in Latin America and elsewhere—a dynamic echoed more recently in the connections between Latin America and the emergence of a post-Franco historical consciousness in Spain. This is an example of the ways imperial or neo-imperial complicity is too blunt a conceptualization for the function of texts, even those produced from an apparent position of power. Lindsay (2009, 98) highlights in political texts, for example, the dual effects of the desire to possess and utilize knowledge of people and places alongside the creation of testimony and archive.

Some characteristics of the idea of Mexico that seem to constantly reappear with different features are not so easily connected to past and present structural inequalities. A sense of independent identity, which we see the complications of in the case of Mexican nationalism, has nevertheless been a defining feature of Latin Americans' own engagements with the idea of Latin America. Another of these features is internationalism, in constantly mutating forms. The Americas, since the conception of the world system in the sixteenth century through the connection of Eurasian and African trade to the newly accessible American economies, have had no exit from globalization, nor even a sustainable illusion of one. In some cases, this internationalism has taken the form of following trends from overseas and perpetuating local inferiority complexes, but in other moments it has been the source of a transformative sense of interconnectedness and solidarity—a dual uncertainty and potency that should not be oversimplified through developmentalist categorizations of global difference.

Latin Americans, with their shared histories (what Mignolo [2003] terms their "colonial difference"), shifting borders, continental exchanges of exiles and of migrants, common antagonists, and semi-common interests in the face of globalization, are building their own sense of a common America. It draws on local traditions of Bolivarianism, pan-Americanism, and historically variable ideological solidarities, but also on the functional patterns of political and economic exchange, family, and familiarity (as well, of course, as histories of internal conflict and war). Transnational continental mobility is a constant of life across the region. The late twentieth century saw the progressing democratization of Latin America, with a simultaneous expansion of the middle class; improvement in services, education, and health; and semifunctional integration of the representatives of previously destabilizing ideological extremes. In the early twenty-first century, then, it may be that the international orientation and transnational continental strategic vision of Latin Americans has the potential to be of enormous benefit for Latin Americans themselves.

For Mexico, the forms of its internationalism have been complicated by its location. Historically, Spanish- and Portuguese-speaking America presented a dichotomy with mostly anglophone North America. Mexico, however, has had the burden of defining the limits between the two, its border with the US both physically and conceptually extremely unstable. Mexican politicians have at times sought to position themselves as mediators, and often Mexican culture and Mexican people themselves are the filter through which ideas of the English-speaking and the Spanish-speaking Americas pass from one to the other. These circumstances also exclude Mexico from some of the continental regionalism to the south. Furthermore, the US itself is blurring the dichotomy (despite frequent nationalist political rhetoric), rising as it is through the ranks of the top five Spanish-speaking nations in terms of population and with its domestic and foreign policies increasingly driven (through both hostility and necessary integration) by the social reality of the consequences of this cultural mix inside its borders. Both these factors and significant structural interventions like the North American Free Trade Agreement (NAFTA) have served to contribute, according to Abellán (2009, 12–14), to the emergence of new regionalisms. Mexico is grouped with North rather than South America, and its fortunes tied more to the US and less to South American powers.[31] Mexico is caught between the sometimes disastrous consequences of its economic linkage to its northern neighbors and its conceptual "southernness" as a violent, poverty-ridden, and non-anglophone country, with the demands of both licit and illicit markets within the former serving to perpetuate the latter.

On top of these complex regional alliances and identities, Mexico has its own internal dynamics of mobility, community, and otherness. Lindsay (2009, 84) highlights one example with her exploration of the Mexican concept of *fuereñez*, applied to a stranger but not a foreigner. It is a way of referring to unknown others that disrupts some of the assumptions of cultural continuity inside a national whole and of foreignness defined mainly by borders or by ethnolinguistic difference. This is an example of a different kind of imagined community and rhetoric of exclusion. As with any other concept of identity, it is a local response to a specific situation with its own racial and class dimensions rather than a potentially universalizable theoretical abstraction. The shifting sense of Mexico's place, transnational ties, and the resonances of mobility and otherness inside Mexico's borders are conditions that necessarily underpin any understanding of travel to and writing about contemporary Mexico. The ways Mexicans themselves have responded to the compromised politics of travel writing provide some insight into the implications of representing Mexico in travel narrative. The role of travel writing in Mexico creates a framework for comparison for the analysis of travel writing from Spain *about* Mexico. Through this comparison, some differences in the experience of colonialism and modernity between Europe and Latin America come to the surface, differences that still underlie the representation of encounters in transatlantic spaces.

In describing the complex relationship Mexican writers themselves have to the travel writing genre, Pitman (2003, 57) writes of the "surplus of representations" that intervene in the construction and consumption of travel writing, particularly with reference to hyper-mythologized sites like Mexico City and others described by many travelers to Mexico. Features marking hyper-mythologized sites include intertextual references that create a map for the reader to understand spatial distance, and descriptions comparing visited sites with iconic places whether imagined, historical, or still familiar today. Modes of engagement with the travel genre by Mexican writers, with Iberian referents and responses to European artistic and literary traditions, also bring home the extent to which travel writing as a colonialist genre has required Mexicans—and other "periphery" dwellers—to deal with Europe and European worldviews, whether through the absorption of imposed categorizations or through more disruptive and critical responses. Pitman (2007) discusses the complexity of Mexican writers' responses to the influential—and often disparaging—accounts written by foreign travelers to their country, noting that they have contributed to reinforcing Mexico's role in the travel genre as host country rather than point of departure. Since the 1970s, different relationships to travel and travel writing have emerged inside Mexico, challenging aspects of the imperial legacy of the genre as well as its traditionally authoritative authorial voice.[32]

This challenge is not easily reduced to a local outcropping of postmodernism, which cannot be straightforwardly laid over Latin America given the context in which the concept was produced and its elisions regarding global power. Similar tactics are found in some anti-imperialist cultural maneuvers, encompassing rather a more generally contestatory attitude relating to both past and present subaltern experience, more in line with principles of critical subalternity or border thinking that disrupt the dichotomies and categories of thought inherited from Eurocentric modernity. This contestatory position opens Mexico's own travel writers to "more heterogeneous Mexican postnational identity, possibly including a more or less overtly political commentary on the effects of globalisation in the region, and on the relationship between self and other" (Pitman 2008, 96). This prescription, as Pitman acknowledges, is never entirely filled out, with most contemporary Mexican travel writing still acceding to the realist model. The genre remains mostly conservative, in Mexico as elsewhere, though uneasy combinations of postmodernist and postcolonialist sensibilities may manifest in response to the actual context of contemporary travel. Potentially critical positions emerge through the modes of narrative employed to engage with conditions of industrial tourism and globalized communications, as well as colonialism and Occidentalism and their legacies in the construction of a sense of globalized historical consciousness as well as belonging. In the process of exploring Mexican writing, however, Pitman has also identified some commonalities in travel writing in a posttourism world, strategies that apply to narratives written in different traditions, and indeed to the limits of looking at texts through national categories. "It is impossible to keep travel writers in a particular national box and to ascribe their tendencies and preferences solely to their national origin. The current chronotope foregrounds an increasingly complex dance of transcultural relationality" (Pitman 2008, 179). It is simplistic to define a corpus solely in terms of Spanish origin and Mexican destination, given the problematic significance of these categories when discussing global mobility and contemporary conceptions of community, identity, and location. For that reason, textual analysis should employ other models for thinking about Spanishness, Mexicanness, and place, such as through the contestability of borders and regions, the nation in relation to state power and in relation to transnational and global relations, and the individuated complexity of belonging to and moving through places expressed by different authors.

Through the histories of both travel and travel writing in Spain and Mexico we can see some of the features—both common and divergent—that have shaped travel as a practice and as a concept in and between these cultures. To approach the contemporary Spain-to-Mexico journey and its resonances in the narratives that describe it, the material influences on travel economies and touristic interventions in destination images have necessarily been combined with more abstract developments in travelers' geographical imagination. Travelers are complicit in reproducing inequalities and reinscribing privileges that influence whether travel writing as a practice only reinforces such power flows, or whether it has the potential to achieve a more complex and nuanced response. Shifts in the nature of travel and the possibilities of writing between Spain and Mexico explored in this chapter establish some terms of encounters for Spaniards in Mexico toward the end of the millennium, and the pre-existing ideas of Mexico, and of Spain, that shaped their recounting.

CHAPTER 2

Memory, Text, and Expectation

The changing Hispanic transatlantic, shifting modes of mobility and writing, and evolving embodied and literary ideas of Mexico and Spain are all important for understanding the interventions made by contemporary Spanish travel writers. Contemporary travel narrative is explored in relation to the material and economic dimensions of travel and the discursive structures that support that material and economic system. The detailed examples presented in this chapter, from books by Francisco Solano and Eduardo Jordá, show elements of the explicitly literary style of a strand of travel writing in the European tradition. Their narrative approaches, though different, both incorporate space for reflection on the writer's sense of self and offer reflective abstraction on the nature of the past through memory as well as historical thinking. This contrasts with many of the texts considered in later chapters, which connect ethnographic and reflexive modes of writing more explicitly to the effects of globality and subalternity in Latin America and also demonstrate some of the problematics of journalism and chronicles and commercial functions of professional travel writing. The relatively narrow autobiographical focus of Solano and Jordá and the fairly straightforward positioning of their works within literary travel writing is fruitful ground to explore their sense of Spanish (or otherwise) belonging, how memory relates to Spanish history and Spain as a point of origin through its democratizing,

Europeanizing late twentieth and early twenty-first century, and the elements of intimacy and of distance from Mexican experiences the writers present in their texts.

European writers demonstrate a wide range of modes of historical thinking, combined with politically engaged commentary or the submergence of ideological function that remains more possible for European writers, even after formal colonialism. Many contemporary travel narratives still mix defense and critique of European cultures, including the often-silenced underlying condition supposed by the economic privilege of access to self-actualization through international travel and to written authority. Silence regarding how rarefied travel and writing remain, on a global scale, has a normative effect regarding middle-class construction of the self. This is evidence of the economic class alignment between the international tourist market and the readership for travel literature as a popular genre. Indeed, the assumed equation of travel with freedom, as Holland and Huggan (1998, 4) have argued, obscures the economic privilege of voluntary mobility. It is important to recognize, however, that privilege does not equate to absolute freedom of thought and action. As Karen Lawrence (in Clark 1999b, 223) observes, "travel literature, by both men and women writers, explores not only political freedoms but also cultural constraints; it provides a kind of imaginative resistance to its own plot." The story the writer tells about one place almost always speaks on as profound a level of the stories they are not consciously telling: the story of their own origins, beliefs, and expectations, and the story of the others acting at the edges of their awareness. Terry Eagleton's ([1976] 2006, 89) comment springs to mind here—"ideology is present in the text in the form of its eloquent silences." The style, subject matter, and orientation the author selects deeply influence the way the intersecting cultures of Spain and Mexico can be imagined by the reader. A deeply personal narrative voice, frequent intertextual reference, and a preoccupation with memory may displace more structural critique. However, intertextuality and memory are not intrinsically depoliticizing and may provide a starting point for gently prompting reflection on historical origins of contemporary problems. Nevertheless, the tension between this potentiality and the consumption of travel and travel writing as products in a global tourism/culture economy remains.

In the same way the political utility of travel writing is submerged in a silent struggle over the meaning of what is described and remembered, so too the significance and impact of individual texts has shifted from earlier travel narrative forms, such as utilitarian intervention in debates over government, as was the case in narratives from the Spanish colonies directed back to the monarch and the ruling class, or scientific writing that assumes the possibility of neutral observer. Travel writing as a popular contemporary genre belongs to the public sphere of media and publishing, where travel narratives, as a form of entertainment, must compete for attention with each other and with all the other noise in which global consumers are constantly immersed. This guarantees contemporary travel narratives neither the audience and influence over place-image of other media like film and television or news, nor a memorable place in the tradition of travel literature given the proliferation of publishing outlets and texts. Their individual impact may be limited. With a textured analysis of the terms of the encounters they describe, however, they can express some of the discursive tensions and conditions of mobility that are played out across cultures and locations. Perspectives from human geography suggest alternative ways of thinking about place. Built and natural environments interact with the description of those environments, their action upon those who inhabit them, and the way inhabitants and environment influence and reconstitute each other. Adams, Hoelscher, and Till's (2001, xiv) concept of "textures of place," for example, "refers not only to surfaces, processes, and structures, but also to communication acts and the multiple contexts that create and are constituted by place." In this context, understanding the significance of contemporary travel narratives involves interrogating the influential and contested ideas about places as well as the historical and material processes that have gone into their creation.

Another shift is the unrepeatability of earlier periods' narratives of exploration and first encounter, nearly impossible in the twentieth and twenty-first centuries. Since at least the early twentieth century, travel writing has been suffused with a sense of its own tradition and nostalgia for a supposedly more adventurous past. The adventure stories written at a time when novelty was still perceived as possible came to define the genre of travel writing in a way that contradicts much contemporary touristic experience. This creates curious disjunctions in contemporary texts between the norms of chronological, exploratory narrative structure and traveler identity construction inherited from past travel stories, and the intertextuality and referential embeddedness that shapes the representation of place today. International travel has also shifted from being the domain of few to the domain of many, and the sensation of following behind is reinforced by the hundreds of fellow travelers alongside at every stage of the journey, whether they are personally present or their traces visible in the infrastructure and information that surround every destination. "In the age of mass tourism—and saturation advertising—practically everything that has been said or written about travel and its benefits has long since become a cliché" (Scurrah 1992, 23). New communications technologies have created an environment in which home can constantly intrude upon the experience of away, and total departures—disconnection from all the structures of everyday life—require an act of voluntary rupture. First anythings are now much harder to achieve, one of the likely causes of the rise of personal reflection as a defining theme over the traditional themes of trade, discovery, and novelty. This sense of repetition acts in concert with the shifts in European thought around questions such as social good versus individual happiness and more general postsecularization destabilizations of cosmologies and ethics. Authenticity of experience is now often defined through the uniqueness of the character projected by the writer rather than through the distinctiveness of their experience as such, and it is the effect of this projection in the work of Solano and Jordá that is a primary preoccupation of this chapter.

From this shift to personal reflection and a sense of destinations as known, so that experiences of place are mediated by the experiences of others, and where histories have been reinvented in changing circumstances, we can begin to understand the parameters for contemporary travel writing. The immediate literary context of the texts is also an important factor. Of books published in the last few decades about travels in Mexico, the majority are in English by American and other anglophone writers. The attention given to this abundance often overshadows works in Spanish, especially those by Mexican authors themselves but also by visitors from Spain and other parts of Latin America. During this period in Spain, since the death of Franco and democratization, travel writers have written more about their geographical neighbors in Europe and Africa than their cultural neighbors in Latin America, reflecting both the immediate geographical and sociopolitical environment and perhaps also the lingering sense of Latin America as a space in which to act, not to be acted upon. Many contemporary Spanish travel books are by novelists and journalists who make writing their profession, with a smaller number of targeted travel books focusing on adventure sports, aid work, crime, or other special interest topics to produce narratives with a niche audience incorporating travel readers as well as readers from other markets. There is also a small subgenre of diplomatic memoirs by Spain's ambassadors, which often discuss postings in Latin America including Mexico, but in ways that are of limited relevance to broader audiences interested mainly in the experience of travel.[1] Similarly, other kinds of memoir such as those dealing with stories of migration and permanent relocation also lack the transience and imminent return central for the home readership. In this and subsequent chapters, I focus on works with a limited definition of travel.

Vanishing Empires: Francisco Solano in the Postcolonial Present

Bajo las nubes de México (2001), or Beneath Mexican clouds, is among the more prominent recent works by Spaniards on travels in Mexico. *Bajo las nubes* incorporates an unusual depth of historical context and consciously engages with the history of representation of Mexico, presenting an alternative to other, perhaps more prevalent, modes of encounter in travel writing. This dual interest in historical contextualization and in the history of stories and images of place permits us to interrogate what Solano has to say about Mexico, and in the same way, what his ideas about Mexico tell us of his idea of Europe, of Spain, and the consequent space of possibility enacted in travel from Spain to Mexico. "México," he writes, "wants to seem like Europe, but Europe shows only an empty mirror, a frame without glass that reflects the face of domination" (90).[2] The mirror is a frequent metaphor for the relationship with the other, recognizing that sense of self (and of group identity) does not emerge only from self-recognition but also from the approach to difference. The mirror in such adaptive metaphors thus becomes both unreliable instrument and permeable surface, the distortions or clarity of which depend on surroundings and on viewer. This insists on relational identity, and though Solano's usage is a pessimistic characterization of the limitations of Eurocentric cultural orientation, it does highlight the transatlantic orientations in the constructions of culture. Carlos Fuentes' (1992) iconic use of the mirror metaphor to characterize cultural exchange between Spain and the Americas has distorted identity narratives. However, the mirror metaphor also identifies possibilities for meaningful self-reflection through historicized recognition of the other, and the self in the other. We see ourselves only because of and through others, and, Fuentes might argue, through the mirrors of history and literature together, and the confluences that disappear in, for example, limited nationalist conceptualizations of identity. Solano's empty mirror is one of many and multiplying mirrors, mirrors that themselves look "from the Americas to the Mediterranean, and from the Mediterranean to the Americas," as Fuentes (1992, 12) essayed.[3]

Solano's residence in Madrid and origins in Burgos in Spain's central north create another mirror or multiplied perspective for comparison with writers whose regional homeland diverges from centrist cultural myths of Spain, such as Catalonian writers (well-represented in publishing and media industries in Spain), or authors from the Canary Islands without even territorial contiguity. Distance, of course, does not guarantee a position of critical marginality in response to stories of Spanish history and Spain's place in the world, but it does introduce an extra tension that may act against monocultural conceptions of Spain. Principally a writer of prose fiction, Solano's novels and short stories play with questions of narrative reliability and fractured realities, as well as engaging structurally and stylistically with the nature of different kinds of texts (letters, memoir, fiction). These persistent interests in his wider oeuvre offer some context for his engagement with notions of verisimilitude, reflexivity, and textuality in the narrative nonfiction work *Bajo las nubes de México*.

Part of understanding historical awareness in Solano's writing pertains to the context of destabilizations of Spanish cultural identity and national narrative. This is a topic in which he has shown interest at least since his 2008 novel *Tambores de ejecución*, with its early postdictatorship setting. Spain itself is still in the middle of a struggle over history. At the center of this struggle is the lingering damage caused by the Civil War and its aftermath. However, wherever there is a revision of national narrative, broader questions come into play. These are questions not only of what precisely has happened, but also of what came before and what will come after. In short, what do Spaniards themselves believe their country to be? To enhance analysis of the work of historical imagination in *Bajo las nubes*, it is helpful to trace some of the tensions and destabilizing factors inflecting contemporary discourses of Spanishness. This instability is a catalyst for transforming possibilities of historical thinking and awareness of otherness for Spaniards both inside and outside of Spain.

The still-passionate debate in contemporary Spain over the blackouts and silences of the Civil War and of Spain under Franco is vital for understanding Spain's recent history and current identity, and the lingering damage caused by the destruction and division of Spain's twentieth century—destructive to the imagination as well as the lives of millions. What such a public interrogation of the past can also produce, however, is a set of tools for rethinking other historical discourses. Nationalist ideologies rely on mythologizing interpretations of a country's unifying national history, and this story, of glory or violence or both, is what is at stake in contemporary Spanish debates about history. Spanish travel writing about

Latin America offers one arena of confrontation between twenty-first-century Spaniards and their sense of the past, as the decision to write encounter creates the potential for a process of reflection on the various spaces inside Spain's borders as homelands, and the incongruity of experience with Spain's own national narratives, or with prevailing narratives of globalization as progress. This process of reflection is not intrinsically negative. It does not demand a constant posture of apology nor perpetual burden of shame or blame for the past, despite the way some critics choose to characterize it. The most meaningful historical reflection engages as much with the present, in the case of travel writing through the postcolonial, late-capitalist realities of host environments. Travelers may perceive their own roles in those environments and in some cases like Solano's, explicitly interpret the significance of both history and myth-making to a sense of cultural identity.

In the first years after the death of Franco an impetus to silence and forgetting largely prevailed in the public sphere. Over the years, however, a powerful will to reveal and reframe Civil War and dictatorship stories arose. Debates on these questions have not been limited to discussions of the facts and unknowns of Spain's twentieth-century war crimes, but also extend to a sense of Spain's historical conscience and national story. When some new action or discovery brings the controversy to the fore, the divided ideological positions and the historical premises upon which such positions are based compete for space in public discourse. Over questions like recovering and identifying remains of the Civil War dead, sentiments vary from vindication to inflammation. Relevant to how such contention over history triggers broader modes of engagement with historical stories, however, is the way that critics of such projects quite often expand their interpretation so the new developments constitute an attack on both living people and on a whole way of thinking about Spain's past, associating Civil War histories with the history of conquest and empire, as well as with the postcolonial turmoil of Spanish-speaking American states. One commenter on a news forum wrote sarcastically, "Fine, when we're done with this we'll start with the Hispano-American genocide, I think we'll have to seek the death certificate of Hernán Cortés" (*El país* online, October 16, 2008).[4] This hyperbolic remark suggests a level of recognition that historical debates encompass more than questions of fact and geographical location of bodies. Excavating one submerged trauma creates a potential space for many competing historical narratives. Another commenter compared Spain's direction to that of "third world socialist banana republics where the Justice system is at the service of politics."[5] This connects Spain's left to extremist regimes that spring up, funnily enough, in environments with entrenched cultures of impunity. At the wilder end, right-wing readers manifested willingness to launch back into open conflict, one calling for "an urgent cleansing of the principal institutions of the nation."[6] Another declared, "we're ready to once again confront the heirs of terror."[7] Such heated remarks manifest the immediacy and importance of the debate over the interpretation of history in Spain. The debate over Spain's national story is demonstrably not limited to the Civil War, but also encompasses other events—including the *leyenda negra* as well as the transnational political implications of ideological swings and processes of democratization in Latin America. In relation to these, Spain's own history and supposedly fraternal present in Latin America is variously mobilized by competing interests at different moments to cover Spain in glory or to cover her in shame. The role of these interpretations in constituting nationalist and other narratives of Spanishness and legitimizing particular regimes was already mentioned in the preceding chapter, but in linking this relationship to questions of memory and historical thinking in contemporary travel writing, it is possible to see historical narratives intersect with contemporary political discourse and individual belonging and alienation, which are fundamental to understanding the dynamics of encounters with otherness.

The immediate example of identifying war crimes is connected to larger questions about what kinds of stories Spaniards choose to use to define their history. These ongoing controversies in Spain are clearly not the focus of this book. Nevertheless, the last few decades of changing and heavily contested concepts of Spanish history are essential for understanding popular ideas of Spain's past. There is a link between the battle over the nation's historical conscience and the conscience—as Spaniards in Hispanic America, as tourists in global capitalism, as writers projecting the authority to describe—of contemporary travelers narrating their encounters with contemporary Latin America. The present interest in human rights and the memory of violence stemmed at least in part from the international response to the collapse of Latin American dictatorships, which activated a livelier discussion of social justice and an antenna and vocabulary for suffering and trauma. To make a connection between debates about history in Spain and Latin American democratization and movements for justice simply reflects the quite real and practical link between Spain's intervention in and engagement with those transitions and the stirring of action on questions of Spain's own trauma and democratization.

Spanish travel writers' changing historical consciousness, and conscience, is partly expressed in the way their European understandings frame *mestizo* and indigenous cultures and the economic and political implications of racial divisions in the Americas in relation to the history of globalization, and partly in the way Spain itself is mobilized (or ignored) in interpreting experience. Travel writing is the expression of a singular—though not unitary—subject's engagement with the surrounding world, and as such no single narrative aligns perfectly with an abstract political theory or with the negotiations involved in developing a conscious conception of history. Instead, the phenomenology of travel is one space for both embodying and representing historical consciousness and awareness of the geopolitics of power. Hughes (2004, xi) writes of the limit point of the journey that the traveler's "stories take on form in the expectation of the audience he has left and to which he must return. Without that place which does not change, what need is there for story?" (I note the gendered dimensions of imagining an unchanging hearth, presumably alongside a patient Penelope, awaiting the return of the explicitly male voyager—a trope that retains much potency in cultural imaginings of the voyage.) In the work of Francisco Solano, the unstable sense of home as grounding for historical consciousness relates to the acknowledgment or elision of

Spain's past in America and specifically Mexico, the kinds of story it is capable of generating, and what kind of alternative modes of encounter such examples present.

The other important component of Solano's historical consciousness is engagement with representation and discourses of Mexicanness. The two threads—imagined Mexico and unstable Spain—twine together to inform his interpretation of sites in Mexico where, at least for him, history rises to the surface and present and past mingle. When speaking of vanishing empires, the title of this section, it is to evoke this appearance and disappearance of history and the choices the writer makes in coming to terms with it, as well as Spain's crisis of identity with the loss of the last of her colonies, a crisis that was a factor in the rise of the competing ideologies of participants in the Civil War. In *Bajo las nubes*, Mexico's change of government in 2000—the first since the Revolution—echoes the fall of empires, and is a revelation both of the failures and corruption of what has gone before and of the capacity of people to imagine something better. As he puts it, "The imagination projects brighter spaces, a more just life, better-shared riches, and a way of laughing that is no longer sarcastic" (93).[8] Solano describes here "the fall of hegemony."[9] Though the result may not have been unreservedly positive, the formulation recalls both Spain post-Franco and earlier falls—the Mexican Revolution, independence from Spain, symbols of freedom and hope quite distinct from Solano's representation of the impact of imperial and hegemonic government, both of which he frequently refers to in his comments on Mexican history.

Of course, travel writing does not necessarily foster consistency or the maintenance of considered theses throughout books or even scenes. Solano occasionally employs historical clichés, like Cortés' small band conquering the mighty Aztec and Cortés burning the ships at Veracruz to prevent retreat. However, these are usually balanced by shifts in point-of-view to take in alternative perspectives, such as his comments about Mexican Spanish's "melody of the Spanish of the Golden Age,"[10] which may seem trite but are in equilibrium with the space he gives to other languages such as Náhuatl and his descriptions of languages as spoken and alive. This contrasts with tendencies for travel writers to use dialect variation for comic portraits. He also employs some problematic and contested othering frameworks, such as that of Mexican nonlinear time as opposed to European "chronological, accumulative" time (57). He uses these mostly to interrogate the possibility of Europeans' confrontation with their own losses, with their attachment to and possession of land, and secular and commercial gods (28). By applying these concepts as tools to critique Europe, Solano is ameliorating somewhat Europeans' tendency to freeze Mexico and her peoples in a distant, unchanging time.[11] Indeed, in describing the ongoing confluence of peoples in the Oaxaca valley, Solano interprets it as a marker of the future than a frozen past, and not necessarily the dangerously Occidentalist future that posits America as daughter of European glories or as utopian laboratory. Oaxaca also represents for Solano "a state of awareness of what Mexico was before the Spaniards . . . of the colonial era . . . and of the present day" (139).[12] The past is not a distant land or finished story, but something that remains a part of immediate environments and experiences.

While Solano occasionally makes claims for the whole of Mexico, Mexican people, and culture, a reductive vision that is a virtually omnipresent feature of single destination travel writing, he also displays the capacity to recognize internal difference. This is regularly evident in his descriptions of different cities (the urban dominates the rural throughout the book), and most clearly expressed in Solano's description of the Yucatán, where he once again uses history to explain the present, in this case attributing the Yucatán's cultural difference and sense of distance from the rest of the Republic to the difficulty of its conquest, its separate government in the imperial era, and its geographical distance (188). All of this contributes to an environment that promotes an ongoing encounter between the European travelers and Mayan people, rather than the layers of *mestizo*, Americanized, and Europeanized cultures that intervene more markedly in other regions. Solano also, and this is perhaps even more rare, recognizes the extent to which tourism itself can neutralize this difference and act to erase the past when he comments on the souvenirs for sale at Palenque, which are identical at the Maya site to those at Aztec sites, and the vendors who are performing indigeneity but whose real stories are opaque to and elude the control of the traveler's gaze. "The arrows are the same as those for sale to tourists at the Calzada de los Muertos in Teotihuacán, 700 kilometers away; so it is fake Aztec craftwork and fake Maya craftwork, and I suspect that they are also fake Lacandones" (179).[13] It is disturbing that Solano establishes himself as an arbiter of the ethnic authenticity of the vendors; the promising effect however is the extent to which these people have a presence in Solano's story but are outside of the story's—and the writer's, and the reader's—ability to interpret and therefore define them in comfortable terms. Rather than a reinforcement of primitivist mystique, this kind of passage exposes something of the economic and cultural structures hidden beneath such mystique. Historical consciousness has also, as in this example, the potential to create new understandings of the tourist/host encounter and of the impact of tourism, which speaks to its productive rather than divisive potential.

One final example shows the extent to which historical consciousness influences the traveler's understanding of his present experience, as well as the histories of his destination and of his own country, to enable a kind of traveling with conscience. When he visits El Edén, a mine in the old silver region, he makes a direct link between Spanish imperial finances, "the silver they admired in Europe's salons" and the place where "six-year-old children exhausted themselves or fell dead in pools with coppery reflections" (71).[14] This is not designed to suggest that European travelers in postcolonial destinations must engage in acts of national flagellation and shame, but rather demonstrates the way Solano uses the horrors of the past to reflect on the present, to suggest for himself and his fellow travelers that this environment, where history surges up into the now, offers awareness, "a general understanding of the sufferings of the indigenous people. . . . That, and the sense of shame driving us not to show ourselves unworthy of their memory."[15] As Solano himself makes clear, it is not a petty bickering or a will to arouse bitterness and resentment that is at stake in interpreting history, despite what present-day critics in Spain's popular debate might imply, but the creation of a consciousness and a conscience that fundamentally underpins how we choose to behave now—in other words, the future, not just the past.

The history of suffering is, often enough, transformed into tourist spectacle, a process that can be perilous and that has the potential to evacuate the past of meaning; what historical consciousness offers is not the past as spectacle, but a sense of the interconnectedness of past and present and the importance of present actions in light of past wrongs. Solano explores his consciousness with a largely positive interweaving of history with present experience. Rarely enough for a travel writer, he recurs more to Mexico than to himself for his interpretive framework. Solano is a telling example because of this difference. *Bajo las nubes* has an unusually sustained engagement with the inheritance of history. Pratt (1992, 217–18) identified the contrasting tendency as "monarch-of-all-I-survey" scenes in contemporary travel writing, describing the manner in which writers often display a sense of power over their environment within their narration while simultaneously distancing themselves from responsibility for it:

> The impulse of these postcolonial metropolitan writers is to condemn what they see, trivialize it, and dissociate themselves utterly from it. It is as if there were no history tying the North American Theroux to Spanish America or the Italian Alberto Moravia to Africa, despite the fact that much of what they are lamenting is the depredations of western-induced dependency. There is perhaps a future implied in their texts, one of violence, by and against themselves.

These actual depredations will be discussed more in Chapter 3 with reference to the representation of contested geographies, conflict, and violence, but in the context of reflexivity and history in travel narration, Solano offers one partial counter example. For Spain, at present, the principal process of historical reconciliation is with the events of the Civil War and its aftermath, but no revision of history deals with events in isolation. The flexibility and will to actively interrogate the past and a citizenry with the tools to understand the impact of historical conflict on following generations are inseparable, and both collective and individual will is required to develop new relationships with not just domestic histories but with all histories of violence, including those being inscribed right now.

"UN VIAJE QUE HUYE DEL TÓPICO"?[16]

Following on from the way historical consciousness relates to a sense of Spain's past and present and a traveler's conscience as participant in a world with an interconnected global history, we arrive at the way Solano engages with the conflict and domination he experiences and encounters himself. This includes his engagement with the act of representation and with his reflexive sense of his own relationship to discourses of place and the power enacted through his narration. *Bajo las nubes* begins with a description of the writer as traveler, interrogating the significance of travel in an age of globalization and global mobility of people. Solano also references travel as commodity through the concept of "touristic emancipation" (16), referring to the prospect of relief from the routine and the weight of the roles played in everyday life. The introduction to the book also displays an unusual level of reflexivity as Solano considers the impact of the traveler's origins on the voyage, as well as his individual character (supposedly "reflective and austere") and his spatial orientation determined by his history of movement and of dwelling in the "chaotic geometry" (16) of Madrid and past movements beyond the borders of Spain.[17] (Outside of Europe, the only destinations directly mentioned in the narrative are Buenos Aires and Mexico.)

Solano's opening gambit also offers a glimpse of his expectations, or lack thereof, for the destination. His framing of his qualities as a traveler suggests rather an absence of temptation and a certain emphasis on his comfort in his own routine: "tends to sedentarism ... to repetition" (17).[18] Despite Solano's emphasis on physical mobility within this routine, through his description of everyday transit and self-image as a "walker on firm pavements ... metro and bus user ... pedestrian" (17) he does not assume the traditional stance of the travel writer as an unquiet wanderer, beginning from a position of lack and desire.[19] Most importantly, at various points throughout the book, Solano clarifies the conditions of his visit, his admission of class and economic advantage, of geographical distance. He also attempts to acknowledge the cultural capital of his informants.[20] He further recognizes that the popular visual symbols of Mexico, such as pyramids and *charros*, serve the image of the place but not necessarily its reality (18). (Due to the transformation of Spain into one of the world's premier tourist destinations in recent decades, as discussed in the previous chapter, this disjunction between the perceptions of the external market and the experience of the inhabitants may be especially evident to Spanish travelers.) Indeed, his conception is of "a country that multiplies itself," the interpretation of which depends very much on the point of view of the teller, what Solano describes as "an intonation of words, according to whether the emphasis falls on the fable or on the plot that governs the mirror that looks back at us" (19).[21] The realities Solano prefers to emphasize are the reception by Mexico of Spanish Civil War exiles and Mexican music, a presence in the author's life since infancy. The latter is an effect of personal circumstance, but the former is a circumstance with consequences for the whole of Spain. It is, as discussed in the previous chapter, one of the defining circumstances of the two countries' contemporary relationship, if not politically or economically (though its influence in those spheres has been considerable), then certainly in the memory of Spaniards.

It is not only the specific historical relationship between Spain and Mexico that drives Mexico's place-image for Spaniards. Broader global tropes of Mexicanness as well as American histories generally also contribute significantly to Spaniards' expectations about Mexico. Mexico City is simultaneously one of the most overmythologized and oft-elided places in travel writing about Mexico. It necessarily remains an organizing locus whether as point of first contact or as ultimate destination, or in negative ways such as through tourists' determination to avoid it in their consumption of Mexico as coastal paradise. The construction of international air and sea ports in beach resorts as well as quick transfers to domestic flights and deluxe intercity coach services at Mexico City's own airport speak to the ways tourist economies attempt to evade the city's weight both conceptually, in the popular imagination about Mexico, and functionally, in terms of its indisputable role as the center of government, infrastructure, urbanization of the Mexican population, and other significant aspects of contemporary Mexican life. This is not exclusively externally imposed, as some conceptual separation of the capital from the rest of the country is inscribed in both domestic tourism and everyday life in Mexico.

Distance from everyday routine is underscored by the way Solano frames the physical reality of the trip. At the airport in Spain he mentions that his flight is the only one departing for a Latin American destination (21–22). This reflects Spain's tight enmeshment with Europe and the still significant barriers to intercontinental mobility for many, even for wealthy (in global terms) middle class Spaniards. Meanwhile, Mexico itself is presented as an international city with flights to and from all perceived centers of European and Anglo-American civilization. Symbolically as well as practically, Europe appears more important for Latin America than the reverse, even in the case of Spain with its claims to a transnational *hispanidad*. Nevertheless, when confronted with the polluted and dispiriting actuality of Mexico City, Solano exhibits some of the imaginative force that is required to view the past, but the past is envisioned through the landscape, not its connection to living people (25). Later, this pre-Columbian vision is represented as an absolute otherness through the author's encounter with the Museo de Antropología. The very practice of museums of civilizations, however, is a European one, which often freezes them in time or reduces them to material traces. Solano himself defines anthropology as offering its audience, in this case Europeans, a confrontation with their own loss of magic (28). European belief is instead attached to materialism, possession of land, and secular and commercial gods. There are few museums that evoke thoroughly convincing long connections between the past and present, and the Mexican Museo de Antropología, while extremely engaging, is not consistently among them. In describing the contemplation of this isolated past, Solano does mention the Spanish role in Mexican history and the Conquest, though he does not specifically name the conquerors, repeating instead the cliché comparison between the sprawling might of the Aztec Empire and the few wily Spaniards (29).

More unusually in comparison to other travel writers, however, when Solano does connect this past to the present it is from the perspective of indigenous Mexicans, through the continuity of Náhuatl as a spoken language. He also refers to the limits of European knowledge and the opacities of pre-Columbian civilizations: what is "astonishing about them is not what we know . . . but all that we don't know" (152).[22] Nevertheless, perhaps as a result of the awe and romance attached to this mystery, while he identifies Náhuatl as still living he simultaneously and rather strangely uses it to encapsulate the vanished past (30). In discussing history, despite Solano's elsewhere demonstrated sensitivity to stereotype, it is difficult for the travel writer to avoid the pernicious tropes of otherness. Other limitations to Solano's recognition of the problematic connections between the present and the past can also be identified. For example, in referencing Bernadino de Sahagún, Solano creates distance between his own act as an observer describing his perceptions of indigenous American peoples and the acts of perceiving and describing undertaken by the first Spaniards in Mexico. He uses Sahagún's profound knowledge of the peoples he lived among without specifying Sahagún's agenda and his historical responsibility, or what it means to contribute to the historical record.

Part of the paradox in Solano's representations of Mexico and Mexico's history comes from his stylistic instinct toward symbolism in tying together the past and the present. For example, in one passage on Guanajuato, the city is "so weighed down with historical reality that, to support its weight, the mixture of its mineral-rich soil is capable of mummifying a cadaver in five years. . . . They clump together, solidify, and become converted into mummies of an *avant-la-lettre* Hollywoodian gore" (69).[23] Not only the obvious intrusion of mortality and the past represented by the mummies (and their conversion into consumables of tourism), but also the illusions both collective and individual that unify historical narratives of Mexico collapse into the fragile body of the disinterred dead. The gory history of the mummified people is subsumed into special effects horror. Historical suffering and violence contribute to the construction of the myths of Mexican character and the nationalist visual language of artists like Orozco. (Solano describes Orozco's theme as the "mythological suffering caused by the arrival of the Spaniards" [65].[24]) Similarly, but with more explicit reference to the processes and consequences of storytelling, Solano picks up on mythmaking around the revolution and individuals like Pancho Villa: "Converted into a hero, a symbol, an object of historical preservation, of Villa now we remember less his stubbornness and his spectacular defeats in Celaya and Aguascalientes than we do the victorious revolutionary, head of the Northern Division, who sat in the presidential seat. Memory stylizes controversial figures" (75).[25] Solano refers to group memory, but the distillations and erasures or occlusions of elements of experience cross over to any making of stories out of the messiness and banality of life.

In an inversion of his usual attention of the eruption of past into present, Solano also sinks contemporary Mexico into its proximate past by examining old photographs; in this case, once again, images of death (32). Through this examination, Solano also recognizes the extent chance can determine what survives. In this passage, there is a fascinating echo between this recognition and the travel writer's own impetus to story building in the process of retrospective reflection, an impetus that can too often mask the partiality and limits of the record of the past. Hughes (2004, 4), drawing on the imagery of the Russian poet Brodsky, writes, stories "creak like boards laid over a chasm." The abyss that can be sensed behind every story is the abyss of forgetting, the most necessary component of coherent memory. Forgetting is what allows both a sense of causation and meaning, and for dramatic recreations and revisions of the past to serve the interests of the present.

Solano himself acknowledges the peculiar relationship between experience, memory, and the reifying power of the written story, noting, "only what's written is real. But what's unwritten is also alive, and it stirs in the dregs of memory like ungraspable fish" (198).[26]

The unwritten is not only the forgotten and the submerged, but also that which *cannot* be written, cannot even be said. "For those of us whose world is built by words, our lifeline is always a bustle of syllables, and the rest is silence, or a devotion of closed lips before the white space that exists between two words" (56).[27] This unspeakable silence and the chaos that lies behind is part of what triggers the will to construct tales. For the religious, as Solano also notes, that which is beyond the verbal and all the chance and treachery of experience can be attached to the mystery of god, but for writers the making of meaning and of order is through story (55). In *Bajo las nubes* it plays out as a sense of restriction, of devotion to shaping something, something with its own will to emerge into being in a form with more or less resemblance to a reality that is beyond the reach of words:

> Writing, above all, is a continuous decision making. . . . There are words that attract each other, through sympathy or habit, and one must accept their linkages that sometimes are more like infections; the order of discourse cannot be turned aside, it imposes its currents and excludes cities that lie too distant; the narration of a journey is like the obsessive worship of an actress, a public infatuation. (198)[28]

This transparency about the inventions, interpretations, and amnesias of narrative is unusual in a genre that usually still depends on its claims of truthfulness to attract readers. Solano makes clear allusions to the fact that the act the reader is witnessing is not the voyage itself but the writing of it, from his comment that "to see is to interpret, and sometimes to invent" (119).[29] This idea destabilizes even the certainty of the role of the witness in the moment of seeing, right through to the very last page of the book, where his voyage concludes not with a classic departure or return image but rather with "the final line and the final key stroke" (199).[30]

Bajo las nubes's erosion of the reliability of the travel narrative itself creates some of the same productive complexities that were evident in Solano's relationship to history and historical responsibility. In one passage describing a literally hallucinatory experience, he outlines the limits of description: "What does it mean to say *good*, to say *interesting*? . . . Any word is inferior to the experience it names."[31] Language and telling are part of the business of being human in the world, and even though narration may itself incorporate anecdote, memory transfused into language, interpersonal communication does not assume the irreversibility of written narrative. In *The Predicament of Culture*'s influential critique of power and representation in the encounter with the other, Clifford (1988, 167) cited Leiris's diary note: "But a voyage must be told. It cannot be a heap of observations, notes, souvenirs—the pieces are displayed in sequences. A journey *makes sense* as a 'coming to consciousness'; its story hardens around an identity" (original emphasis). This has long been a fundamental assumption of first-person narration, which places at its center the transformations of narrating subjects through their responses to external circumstance. Solano, by extracting some inevitability from history and some verisimilitude from storytelling, gradually contributes to the construction of an unstable narrative self. Through elements like this, it might be possible to argue for certain continuities between writers in the face of the fracturing pressures of globalization, despite the different local histories that inflect their terms of encounter and their individual positions within the matrices of power.

"Everything, clearly, depends on the spirit of the traveler," Solano writes (164).[32] With this phrase, which refers explicitly to the mutability of place according to visitors' imaginative horizons, Solano encapsulates the way travelers' desires and expectations shape first their journeys, the sense of place and other, and ultimately the construction of narrative out of experience. It is not unusual for travel writers to recognize that different versions of a place are apparent to different visitors, but this realization, coyly shared with their readers, more often serves to reinforce claims to perspicacity and privileged insight. Solano, on the other hand, is clearly aware of travel's performativity, and that the travelers themselves are not the only ones to gaze, nor is their encounter with place definitive. This sometimes takes the form subtle references to the action—and the self-delusion—of foreigners in Mexico, as in one description of "extravagant characters with fatuous social drives, with an 'I' lit up with the need for redemption'" (167). There are also more explicitly performative vignettes, like that of the "couple dressed up as explorers, in the style of *Out of Africa*, so cinematic and dapper that I expect, with total conviction, that they will offer me a nip of whisky from a silver flask" (85).[33] His critical eye for tourism's pernicious elements does not miss Solano himself. He inverts the gaze as in this moment where a Mexican silently judges the action of the intruder: "We thought ourselves alone, but an *indio* with a mute dog had seen our whole fantasy" (83).[34] In other moments, he even more explicitly includes himself in the dynamics of an industry from which no travelers, however high-minded or well-intentioned, can materially extract themselves, using a "we" that problematizes his own act of travel: "Neutralized by touristic indistinguishability, we are all gregarious or stupid, and until we get in the car, ridiculous too" (153).[35] This reflexivity extends to references to the complex consequences of tourism, for example in the production of indigeneity as spectacle. In the following passage, Solano goes a distance toward portraying the damage created by a search for authenticity that frames ethnicity as a consumable element of place, founded on an underlying assumption of essential racial difference: "These *indias* bring out a false local color, they are living archaeology for tourists. . . . They tolerate their presence, which colors the environment, they are the link to the heart of Mexico, but they must not go too far with the whites" (142).[36] Solano's acknowledged unstable position and efforts to invert the usual direction of the gaze contribute to the portrayal of a traveler subject to transformation, a transformation not at the service of constructing a classic narrative arc as is the case in so much travel writing, but that interrogates the terms of the traveler's own power to represent the other.

Bajo las nubes is unusual in the author's explicit situating of the text within traditions of writing about Mexico. He recognizes that the idea of a place is as important to the traveler's perception as the embodied experience. "Mexico too has been made out of words. . . . Mexico becomes more transparent as, through reading, the bewilderment provoked by a current situation that both transforms and perpetuates itself in the present eases" (91–92).[37] He cites a very specific genealogy of representation from outside arrivals like Cortés and Bernal Díaz del Castillo through to the self-representation of twentieth-century writers like Elena Poniatowska and Juan Villoro. He also references the impact of the Spanish Civil War exiles on the evolution of the idea of Mexico in literature. Solano rates the influence of these and other writers very highly, writing that "a country is shaped by its geography, its history, and the memorable texts that attempt to cover its world of prophecies, failures, and secret passions" (89).[38] This intertextual focus tends to an abstraction that limits critique of economic realities in people's daily lives. However, the perspective is effective in acknowledging the role of both change and contingency in ideas of place in ways that representations drawing more exclusively on geography, landscape, or sensory encounter do not. Solano alludes to both the multiplicity and the fundamental interminability and incompleteness of ideas of place, describing the experience of Mexico as being "within an unfinished dream, a dream that is being dreamt" (89) and asking in light of the textual rendering and rerendering of Mexicanness, "which Mexico are they writing these books about?" (90).[39] *Bajo las nubes* allows for the Mexico of its author's literary imagination, the Mexico of his experience, but also the many Mexicos that are beyond his reach, including the Mexico that is becoming, since in the act of narration he signals that he is already engaging with a place that is past.

He demonstrates a consistent awareness of the influence of intertextuality on representation of place. Despite his preoccupation with poetic and literary abstractions, Solano's writing also displays a reasonably nuanced engagement with historical inequalities and with his own role in both intertextuality and inequality. Nevertheless, *Bajo las nubes* is far from giving us a travel story that radically disrupts or cleanly critiques the problems of contemporary travel in and travel writing about Mexico. Romantic cultural stereotypes and generalizations sometimes prove too hard to resist, as in the following comparison: "Like drunks and women resigned to abusive marriages, Mexicans prefer the melodrama of life, which is always a story, to life itself" (62).[40] At others, Solano stays at the surface of things, and what he sees passes into his possession as images that blur into a sense of place over which his own asserts control—at least until the images repossess his imagination: "A Tzeltal girl crossing the road, three peasants drinking pulque at the foot of a maguey, a stone serpent, the lizard shows its head on the fallen column, an amber face, the *huipil* on the pavement to muffle the coins, everything seen, recorded in a moment, shone again in the light of dreams" (97).[41] In this passage the texture of place, the individual stories and embeddedness of each person, each artifact, and each animal, are lost to the wash of the visual and reduced to signs. Solano is not here imposing his own interpretation on them as symbols of cultural identity or geographical place, but given the already mentioned focus on narrative construction throughout *Bajo las nubes*, we must also be aware of the act of selection in the seeming naturalness of the flow of imagery.

These signs of Mexico may at times fit within a narrative of sensitivity to historical violence, as in one of Solano's references to the Rarámuri: "The Tarahumara, the true owners of these lands, now superimposed on the landscape like melancholy signs for remorse in cultural conscience" (77).[42] Although here the indigenous presence impacts the traveler as a kind of cultural conscience/consciousness, this ambiguous metaphorizing of indigenous presence remains a form of reinscription of the trope of indigeneity as sign rather than subject. In his passage on the hallucinogenic drug pioneer Robert Gordon Wasson's encounter with rural Mexico, Solano writes, "like all discoverers, he had to bring them out of obscurity and at the same time contribute to their annihilation" (125).[43] This is the paradox of discovery narrative, and a debate that is far from academic as we see in ongoing conflicts over natural resources and indigenous peoples. The circulation of specific narratives of indigeneity may link to mobilizations to protect the Amazon or other resource-rich regions subject to extractivist violence, but the modes of representation often remain highly problematic.[44] This danger also attends more generally the act of writing about the presence of cultural others in the general rather than the particular case, and it is a danger that Solano, for all his insights into the problems of representation and of the historical implications of inscribing Mexico through travel narrative, is unable to avoid.

The influence of past representations and discourses of place over the experience of encounter is clearly very important for Solano, as for many other travel writers. Intertextual references are among the clearest indicators of the importance of experience in travelers' perceptions, and especially the importance of the past in processes of narrativization and reformulation of perceptions into story. This is certainly evident in the contemporary perpetuation of many of the tropes of discovery and adventure, but the personal history of travelers is also significant for the ways their origin and personal geographies shape their sense of place, though they may not themselves explicitly explore the idea of home within their narration of journeying and away. While Solano demonstrates sensitivity to the instability of identity and the variability of ideas of place, the application of this understanding to his sense of home and familiarity in comparison to mobility and strangeness has only a limited presence in *Bajo las nubes de México*. The following section explores ideas of home and, particularly, memory in the work of Eduardo Jordá, and their intersection with the kinds of intertextuality and dynamics of journeying thus far explored in this chapter.

Between the Lost City and the Unchanging Place: Eduardo Jordá from Mallorca to Mexico

Travel writers have long engaged in exchanges with previous travel narratives as a fundamental element of their relationship to place. This is most obvious in the subgenre of travel writing that purports to "follow in the footsteps" of past travelers, a sustained example of which, Eloísa Gómez Lucena's *Del Atlántico al Pacífico: Tras los pasos de Cabeza de Vaca*, will be discussed in Chapter 4, because, despite its intertextual premise, it does not dwell on textuality or memory and expectation the way the works discussed in this chapter do. Eduardo Jordá's *Los lugares que no cambian* (2004; Unchanging places) collects a selection of such followings undertaken by the Mallorcan writer. Virilio (2005) theorizes mobility today partly through the repetition of past itineraries. We can connect the "footsteps" subgenre to the sense of loss attached to the idea of an already known world that was described in the introduction. This characteristic creates in the narration of travel a reiterative quality. A place is not merely retold; the operation—travel—that produced the original telling is repeated, and each iteration incorporates inconstant, unpredictable variables. As a communicative act, travel writing is not so much a meditation on knowledge or images of places that purports to give readers access to the past. Through Jordá's particular act of following and production of a reiterative narrative, it is possible to make out some of the tensions between the idea that we can know what is distant (or even what is near) through its representation in writing, and the actual embodied and inscribed enactment of the journeys that produce such representations.

Jordá's narrative displays some thematic continuity with Solano's, in that his literary preoccupations and aestheticized poetics of place contribute to an unstable traveling subject and a subjectivity contingent on place. Both are interested in travel not as an act of witnessing to gain authority about what they are reporting but as something that threatens their sense of self. In Jordá's case, this is primarily defined through his spatial subjectivity as it is performed in his routine and his relationship to his personal history, rather than the wider histories that preoccupy Solano. As Musgrove (1999, 31) writes, "In travel, the *territorial* passage from one zone to another, the border crossing, represents a critical movement for the identity of the mobile subject" (original emphasis). While Musgrove goes on to privilege the link between seeing and understanding in a way that is problematic, his exploration of journeying as a form of psychic "unsettlement" is a useful one for considering how, in the departure from the familiar, memory and expectation play out with the elements of otherness that cannot be reconciled to them. This unsettlement offers a contrast with the classic power of the gaze of the traveling subject, that power that lies at the very heart of the problem of travel writing as a genre that represents unequal relationships. In Clark's (1999b, 212) analysis of Jonathan Raban, he describes the enormous degree of authority and certainty afforded by the imperial dynamic. Travelers from the old empires are no longer the privileged observers of yore. Europeans are now, arguably, in a position of supplication in relation to some of the more recently ascended empires, though Latin America does not confront the Spanish traveler with this changed polarity in quite the same way that the United States confronts the English. Still, the travelers of today are responding to a tradition that carries with it histories of writing within and against evolving geopolitical systems, whether they choose to address these explicitly in their writing or not. This section analyzes Jordá's *Los lugares que no cambian* as an example of a form of contemporary Spanish travel writing that is densely and deliberately intertextual and therefore can only be understood in the context of its relationship to the literary traditions of its genre, as well as the histories of mobility connected to its routes.

Los lugares que no cambian falls within the subgenre of travel writing that relies on previous textual journeyings or travels through literature, taking an explicit or implicit premise of following past travelers. The tales such works recount rely on an assumed coincidence between the writer's literary education and readers' at least minimal awareness of famous writers and travelers past, if not their own reading of their works. The subgenre is expansive, with books promising to follow the footsteps of such diverse and variously mobile travelers as Marco Polo, D. H. Lawrence, Bruce Chatwin, Freya Stark, or even Buddha. Jordá's book contributes therefore to a trend in contemporary travel writing in which writers filter the experience of place through literature and through poetic sensibilities dependent on memory, and therefore emphasize the centrality of the qualities of the individual subject in encounters and traversals.[45]

In Spanish-language travel writing, it is noteworthy that the works referenced are as likely to be originally published in English as Spanish (whereas the reverse is certainly not true). As discussed in Chapter 1, for Spain, and to a degree Latin America, the preexisting descriptions with which later travelers consistently contend are in many cases from works by anglophone writers, plus those of a selection of especially influential continental Europeans. This is, perhaps, a reflection of the tradition of travel writing as it has developed through the nineteenth and twentieth centuries in connection with British imperial expansion. The English-language scholarship that has emerged around British imperial discourse in nineteenth- and twentieth-century travel writing has reinforced the primacy of this tradition. Focusing exclusively on the impact of this tradition, however, as is evidenced by the many critical works that contest this Anglocentric genealogy, occludes the diversity of narratives produced through, for example, the ties between Spain and Portugal and the Americas, through imperial relations, familial ties, linguistic commonality, flows of migration, and so on.

What English-language and other European narrative traditions do offer the Spaniard traveling in Mexico, or other ex-Spanish territories, are voices with different relationships to the history of Spain itself. These alternative intertextualities may offer more literary, individual, and less politically and racially fraught relationships—though not, of course, without their own problematic enactments of power and connections to historical and contemporary violence. It is the individual voice, after all, that is the central illusion of travel writing: a solitary adventurer in the world, often suppressing the presence of companions and the professional and financial motives for travel, certainly all too often ignoring the power relationships implicit in the transactions between travelers and hosts, transactions that have been recognized as having, fairly regularly, a neocolonial flavor. This is rather more difficult should a Spanish writer choose to comment on the Spanish tradition of writing about Latin America, as Solano did, with its origins in the dispatches of Conquistadors, followed by the writings of members of religious and diplomatic missions. The Spanish tradition more rarely mobilized the framework of scientific detachment, which was what allowed nineteenth-century British travelers to create the illusion of a separation of their endeavor from the military and mercantile purposes of the general flows of travel of their era. That illusory split was the precursor to the adventurous twentieth-century traveler striking out as an anonymous stranger to distant lands, with neither care for their new environment nor baggage (of any kind) from home. Referring to these non-Spanish works, therefore, is potentially rather less complicated for a Spanish writer who wishes to sustain a focus on an individual perception of the destination and his or her relationship to journeying, rather than tangled transatlantic histories.

Certain styles of thinking about travel, present in the different travel writing traditions, have a specific resonance for different authors, suggesting the reasons select narrative approaches appeal to Jordá in particular. In his career he has actively engaged with questions of violence and the history of power. For example, in one parallel, Jordá was the translator of a recent Spanish edition of *Heart of Darkness*, that seminal—though not irreproachable—critique of the colonial project, and it was Conrad he read before going to Burundi on the trip that would inspire his novel *Pregúntale a la noche* (2007; Ask the night). His creative engagement with the complexity of historical violence is present in his insistence that some of the poison associated with the divisions between Hutus and Tutsis was created by the colonizers, a historical contribution that is sometimes sublimated by the extremes of violence and retribution that have characterized the lengthy civil conflicts (Blasco 2008). Regarding these issues, he thinks, most Spaniards are living in what he describes as "a kind of comfortable daydream" (in Valenzuela 2007). In this context, theories of memory as opposed to history are useful—the idea that humans construct a collective conscious awareness of a limited number of ideas, and that the ideas retained are often determined by what is useful to us pragmatically in order to be able to adapt to the world in which we live.[46] For this, and other reasons, blanket critique is not a meaningful response; as Jordá himself cautions, corruption is not universal but individual, and both Europeans and Africans may be corrupt. The difference is once again one of power and representation. This dual perception of influence and of individuality is representative of the tension Jordá often explores between the past, especially as it is represented in literature, and the way these histories work on the imagination when it comes to interpreting the experience of the present.

Jordá also has a close connection to other tensions around belonging and expression in connection to place and global, national, and regional relationships. As a Mallorcan, Jordá, like many writers from

Spain's non-Castilian-speaking regions, has been criticized for writing in Castilian Spanish instead of the native language of his community or the regional language of Catalán. It is worth noting that Jordá's university education was in Spanish philology, suggesting a long process of internalization and accommodation of *castellano*, also the language of Jordá's poetry. The intense promotion of regional languages forms part of a politics of the center-periphery in Spain. This politics is a fascinating case study for issues of regional and linguistic identity construction, given Spain's past imperial dominance, subsequent eclipse, and present economically destabilizing but politically moderate influence in the European Union, as well as the way Europe's relationship to regions sometimes circumvents nations. Parts of Spain's national myth are built around unification and solidification of long-fluctuating borders—issues that reappear in the later discussion of detailed aspects of *Los lugares que no cambian*.

Richard Sennett (1999, 23) draws on Arendt to suggest the potential role of geographic places as alternative sites for the formation of community given people's "dislocations and impoverished experience in the economy." This tendency offers a contrast to the broader theorization of the effects of globalization offered by Zygmunt Bauman (2000, 11), who argues that "the difference between 'close by' and 'far away', or for that matter between the wilderness and the civilized, orderly space, has been all but cancelled." Bauman, however, is talking about the operation of *power*, for which the kinds of allegiances of affection and trappings of identity mentioned by Sennet may be mere camouflage. Regional affiliation in Spain has many specific historical causes, but one contemporary condition that intensifies the situation is, as Sennet proposes, the rise of those very supranational forces that Bauman describes as "extraterritorial power" (11), which drastically influence the fates of nations and regions. Against it, Bauman suggests, the "valiant defense of community" (169) has but a weak and disintegrating base on which to draw. Extraterritorial power, in the context of travel and tourism, contributes to the evanescence of places while simultaneously curating them as consumable museum spaces.

This ambiguous semi-peripheral, semi-imperial perspective aligns with Jordá's nuanced portrayal of the blurriness and permeability of borders and allegiances and his interpretation of the effects of the expansive influence of something that might be termed global Euro-American culture. Tanger, for example, he describes as "floating in no-man's land, not belonging to any continent, any civilization" (in de Villalonga 1996, 17).[47] This characterization of the iconic, cosmopolitan zones of passage, perpetually filled with both the strange and the familiar, is perhaps something of a cliché; however, Jordá extends this sensibility to critiquing his own preconceptions about Euro-American civilization and wealth. He notes his own shocking encounter with Manila, which his vague association of the modern Philippines with the US had led him to believe was somewhat prosperous but which he found to be surrounded by shantytowns (*Adn.es* 2008). Both these characterizations suggest an ability to detach places from their preexisting geographical and cultural associations, to reinterpret them based on their subjection to altered circumstances and different times. Mediterranean islands like Jordá's home are themselves charged with the history of trade and shifting power while also creating the peculiar condition of island experience, which promotes a sense of geographical isolation and invariable borders.

As a writer, Jordá simultaneously draws on the powerful emotional quality of proximity and belonging for the individual and recognizes its debility against the losses and turbulence of time and the wider world. He has also reflected on new realities that have transformed travel as well as the project of producing art: the rise of terror. Jordá edited (with José Mateos) the poetic memorial that was released as a tribute to the victims of the May 11, 2004, Madrid train bombings (11-M), an event that shifted the ground in Spain for contemplating fear and Spanish authorities' territorial control. Terrorism in Spain before 11-M was associated with those very regional affiliations mentioned previously—actions that were abhorrent but driven by motives that were familiar if not sympathetic. 11-M, the work of an Islamist extremist terrorist cell, steeped Spain in the deterritorialized fear and uncertainty that has emerged as a major price of globalization's ascendancy of speed and fluidity over geographical limitation. The forces of the global shape the intimacy of feeling and how feeling intersects with places, local and remote.

Jordá's explorations of space and memory and his intertextual engagements with past stories of travel are subject to both the precarious privilege of the voluntarily mobile global traveling class and the potent operation of the memory of home. Specifically, in his travel writing distant places are mediated through literature, literature that assists in the construction of expectations of the yet-to-come despite being inflected by the past and most particularly by the moment of writing. Travel, therefore, is narrated by way of an exploration of stories consumed and digested in stillness, at home. The lost city of Jordá's childhood (*La ciudad perdida* [2001], or The lost city, being the title of Jordá's memoir of Palma de Mallorca), on the other hand, is mediated through movement and traces of remembered trajectories, the child being the blank slate on which a place can inscribe itself. In *La ciudad perdida*, he writes, "Beyond that house, beyond that triangle of streets that reappears in a dream, beyond a few friends, a few streets, the city is just an administrative entity that appears on maps, nothing more" (2001, 12).[48] The connection between travelers' sense of home, their sense of identity, and the experience of dislocation or of passage, therefore, is determined not by the abstract characteristics of place but by the sedimentation of memories and the extent to which new experiences can be accommodated within that framework. What is important is that the personal journey does not supplant the sense of place, which is one criterion used here to distinguish travel narrative from other forms of diary or memoir, but rather enriches it; each transforms the other.

Among contemporary travel authors Jordá is unusual, principally a poet by trade rather than a writer of fiction or nonfiction prose, and thus takes considerable care with the language he brings to the evocation of place. His attention to the narration of experience, to the delicacy and specificity of the fleeting encounter with its origins and consequences dispersed through time, is the complement of his poetry's emphasis on what reviewer Fernando Menéndez (2006) has described as the protagonism of places and landscapes. Menéndez compares Jordá's poems collected in *Mono aullador* (2005; Howler monkey) to postcards, and their reading to a "tour of Europe and other lands" (10).[49] As a travel writer he is similarly alert to images and other senses of place that may escape more typical narrative temporality.

Jordá's ode to Palma de Mallorca in *La ciudad perdida* is testament to his reflective relationship with the concept of place in relation to, in this case, home. He writes, "Seen from within, with memory's eyes, Palma was a livable and pleasant city, although I guess that any city in which one is born and grows up ends up becoming, with the passage of time, the illusion of a livable and pleasant city" (2001, 55).[50] This condensed, imaginary city is the product of a blending of memory and desire, that is, what we have lived through and what we wish for. Palma, in which Jordá no longer lives, is reduced to his memories of its topography. Jordá is making a claim for the formative character of childhood spaces and trajectories and for their staying power in the imagination of even those adults who have, at least physically, left those spaces and trajectories far behind them. Luis García Jambrina (2005) suggests that Palma de Mallorca and the memory of childhood is "the only homeland the author considers his own."[51] Jordá (2001, 57) himself says "What happens is that the passing of time envelops even the least memorable things in an ennobling aura," suggesting the impossibility of the present equaling the nostalgic past.[52] For Jordá, memory is indelibly marked by proximity to the sea, the classic and inescapable homeland of the traveler as well as the default imagery of the island dweller's formative environment. Jordá then matches the intensity of his connection to Palma de Mallorca with an insistence on mobility for both his characters and himself; "my characters usually live elsewhere, far from their place of origin" and the "only homelands that are worth it are those that one can choose" (in Martínez Zarracina 2006).[53]

In contrast to this poetic evocation of the importance—and subjectivity—of memory and the contingency of place, it is worth commenting briefly on the travel narrative of Javier Reverte, to understand Jordá's alternative stance on the nature of experience and orientation toward mobility. Reverte is perhaps the most popular contemporary Spanish travel writer. Although he has not written much about Mexico compared to other destinations, in a discussion of the changing meaning of travel for Spain, it is impossible to pass him by completely and hope to have suggested something of the processes of interrelationship of travel and writing in contemporary Spain. A brief comparison of Reverte's evocation of Spain, especially the Spain of his childhood, with his narration of Mexico among other adult destinations in the volume *La aventura de viajar* (2006; The adventure of traveling), serves to relate this preeminent contemporary travel writer to Eduardo Jordá through understanding different possible influences of past cartographies on present interpretations and experiences of place. Structured partly like a memoir, *La aventura de viajar* combines in a single volume (unlike in Jordá's case) Reverte's meditations on the constitutive effects of childhood memory and his outbound so-called adventures. The reflections on Spain also offer a much more explicit engagement with post-Franco transitions and new meanings of mobility, as well as the imaginative geographies inscribed during the Franco era, thus overtly defining the background for the traveler's sense of the world. These geographies evolved through spaces actually physically marked by conflict, as evident in Reverte's reference to the remnant presence of the Battle of Madrid in the "buildings wounded by bombs, artillery mounts, little bunkers and machine gun emplacements in clearings.... That shabby Madrid of the postwar was an emotional universe, because it let us see the traces of terrible battles" (18).[54] Later, he writes of the end of the Franco era and the transformations it wrought both in the practice of his profession of journalism as well as in the nature of the stories that could be communicated, given the awakening of a "Spanish society that was starting to demand truthful information" (72–73).[55] This awakening occurred in the wake of years of censorship and propaganda.

Reverte's book overall creates a sense of vacillation between the expectations built up in advance of travel and ambivalence about what constitutes putative real travel. From his literary precursors and the existing representations of place "is born a good part of my nostalgia for that which I don't know" (163).[56] Eventually, drawing perhaps on his emphasis on the invention (in life as in literature) of the traveling subject as hero of his own story ("One must try to give one's own biography a certain epic flavor" [41]), Reverte questions his own self-definition as a traveler: "in a certain moment I had the impression that despite all the flights, the hotels, the palaces, so much of the world traversed, so many displacements with kings and presidents, I had never travelled" (139).[57] Here he is developing a particular definition of supposedly authentic travel, privileging interpersonal encounter and the exploration of spaces of difference. Reverte's actual travel stories, perhaps because of his foregrounding of these kinds of categorizations of travel and narrative tendencies, adhere more closely to the generic conventions of the travel story that have been so thoroughly critiqued in studies of travel writing than do the slipperier stories explored in detail in this book. Although he frames his text as a journey conditioned by journalism in a similar mode to Alfredo Semprún, whose writing is discussed in Chapter 3, Reverte's conceptualizations of travel, its appeal, and its narration remain more conventional, which may be usefully taken as a kind of norm for travel writing as a popular, middlebrow genre. The stories presented in *La aventura de viajar* have moved much further away from the circumstance and temporality of journalism than those written by Semprún. For the purposes of this book it is obviously most relevant to take an example from stories Reverte tells about Mexico, which in the case of this collection are based on trips he took as part of the press gallery accompanying presidents of the Republic. What is peculiar, however, is the dissociation between his different themes: comments on Spanish politics transposed to airplanes and press conferences that happen to be in Mexico, local color anecdotes, and a trite passage repeating the already exhausted conflation of Mexico with surrealism, which Reverte illustrates with images from Tijuana of the donkeys painted for the benefit of scenic photographs and of a mistranslation on a menu with a peculiar effect (135-36).[58] These images suggest the effects in that town of commodification through tourism rather than the surreal undertow of Mexican life.

In contrast to these observations and anecdotes, which place the object at a remove from the traveling subject, throughout the multi-genre oeuvre of Jordá what we see is an ongoing searching through the connections between the memory of words and the encounter with place, between expectation and experience. Jordá's writing incorporates the slippages and ambiguities around the nature of narration of place and the categorization of travel writing; his inclination has been described as exploring a "border genre incorporating autobiography, fiction, essay, and chronicle."[59] But how successfully do his literary preoccupations and foregrounding of memory translate to travel writing, especially travel writing predicated precisely on a memory of reading? Especially in the case where that memory does not awaken a possessive hunger for the thing described, as it did in the case of Reverte, but rather positions reading as part of the process that changes the reader, and changes their ability to perceive their reality. The particular focus is the specific dynamics of travel in Mexico within this interplay of memory and mobility. The collection of travel essays in Jordá's book *Lugares que no cambian* is part of a series that, despite its name, *Trayectos*, suggesting a preoccupation with travel, is focused on more personal journeys, tending to semi-memoirs centered on explorations of film and music. The cover, unlike the picturesque photos or images symbolic of places that so often grace the jackets of travel books, is a rather shadowy photo of an immobile and nonspecific train.

As an epigraph for *Los lugares*, he has chosen lines from W. H. Auden's "In Transit": "Somewhere are places where we have really been, dear spaces/ Of our deeds and faces, scenes we remember/ As unchanging, because there we changed" (11). This reminds readers of Jordá's poetic vocation and his emphasis not on exoticism, which he abhors, nor even novelty or difference, but on memory and the construction of the self. *Los lugares* itself is fundamentally intertextual, dealing with places that have a previous hold on the imagination through literature—mythic places—and hence with the simultaneous impossibility of changing that imagined place and the impossibility, as the summary on the cover suggests, of any true concordance between the literary and the real. A reviewer in *La Vanguardia* (2004, 13) proposed that the actual purpose of the book, in fact, was "contrasting his readings with the direct observation of the settings that inspired them."⁶⁰ In his piece on Puerto Escondido in *Los lugares*, Jordá gives an accounting of the place as a site for famous travelers—poet-boxer Arthur Cravan, Paul Bowles—such that his own experience there is a sort of null zone of transit between the imaginary historical place through which they moved and his own conjectures about a future characterized by the depredations of tourism (101). He engages in an extensive speculative description of his imagined retirement based on his long-past experience of Puerto Escondido, and this, in combination with his nostalgic evocation of the past visits of others, generates a peculiar temporal fusion made of an unseen past and the anticipated losses of the future. His writing, therefore, is not occasioned by his own visits or revisits, but by the impossibility of revisiting and by the gradual homogenization of places—the erosion of their uniqueness—through the forces of globalization: "if I ever return, Puerto Escondido will be a perfected version of any place on the Mallorcan coast." (104).⁶¹ Time, then, and its compression in our present era, bring places closer together and change them irrevocably, while also changing the traveler. "We can never go back to the same place. Even if the place isn't unrecognizable—which is progressively less likely—the passage of time has made *us* unrecognizable" (101).⁶² Here again is Jordá's preoccupation with the memory of our past selves, selves who become strangers but strangers who are the guardians of our only possible connection to a sense of place.

The passage of time alters both the destination and the native milieu and sense of home of any possible visitor. Neither home nor away can ever be the same as for a past traveler. The travelers whose paths Jordá follows came from and passed through a different world. Jordá's work is so infused with the sensibilities of these past travelers and past selves it is perhaps inevitable that he falls occasionally into Eurocentric tropes, treating whole peoples as having a uniform type, while reflecting for himself as an individual on the personal benefits of the societies and places in which he finds himself. On one notable occasion, the Zapotecs are collectively branded as having a peculiar pacifism resulting from an intensive identification with and attachment to their women (103). Later, the indigenous people of Chiapas are compared in one single passage to different animals, and Jordá attributes to them several animalistic qualities (109). There is some slight counter in his description of the guerrilla resistance in Mexico's south, the motive for which Jordá sees as merely a minimum of respect and of dignity for groups of indigenous peoples too long ignored (110). In an evocative passage, he describes the interaction between the kind of silence profound enough to be felt, the encroachment of the jungle, and the symbol of an abandoned roundabout representing the interventions of outsiders in the life of the people there, before closing on this possibility of a just eruption of noise or violence. This seems flimsy in comparison with the previous reductionist descriptions, though it is a rare outsider travel story indeed in Spanish or any other language that does not stumble somehow into offensive cliché when describing indigenous peoples. In Jordá's case, it can perhaps be attributed to his inheritances from the writers he so admires, though not the admirable ones.

His relationship with these past narratives influences his whole project to a marked extent. In Oaxaca, Jordá (107) is detained by a newspaper he finds left behind under his bed. This chance intervenes in his immediate impression of the place, with its sudden insertion of a tale of kidnapping and murder. The Hotel Francia itself, which occasioned this sudden interruption, was chosen for its connection to Malcolm Lowry and to D. H. Lawrence. While he mentions the hotel's present discomforts, the squeaks of the bed and the strange noises from a toilet upstairs, it is only to reject their importance compared to the intensity of his relationship to Lowry's and Lawrence's books. What he wanted—why he came, in fact—was to discover "what remained of all that of which I had read many years before'" (107).[63] Jordá's temporal reference for relating to Oaxaca is the past moment when he first read about it; neither the immediate context for the composition of the books—the different authors' times—nor the time of the composition of his own book, really enter into his feelings. The news of violence, lurking under the bed, was not able to intervene in his present experience to the same extent as his literary education. Physical reality registers in the details of the narrative, and to this extent Jordá is acquiescing to the conventions of travel writing, unlike voyagers such as his purely reflective contemporary Agapito Maestre, who barely pens a single descriptive word in his nominal travel story about Mexico. Chronological progression and physical movement do not provide the logic for the book, however, which is preoccupied with the function of memory and the influence of the past over our present perceptions. Jordá's work is embedded in the past, while containing a degree of acknowledgment of and melancholy for the pace and the perils of the present. His artistic project is extended through sustained interest in the fundamental intertextuality of travel narratives, through the retracings he enacts, the retrospection, and the collation of memories, texts, and sights.

One of the principal preoccupations of this study is the extent diverse examples of contemporary Spanish travel writing engage with or avoid compromised modes and histories of representation. It is quite common for Spanish travel writing, at least in texts that are not explicitly political, to take a reflective, literary approach, and the works of Eduardo Jordá are an engaging example of this style while simultaneously displaying the flaws of hyper-textualization of place. In Jordá's work, commenting on literary representations does not automatically equate to negating the historical forces and current socioeconomic realities that shape the places through which he travels—although it would be fair to say that the appeal of literary history is, at times, his only interest in a particular place. Jordá's travel writing in *Los lugares que no cambian*, when read in the context of his reflection on the constitutive character of home and memory in the memoir *La ciudad perdida* and the postcolonial critique in the novel *Pregúntale a la noche*, offers an example of the uneven effect of literary nostalgia as a method for interpreting place, when combined with sustained sensitivity to the effects of time.

Rather than echoing the grand modern narratives of discovery or of adventure, Jordá's reiterative travel, determined by existing texts that define how a journey is to be understood and establish the wayposts, has something in common with the premodern mobility of the pilgrimage. As Lutz Kaelber (2006, 280) notes, "Established religions are not the only entities that lay claim to a sacrality of place, and those who commemorate and recreate it in pilgrimage are not confined to established religious communities." The personal and historical resonances of places have the potential to create a spiritual and emotional dimension to travel. For Jennifer Selby (2006, 165), this is a fundamental dimension of the function of Urry's tourist gaze; its transformation of the ordinary material encountered in transit into sacred and transcendent experience. While travel writing in the forms we encounter today emerged in parallel with imperialism, middle class access to travel and the cultural appeal and economic systems around established travel routes make pilgrimage in some ways a more relevant model. In a work like Jordá's *Los lugares que no cambian*, the existence of previously documented journeys, the centuries of repetition and narration increase the weight of a place—at least, the weight of the *idea* of a place. The danger of this, however, is that the infusion of the past and of the textual renderings of place into the physical encounter may serve to abstract the traveler from the immediate meaning and consequences of their touristic encounters. At least in Jordá's case (less so in Solano's due to the broader and less personal spectrum of his intertextuality), the elevation of the intertext almost precludes a meaningful engagement with what travel means in Mexico today and how the author's own journey is connected to wider political and economic circumstances. The following chapter addresses texts that directly discuss the effects of globalization through select Spanish authors' responses to the conditions of contemporary travel, including their engagement with the forces that are now limiting the mobility of some groups while increasing that of others.

CHAPTER 3

Violence, Instability, and Danger

Travel narratives encompassing reflection on the traveler's expectations and their knowledge of existing texts often include hints of awareness about the problems of representing other cultures. In their transparent textuality, they gesture toward the constructedness and partiality of stories. They suggest the complicity of travelers and travel writers in perpetuating cultural stereotypes, and the failures and limitations of subjective experience for narrating otherness. This awareness also extends partway toward narrating place and difference in relation to consequences of historical and current oppression and violence. Nevertheless, the travel narratives discussed in the previous chapter rarely interrogate deeply the meaning of travel and the role of a European travel writer around the turn of the millennium, in terms of the actual material and political implications of tourism alongside other forms of mobility. Forms of literary nostalgia and consumer topophilia fail to provide a convincing response to the problems of acceleration and homogenization of place described by Bauman (2000). Global elites—including those with the freedom to travel for pleasure or for art—experience the collapse of distance as access, whether to information, to new experiences, or to personal security. Subalterns, on the other hand, are themselves accessed *by* global capital, the agents of which reshape their local economies but the masters of which are mostly beyond their reach. All enter Marc Augé's (1995) anonymizing community-less non-places at times, whether in antiseptic luxury or degrading slum, and live with the dehumanizing effects of globalization in their daily lives. However, globally determined places have very different consequences for different groups. Joseph Pugliese (2009, 664), in his critical work outlining the intersection of law, power, bodies and space, describes the abuttal of tourism economies with other forms of mobility via the "violently disjunctive accounts and experiences of (the same) space." This radical disjunction can productively extend the application of Augé's concept to places that are defined by human mobility, where the details of human experience are subordinated to massive transnational economic and legal forces. Specificity—the value of life—tends to disappear. In Pugliese's example, tourist accounts of Lampedusa evoke "a 'place of fable' with a 'fairy tale sea,' an 'unforgettable postcard place' and an 'island of dreams.' Reading these reviews, I experienced an acute sense of disorientation, as my vision of Lampedusa is of an island infamous for its overcrowded, traumatizing immigration detention center. It is a harrowing site that has witnessed the unsolicited arrival of hundreds of dead bodies of asylum seekers and refugees" (663).[1] Pugliese argues that this dissonance is a structural component of the transnational in the contemporary world, an argument borne out by the ease with which one can identify such examples throughout the globe.

The examples of travel writing in this chapter show how some of these dissonances emerge in texts that bring a privileged European subject into contact with the material traces of power and the individuals subject to its mechanisms that are not otherwise designed to touch the lives of these same Europeans. Peñate Rivero (2012, 319) suggests that in what he terms the third stage of Spanish travel writing it is quite common that "the critical or even condemnatory content appears pretty clearly."[2] This remark refers specifically to *El rumor de la frontera*, in which Alfonso Armada (text) and Corina Arranz (photography) travel the Mexican-US border, a site par excellence of the involution of global capital, economic and ethnocultural division, and mobility. In *Viajes desaconsejables*, the second example explored in this chapter, the news media cycle and the scales of relative impact and relevance for Spanish readers determine the trajectory of journalist Alfredo Semprún.

Alfonso Armada and Corina Arranz's Mobile Frontiers

The US-Mexico border is of monumental importance in the destiny and current identity of not only Mexico but also the USA. The push-pull around this border is the effect of conflict between views from the north and the south. José Saldívar (1997, 1) notes the shift away from nationally bounded understandings of culture, proposing a multifaceted approach. Linking this border to Spanish transatlantic histories and trans-Mediterranean pressures, as well as Europe more generally, offers a valuable point of contrast to a purely US-versus-Mexico spatial poetics. It still, of course, falls into the category of literature *about* the border, telling a journey *to* the border, rather than literature produced on the border by border dwellers, a distinction María Socorro Tabuenca Córdoba (1995, 161) reminds us is important. Stories of visiting and crossing are not the same as stories of dwelling, however precarious the dwelling might sometimes be. This type of text narrates a trajectory, from somewhere and through elsewheres, evoking a highly contingent and temporally bounded sense of place. Such stories are the product of their conditions, moment, chance encounters, logistical mischances. They are also records of intercultural contact. As part of revising a concept of travel writing that is over-reliant on equating place and identity with nation, we can also note the intercultural interventions that Armada and Arranz have made, as travel writer and photographer, passing great stretches of their transnational lives outside of Spain, engaging in processes of reflecting on the world they encounter and interpreting it for mixed audiences.

The resonance of Pugliese's Lampedusa example of place dissonance for understanding the dual function of the Mexico-United States border region as tourism site and migration channel is obvious. The conflict between differing experiences of mobility echoes the Mediterranean case. The interconnectedness of global capital, mobility, and economic and cultural difference become material, or as Bob Hodge

(2002, para. 12) terms it, real: "Borders are created as reactions to the monstrosity of chaos, and monsters are created by these borders, in a dialectic process in which both borders and monsters acquire material dimensions, becoming 'real,' having 'real' effects."

What is the capacity of language to engage with those real effects and what are its limits? While referring to this place as a crucible of globality and as an example of the confluence of mobility and power, it must remain perfectly clear that borderlands are not a symbol; they are an ongoing human tragedy. Hyper-theorization of such sites obscures real suffering, as in Youngs's reminder of the potential dysfunctions of metaphor. The representation and abstraction in language, with its potential to gloss over embodied experiences of suffering and joy, recreates the world as a narrative owned by its author, a possession then reinforced through reading. If stories become too abstract, materiality—with its specificity, violence, mourning, and human vulnerability—gets lost. But the stories told about places are important, and places, in any human sense, cannot exist without them. As Price (2004, 3) describes it, "narratives about people's places in places continuously materialize the entity we call place." It is increasingly important to consider narratives about movement as well, and how they materialize place, as another possible response to the effects of globalized mobility that Bauman has described. Many places are products of transit as much as stasis, and *El rumor de la frontera* describes the intersections between going and staying, for the author himself, the people he encounters, and in the traces left by the people passing through.

In this story, as in many other stories about this region, the most powerful force is the maelstrom of human mobility that partly defines contemporary Mexico. It is important to remember, however, that the idea of Mexico is also related to the great territorial divisions and political power plays to which the lower North American region has been subject in the past. Many influences go into ideas of Mexicanness, and none of them depend upon or correspond cleanly with cartographical divisions or the details of the organization of the modern Mexican state.[3] One element of the analysis of *El rumor de la frontera* is the identification of those elements of point-of-view that do not presuppose the US-centric sense of the present that often drives discourse even outside of the United States itself and that instead speak to the particularity of the authors' trajectories and orientations, and their narrative and visual construction of the rapidly changing places within this contested zone. The areas both north and south of the current border, part of variously unified pre-Columbian territories, were incorporated into early chronicles around the Conquest and colonization, featured in the definition of Nueva España as well as postindependence Mexico, and therefore were part of the discursive construction of the idea of place through this region in all those periods. Even its partial annexing by the United States contributed to new discourses of transborder identities rather than neatly excising the territories from a historicized imagining of place. The intensity of efforts to physically and symbolically fortify the border testify to its recency and fragilities.

El rumor de la frontera necessarily engages with the presence of the United States as a delimiting condition for contemporary Mexico. Nevertheless, while exploring the looming presence to the north, Armada's text constantly evokes the continuing sway of both pre- and post-Columbian past connections—one of the effects of a Mexico first encountered through European history rather than in adjacency to the United States. It remains imbued with "the unexpired heritage of Spanish explorers, adventurers and monks" (Armada and Arranz 2006, 15). Mexico, with reference to indigenous cultures and its spiritual heritage, is "a country that seems crushed by the weight of its impressive history" (15).[4] This historical perspective is nearly invisible in mainstream Anglo-US discourse, except via images and artefacts of exotic difference, decoupled from their historical and cultural meaning. Temporal distancing has been a significant trope in the representation of Mexico, so the inextricability of past and present characteristic of Armada's text provides a counternarrative. It allows for the evolution of cultural meaning according to changing conditions. The historical imagination as inscribed through narratives of encounters with peoples and places speaks to the connections between past acts of violence and discursive interventions in ideas of place and difference, rather than categorizing difference through temporally marked hierarchies of development.

Armada begins, as many travel writers do, by invoking his point of departure. Tellingly, and unusually for a travel book, this point is not his immediate home but rather his conception of borders as it evolved through his childhood trips to Portugal (11). This is a useful organizing idea since the juxtaposition of a memory of passage through a boundary like the mountains of Iberia with a recently invented frontier such as the United States-Mexico border powerfully evokes the capacity of division to engender tragedy. This is pointed given that the Spanish-Portuguese border (itself long-contested) was partly dissolved in the European Union. The border created at the Treaty of Guadalupe Hidalgo was drawn by violence, not mountain ranges or even rivers, since the river in the United States-Mexico border zone is not what divides, as we see in Armada's discussion of the rivers' many crossings. Somewhere in between these two reference points lies Armada's reference to the Strait of Gibraltar with its share of regular heartbreak as people die trying to cross from Africa to the European Union. Armada evokes borders for their common features while maintaining their local specificity. They are lived places, with histories that transcend the "geopolitical legalism" of the contemporary line between nations, having "long been divided as well as connected along social, political, cultural, and economic axes that predate this boundary" (Price 2004, xiii).

Armada alludes to the ways the global system of racially and economically differentiated experiences of place operates in Spain itself. In one passage, he mentions a Spaniard "fallen" into the Mexican "lot" in the United States: "He didn't have the luck of his brothers who stayed in Spain. . . . He's done a bit of everything, and the last five years has worked as an agricultural laborer" (168).[5] The comparison clarifies one aspect of global inequality in its relationship to the luck of birth and probable destiny, the deviation from which is perceived as extraordinary. It is a subtle critique of the equation of identity with nation, the kind of denaturalizing of the idea of the nation-state that Price (2004, 33) finds to be one of the most powerful potential functions of storytelling.

Such direct invocations of contemporary Spain are few, despite the original domestic audience for the book, but they demonstrate Armada's awareness that while he explores the divisions and connections between Mexico and the United States, Spain does not align neatly with one side or the other. He draws connections between Spain's historical ties to the region and the capacity or incapacity for comprehension of place, such as in the following sentence about the religious missions in the region: "the Spanish missions that appeared like apparitions in lands completely unknown to the Europeans who, centuries later, would still not manage to understand very well what the hell the United States is."[6] Spain's extension (partly religious) into the Americas encompassed areas of the present day United States, though this historical interconnection does not equate to understanding.

Despite its cultural and historical ties to Mexico and its past massive emigrations (and recent economic push factors), Spain, like the United States, is now an immigrant country. Spain's commonalities with both the United States and Mexico are a further testament to the fact that the border zone is not a clear division between two diametrically opposed worlds. The book's blurb may describe the two sides as "two worlds with nothing in common," but that is promotional hyperbole positioning the book as a sellable commodity in the popular discourse about the border, and is not repeated within its pages.[7] Both sides of the border are home to people with shared languages and histories, with Armada going so far as to say "everyone is Mexican whether they were born on this side or the other" (143).[8] The stories Armada recounts suggest this belief is very common, even inside the border patrol itself and its dependent industries.

He notes, as is increasingly commonplace, the demographic shifts showing just how many places in the United States will soon have majority Hispanic populations, notably in states such as Texas (25). In cities like Laredo, Armada (59) claims, the population is already some ninety-five percent Hispanic, and even the border patrol is predominantly so, though not in the same proportions. In addition to referring to data and exploring popular perceptions, many of the descriptive passages in *El rumor* evoke in Texas a similar ambience to that found in states like Chihuahua, with similar inhabitants, preoccupations, and climate, among other things. Armada perceives that north of the border "Hispanic people are an overwhelming majority and Spanish the language saturating like a mudslide the whole reach from east to west, as if quietly reconquering a stolen territory" (15).[9] This, clearly, is not a product only of recent migration and seasonal mobility, but one part of a much longer history of convergence and division, displacement and settlement.

The people to the north and south of the river that tracks part of the border, with their linked stories and family and social ties, are the same people, as Armada explicitly states. His humanizing, tight-focus anecdotes further trace the ways human beings are very much the same everywhere, even beyond the common cultures of the region. Peñate Rivero (2012, 323) argues that the focus of the book is very much on human encounter, with the geography secondary, as a setting for both historical circumstances and human drama. While, as shown below, the geography plays an arguably more significant role at various points in the book, the anecdotes of individuals who variously come to fore in different locales are certainly central. *Tejanos, californianos, arizonianos, nuevo mexicanos* and Sonorans, Chihuahans, New Leonians, Tamaulipans, and Baja Californians are connected, their lives shifting between two languages and cultures, save that some are protected by the powers of their state apparatus and cushioned by relative wealth and advantage, whereas others are constantly subject to the grinding gears of violence and exploitation that are the engine on which the very mechanism that separates them runs. The stories Armada tells emerge from diverse locations along his route, and Arranz's photographs are similarly diverse; however, it is necessary for a work like this one to present its version of Ciudad Juárez, since of the border cities Juárez has most possessed the popular imagination as a symbol of what has gone wrong. "Ciudad Juárez, where all horrors are consumed. Here opulence is concentrated; the bloody and the forgotten, the insatiable and those that put to the test people who have no choice but to live here or who refuse to capitulate. Next to El Paso, one of the cities that, year on year, heads the list of the safest cities in North America" (Armada and Arranz 2006, 104).[10] Ciudad Juárez and El Paso form a single community, more so each year, and Armada's attention to such twin cities echoes the frequent attention in literature both from and about the border to such urban dark mirrors, perhaps most intensely in Gabriel Trujillo Muñoz's writings about Mexicali-Caléxico. Arreola (1996, 356–57) has critiqued the cultural overemphasis on this twinning, which creates an illusion of a kind of balance that does not exist. *El rumor*, with its dual attention to personal stories and to broader historical and cultural narratives, does reproduce border clichés like twin cities, but partially reframes their usual meaning by undermining the line that defines them.

All the social and economic machinery surrounding the border, with its surface functions of security and order and its submerged criminality and destruction, is not something over which any actor can demonstrate clear control (despite nationalist propaganda to the contrary). Armada also reminds his readers that imposition by its very nature invites resistance and subversion. The defense of borders assumes their porosity; borders suppose their own crossing. "The border is also an impulse to go beyond, to modify the fruits of the logic of history, a mask of old iron teeth. Like the wall half eaten away by the sea in Tijuana. The carcass of a political Titanic" (179).[11] Even the strongest walls are an Ozymandian endeavor. This porosity applies not only to the parasitic opportunism of the violent and criminal border crossings but also to other, more humane connections and transgressions that erode the authority of the border.

While it largely transpires in the United States, *El rumor de la frontera* barely touches on the influence of Anglo-American culture from the north. At intervals, the inconsequentiality of the very notion of geopolitical boundaries is underscored through Armada's recourse to geological time and the gradual pace of natural change. While mostly avoiding the erasure of present-day border trauma, Armada uses this tactic of temporal sprawl to diminish the significance of ownership, a concept of space that often perverts rather than draws on the more dynamic sense of belonging with which humans conceptualize their surroundings. This long-view temporality is "capable of laughing at all the historical episodes in which human memory intervenes, our frontier records, our titles of property" (125).[12] Human time, in comparison, is ridiculous, and human cartography is "less than the slightest tilt of the geological clock, which regards us without awareness, and therefore with neither disdain nor compassion" (91).[13] While this temporal concept is useful for creating perspective about human territoriality, Armada also clearly struggles with the distance such a position creates from human experience and the difficulties of incorporating a sense of natural change into the messy business of being in places. "The ancient ocean of the glacial era is now an inconceivable dazzling whiteness. Such purity seems inhuman" (123).[14]

Temporal expansiveness in considering the region he is traversing also gives Armada room to explore definitions of places different from the modern territorial ones and place those definitions into historical perspective. He references indigenous American concepts of place to highlight the relationship between people and their surroundings and the constitutive power of the natural environment. If this power can somehow infuse the sense of place around the US-Mexican border zone, then the relationship between *geo-* and *graphia* becomes simultaneously broader—conceiving the continent as one continuous land—and more humane, allowing for similarity of human experience via human relationships to this continuous space. As Armada writes, "The austere beauty of the Sonoran desert knows nothing of politics: two thirds of it are in Mexico but it extends also through the south of California and Arizona" (158).[15] People, not place, have invented the border, and it is people who therefore determine both its operation and its consequences.

Macro-level division repeats at the micro level. The texture of border life bristles with man-made differentiation and exclusion. Patrol trucks have a "security grille between the front and the rear" (60).[16] Borders are imposed even between individuals, with free humans at the front versus animalized, canine-like humans behind. Mechanisms of border crossing also offer a marked contrast. The whole book is flavored by the experience of Mexicans crossing to work in the north, but it also includes mentions of the daily lives of people who live on the US side of the border and work in Mexico, such as managers of *maquilas*. Their commute is all car-bound tedium rather than perilous chance, and the duration of crossing is significantly compressed in comparison to the northbound direction. In a now almost-cliché commentary, Armada (76) points out that poor migrants and seasonal workers are giving their lives to benefit the US, providing labor for industries like agriculture upon which the United States depends and doing menial work that many US citizens are not willing to do. Arnold (2007, para 6) has made the crucial connection that this inextricable usefulness and loathing is a product of a long-term historical ambivalence in the United States that leads to Mexicans' position as "valued and degraded, crucial to the U.S. economy and yet waging a war on it, upholding family values and yet destroying social welfare institutions and producing too many babies and so on." Few human creations bring pure, unalloyed destruction, however, and Armada also notes that border security has provided some otherwise disenfranchised US citizens with a mission and sense of belonging (138). The tragedy of this mode of identity formation is that it comes at the cost of the exclusion and suffering of others.

The side effect of the book's preoccupation with geopolitics, global capital, and their social impact is that it leaves little room for interrogating the act of narration and the significance of writers' and photographers' roles in producing images of place. Low interiority and impersonal voice characterize Armada's documentary style (Peñate Rivero 2012, 320–21). This absence prevents a degree of personal implication in the geographies and peoples observed and the descriptions produced. While *El rumor de la frontera* is a critical and engaged piece of writing, it does not directly account for its own position in the textual mythologizing of the border zone, nor in any substantial way for the authors' own relationships to the very themes of privilege, mobility, and power to speak with which the book is otherwise so concerned. Furthermore, while space is made for individual anecdote, and some of Arranz's photos show highly particular subjects, the book lacks the evocation of the bodily effects of poverty and disenfranchisement that Saldívar (1997, 135–36) finds most effective in a work like Luis Alberto Urrea's *Across the Wire* (1993).

Extending the focus on discourses of place and the large-scale historical and socioeconomic perspective, Armada shows interest in the myths of the Wild West and their reenactments and reinterpretations in the millennial borderlands. Are these intertextual references and allusions to the romanticizing of violence sufficient for the book to be understood as a comment upon and a reflexively aware and subversive critique of the tropes of the borderland? *El rumor de la frontera*, like almost all travel stories, is laced with references and connections to existing ideas of place. Armada's choice of references, from Robert D. Kaplan to Roberto Bolaño and Cormac McCarthy, are suggestive of his textured understanding of the interrelationship of material effects of economics and the less quantifiable functions of memory and story, even though he does not comment on his own narrative's direct contribution to those functions.[17]

Armada is invested in works that represent very specifically and often with novelistic sensitivities the precise zone he traverses (Bolaño's great novel of the Mexican borderlands, *2666*, McCarthy's border trilogy, Kaplan's *An Empire Wilderness*). He focuses on the way such texts also, in his view, bring out the widespread social failures and cultural paradoxes analyzed by Walter Benjamin. As controlling literary references, Bolaño and McCarthy have in common a fusion of the mythic nature of storytelling with the bleaker and more apocalyptic elements of frontiers, with their suggestion of pervasive evils. Edmundo Paz Soldán (2008, 222) argues that *2666* employs the Juárez *femicidio* "as a metaphor for the horror and evil of the twentieth century."[18] Armada himself is preoccupied with facts, statistics, and the personal stories of the people he encounters, but all set against the epic imaginary of this region and therefore repeating the inscription of the borderlands as a space of transgression and ungovernability, a characterization that is not all that far from the romance of the Wild West. At times, this takes the form of direct acknowledgment. Presidio and the Big Bend area, for example, are "in tune with the legends of the Old West and the mystique of the road" (93).[19] Peñate Rivero (2012, 330) characterizes Armada's focus on the Old West as one of the methods employed to find commonalities throughout the regions explored. It could be considered strategic rather than over-invested in existing myths. Armada also displays some awareness of the potential for romanticizing violence that is so closely connected to this intensively reinvented history, commenting that "Texas, to the point of infantile obscenity, fancies it does everything on a large scale. Even slaughters" (25).[20]

At one point, Armada agrees with one of Bolaño's characters that *Pedro Páramo* and like tales are not fantasy: "even though literature allows a lot of license that reality does not, for some time life in Mexico has acquired extraordinary overtones" (173).[21] Armada's refusal to categorize the extraordinary as magical is appropriate, because as Hicks (1991, xxvi, 22) has argued, magical images become abstracted from the system that produces the daily conditions of life, a move that is profoundly depoliticizing. By absorbing the imagery and potential reality of mythic hauntedness and woundedness, Armada creates a tension in his text between two possibilities. The first and more laudable effect is emotional energy to counter the abstraction that can often occur in the assumption of the authoritative voice of nonfictional narration. The second and more problematic possibility created by Armada's absorption of novelistic imagery is romanticizing the violent elements of the border zone in ways that position them within an adventure-heroism trope. Certain types of stories tend to emphasize the worst aspects of place, reproducing established stereotypes that satisfy rather than challenging audience expectations. Among elements Kathleen Staudt (2014, 472–73) identifies in the cultural reinforcement of accepted negative images of the border is Hollywood films' naturalization of explicit, embodied violence in Mexican territory, where violence in US territory is sanitized or justified. One of the more insidious threads in contemporary travel writing is the connection of the valued commodity of authenticity—always only a projection of the traveler's desire—to superficial encounters with poverty, hardship, or danger, something that will be explored further later in this chapter. The bleak atmosphere evoked by Bolaño and regularly referenced by Armada drifts toward the appeal of exoticism, although Armada, in the main, does not perpetuate the disturbing equation of violence (or at least menace) and authenticity. This successful avoidance of the trap of authenticity is a result of his work's continuous close engagement with the power relations shaping present day textures of place.

US public discourse frequently falls into peculiar contradictions around questions of violence and control, contradictions that are notably heightened in the case of the border with Mexico. Armada mentions the example of the US military's laundering of the clothes and possessions of dead soldiers before their return to their families, suggesting that the effect is itself an erasure of life: "the Pentagon's laundries are so efficient and hygienic that the last trace of life has, with the best of intentions, been erased" (73).[22] The humanity of life—the messiness of human bodies both in the living and in the dying—is occluded, with the personal effects of the soldiers becoming pristine symbols of their office rather than the actual tools of their daily experience. On the other hand, an extremely explicit fascination with death makes up a significant proportion of US popular entertainment; in this fictionalized realm of oblivion, death is casual (as in action films and series) or an intellectual exercise (as in police and medical procedurals). These dual cultural processes—erasure and fictionalization—strive to contain violence and suffering in ways that keep them distant from the everyday business of consumption, which Armada positions as the main function of global capitalism and which reproduces global inequalities. Like the territory between the United States and Mexico, however, trauma and suffering show themselves to be beyond human government. Timothy Luke (2016, 124) has pointed to the way the very failure of security at the border, and the design of walls and fences as symbols of control that function only to redirect flows of people rather than prevent them, "encourages citizens to look away from the raw edge of actual territorial limits and ignore the permanent contradictions between wealth and poverty they often reveal." The fundamental ungovernability of mobility and associated traumas is one factor driving the toxic fear flavoring much public discourse surrounding migration, which occasionally accelerates into paranoia and punitive reprisal. Romantic fantasy and conscious oblivion do not permit any kind of in-betweenness. The barriers between the living and the dead, between the north and the south, are conceived as absolute in order to support myths of national identity, so their creeping failures and the intrusion of the one into the other can only be wellsprings of anxiety.

Although Armada's attention is mainly on towns north of the border, the gravitational center of both trip and story is Ciudad Juárez, where many of the problems of place-image already discussed reach their apogee. This centrality applies both in practical terms—Juárez as the site of slaughter, impunity, people and drug smuggling, *maquila* exploitation, differentiated experiences of crossing—and in a symbolic sense, as Juárez stands in for all that is most perverse about geopolitics and for the ongoing, seemingly unstoppable trauma of the border: "The trip's nucleus, its epicenter, is in a scorched inhabited dump. The border's shredded heart is its largest metropolis, Ciudad Juárez . . . a synonym for junkyard, living example of contemporary society's 'normalization of barbarity,' as Sergio González Rodríguez described . . . where political power and *narcotráfico* mated to birth a mutant that devours human flesh" (115).[23] The imagery around Juárez echoes Heriberto Yépez's (2006) rejection of a celebratory multicultural or hybrid Tijuana, evoking instead a scrapyard of capitalism defined by hate and disgust. Rodríguez (1992, 106) makes a similar point, suggesting that post-NAFTA Tijuana is not at the border between Mexico and the United States but between everywhere and everywhere, a "colony of Tokyo" and a "Taiwanese sweatshop."

Armada identifies positive forms of hybridity on the US side, wedded as benefits often are to the position of economic advantage. The *rumor* of San Antonio, for example, arising from the use of Spanish but also architecturally, gastronomically, and climatically, exudes "a past that combines what is Texan with a seemingly intrinsically *gringo* pride and that has at the same time Mexican roots and a Spanish nature" (19).[24] The cities and towns of the borderlands are ripe with cultural contradiction and the paradoxical exclusion and fusion that characterize borders. The most thriving forms of hybridity to both south and north, however, are not inspired cultural fusions but deplorable abuses and exploitations. The point that Armada is very careful to underscore is that the violence represented by the idea of Juárez is not the product of criminality arising from some millennial evil. The supposedly benign instruments of the contemporary global economy enable and depend on violence. Each violent event and act has individual human victims, but the crimes are enmeshed in globalized exercises of power.

Armada identifies the nature of the crimes and their relationship to power more specifically in the following passage: "high-tech multinational production lines, extreme poverty, the constant passage of emigrants seeking a better life north of the line, organized crime, *narcotráfico* with all its ramifications exist together, and those who resist do so by organizing themselves at the margin of a state that not only does not protect them but actively appears as an accomplice of wrongs" (121).[25] The sense of place evoked in the book is not just of the *frontera*, but also suggests its origins and the proximate and remote aftershocks it creates. This is a directly critical mode of travel writing, which takes as its object how everyday life is shaped by economic relationships and state power and what is produced at the margins. However, this marginality is not only subjection to power, but also, as his phrasing suggests, a space of potential forms of resistance. The direct critique does, however, displace the sense of place as lived and the resistance in the voices of the inhabitants, even though one of the characteristics of *El rumor* in general is the proliferation of voices.

As a framework for this kind of critical assessment, Armada (82) draws on Benjamin to critique the relationship between human suffering and global power and capitalism. He sees the worst aspects of life on the border as the outcome of the unchecked function of capital and the injustice of a system that seeks only its own perpetuation. Armada again compares the Mexican effects of this system to those seen in Spain. The Spanish economy depends on migrant workers, and as in the United States, this practical reality is in constant tension with the use of fear to political advantage. Armada describes the operation of the border as "an echo of the sub-Saharans deported by the Spanish Government to Morocco, which in turn abandons them in the desert, without water, without food, without shelter" (156).[26] No migrant's plan is to die in the desert; they are responding to the pressures of global capital and the violence and insecurity it produces.

The enmeshment of global power and local suffering is something Armada continues to explore via the effects of changing macro conditions. For example, the September 11 World Trade Center attacks in 2001 changed the meaning as well as the embodied experience of mobility for everybody everywhere. The subsequent wars brought new waves of refugees, states implemented different security regimes and experiences of air travel, and the climate of fear embedded new vocabularies of religious tension into public discourse in many countries of the world. Along the US-Mexico border, Armada shows how the increase of security and US paranoia rhetoric reshaped not only trans-border mobility but also trans-border economics:

> With the border blocked at both points, through an excessive collateral effect of September 11, 2001, vendors from Boquillas del Carmen cross here [near Big Bend] the almost always fordable currents of the river (Bravo for them, Grande on this side), leave on the paths painted stones, copper scorpions, and illustrated sticks next to a can anchored with a rock so that travelers can pay what they think the items are worth. (90)[27]

This local economy should be an example of the free trade fantasy, wherein the market determines worth, but at this micro scale it is precisely what the mechanisms of transnational capitalism attempt to prohibit. When Armada brings his systemic critique down to these kinds of local details, this mode of travel writing much more effectively marries a real sense of place—the lived how of resistance at the margins—with trying to foreground the invisible forces of late capitalism and the myths (like free trade) that support its self-perpetuation. Spatial control springing from heightened discourses of security, paired with liberalization applied only to capital flow, exacerbates the differentiated material effects described by Hodge. Free trade is not for individual, human-level gain, at least not within the confines of the law.

Another such myth is the idea of total state control of space and its inhabitants—particularly illusory along long land borders, as Luke (2016) has argued. While the insidious colonization of communities and environments by the worst effects of uneven capitalism seems unstoppable, with neighbors divided by new blockades reshaping the topography of towns and cities, resistance to control also leaves its mark on the landscape. The human costs associated with crossing outside of the controlled channels—the enormous historical wound of death and suffering—show in physical traces such as the anonymous white crosses erected along the border that Armada describes (164). More mundane but equally chilling are the emergency handsets on telephone towers strung through the desert in Imperial Valley, "so that illegal emigrants can surrender before death hunts them down" (166).[28] Through descriptions of such objects, Armada's critique of global-local power alludes to the failures of control. It is not only a failure of power over people, but it also implies the impossibility of the ultimate mastery of space and nature that was one of the central propositions of European rationalism and colonialism. Armada's focus shifts between the political and the natural spheres, with references to nature a reminder of the particularity of all places and the ways they remain unique and irreducible to units in a uniform global system, while political controls always suppose the possibility of resistance and subversion, though the cost may be high.

As already mentioned, the most significant weakness of *El rumor de la frontera* as an example of the positive possibilities for recuperating travel writing as a critically effective rather than purely neocolonialist genre is the absence of significant self-reflection. Indeed, despite taking the theme of mobility and migration as a focus throughout, the book is not particularly transparent about the circumstances and material assistance from others that actually facilitated the trip, except briefly in the acknowledgments (Peñate Rivero 2012, 318). Despite occasionally recognizing his foreignness and incomplete knowledge, Armada does not deeply interrogate his trip's—and his book's—complicity in or resistance to historical paradigms about Mexico and the border zone. Nor does he fully acknowledge the formation of his frame of reference and the beliefs and expectations that determine his capacity for interpreting the spaces and peoples he encounters. Nevertheless, *El rumor de la frontera* demonstrates sensitivity to the mutability of the meaning of place and the consequences of this mutability for both residents and transients. S-11 is just one of the examples Armada gives of the potential for global forces to change the texture of local experience in ways that are differentiated according to factors like class, ethnicity, language, and distance. The same event can, in a different location, create a sense of sacredness in an otherwise materialistic public life, as seen in the passions aroused around the debate over New York's Ground Zero. That sanctification supposes exclusion, in the dichotomy between what is pure and hence permissible and what is irretrievably impure, an established symbol of hatred or suffering. That moment was also the prologue to a simultaneous reinforcement of borders and heightened hysteria in debates over US national identity, with flow-on effects in Mexico and on Mexicans and Central Americans living in the United States.

Armada draws our attention to similar reconfigurations of sites that have sprung from equally transnational but more mundane causes like economic rationalism. One case he mentions is a mine closure, an example of resources demand building up a town before erratic commodity prices destroy its viability overnight (94). The people who seek work in the boom—or whose incomes are no longer enough given sudden surges in real estate values and other costs of living—are cast adrift, increasing the yawning disparity between privileged and subaltern mobilities. In the wake of such processes lie the half-built infrastructure and purposelessness of capitalism's ghost towns. This mode of travel writing takes a physical space—in this case an uninhabited town—that could readily be presented through anecdote, as a metaphor or in the contexts of intertextuality or personal memory, but instead features it as a materialization of actions arisen out of political and economic ideologies.

Corina Arranz's photographs are similarly preoccupied with mutability and the temporary texture of place, almost by the very nature of her project. Photography freezes time and is extraordinarily contingent on the circumstances of the encounter. The effect of combining text with photographs, Liliane Louvel (2008) theorizes, is that photographs trigger speech out of silence and demand the comment of the spectator. Even more than narration, photography may incorporate details and provoke responses outside their author's control—which may indeed have even escaped her notice. Further, as Barthes (1982) explored, that which is most moving about photographs is not the *studium*, the social context and associative meaning attached to the image, but the *punctum*, the emotional connection some element makes with the spectator-viewer.

The viewing of photographs, when physically included in a book, as is the case with the print version of *El rumor de la frontera*, may also upset the chronology, be presented and/or consumed out of order, and thus create echoes and moments of reinterpretation and revelation as the reader progresses through the narrative. In the book, the photos appear as an isolated section halfway through. Arranz also exhibited them in galleries, creating a life for them with yet another relationship to text. The exhibits were mainly in Europe and North Africa, as was the initial immediate audience for Armada's text, a point of note given the Mediterranean comparisons that occasionally feature. The comparison works in both directions, bringing Mexico into a recognizable framework of mobility and border security and also demystifying the Mexican case and acting against a US discourse of American uniqueness. The published selection of Arranz's photos, which also humanize place through intimacy and communicate the geographical presence of natural and built environments, is balanced between portraits and landscapes of varying degrees of habitation. There are also photos that function somewhere between the two modes, like *Cactus sahuaro*, which features a man turned toward a cactus three times his height that juts into the sky, achieving a monumental scale and diminishing the long line of fencing that appears behind the pair. As viewers we must choose or alternate between plant and human.

Similar compositional effect is achieved in *La Santísima Muerte*, which focuses on a statuette of death, but here the eye is drawn to the smiling face of a young girl, peeping through from behind the statuette at about hip height, shifting the sense of the photo away from the commodification of religious iconography to the specificity of the relationship between person and place. *Cactus sahuaro*, outside, is open to the sky, and *La Santísima Muerte* is interior, cluttered. Arranz's imagery explores tensions between enclosure and openness, as signaled from the first image we see, the book's cover, where the ocean renders the extension of the fenced border into its inhuman and uncontainable waters utterly absurd. The photos are evocative of Price's (2004, 38, 41) critical appreciation of the bordered and inhabited condition of the supposedly boundless and uninhabited desert/West. The portraits, with their humanizing effect, show the region's residents in environments dominated by walls, some of which protect or shelter them. In others, they are figuratively entombed—still living humans lying about in a cell, or the dead represented by memorials even though not all bodies are recovered, and some may lie in the desert, their flesh blistered or skeletons bleached by the pitiless sun. But a tight focus on a single object or person is rare, so the photos provoke viewers to choose, to move the eye and navigate the images in response to our own emotional response—or in flight from it.

The iconography of the West and its cargo of individual masculine freedom appears, echoing Armada's focus on this cultural myth, but is undercut. In a saloon, costumed male servers provide male clients with food in plastic and foil packaging, implying the commodification and packaged consumption of the idea of the West. The final image—one of the few without people—is a highway, the modern symbol of the journey and of the possibility of reinvention. Here, however, it vanishes not into the boundless horizon but appears to terminate abruptly at the foot of a craggy hill. But every road begins and ends somewhere. The fantasy of creating a nation out of the supposedly untamed wilderness depended on the exclusion of Mexico over the border, on ignoring the networks built around cities, and on a feminized, subordinate image of nature (Price 2004, 38–39, 50). Arranz's photos emphasize inhabited spaces and place memories, interconnected geographies, and an environment that is only hostile in its instrumentalization as border, rather than in its nature; places change according to how we live in them.

Classically literary travel writing, including much of the travel-writing canon, often elides or minimizes mutability. Such elisions grant places false permanence and give the writer an authority and power to define places that brushes over the contingency of the singular journey. False permanence is a significant source of the tendency to reproduce imperialist discourse so effectively critiqued by Pratt. Alfonso Armada and Corina Arranz represent the places they explore in the context of the present movements of people that are so reshaping the texture and meaning of the region. This representation is situated in terms of historical myths of the borderlands in general, the myth of the US American West in particular, and the alternative concept of place offered by considering space and geography in nature through geological time. The focus on crisis conditions in travels through and near Mexico highlights the kinds of tensions that often disappear in travel writing representing places and peoples as static, with narrative used as a form of literary adventure with a structure over which the writer asserts total control. Travel writing that presents places as they change can have the dangerous effect of reproducing suffering, poverty, and violence as sources of authentic experience. Overall, however, engagement with upheaval in the experience of mobility disrupts old concepts of global centers and peripheries. By bringing to the forefront Pugliese's disjunctive experiences of place, this engagement foregrounds multiple modes of being-in-place, diverse transnational networks, and multidirectional flows of power. Even though abstraction from life to metaphor and the use of inherited tropes of place persist as nearly inevitable products of the attempt to use narrative to make sense of encounters, this mode of narration foregrounds the ways travel writing can speak to the physical and material conditions of contemporary mobility. Armada and Arranz's evocation of some of the variable—and historically unstable—ways of being in, thinking about, and passing through the border is not wholly free of romanticizing a bloody past and present. It does, however, suggest the significant differentiation in the experience of place and of mobility that is emblematic of our critical experiences with global capitalism. The text is an inevitably imperfect but effective combination of poetics, geography, political critique, and the specificity of interpersonal encounter and human-scale anecdote. This kind of contemporary travel story reflects the nature of mobility in a world ever more compressed, with millions of involuntarily displaced people, hundreds of millions of migrants responding to global-level disruptions that shift patterns of migration, and post-terror security paranoia. *El rumor de la frontera*'s external focus on conflict and change, without ignoring history and lived experience, suggests some of the more promising possibilities of testimonial engagements with place. While acknowledging the work's limitations, especially in the area of critical self-reflection, *El rumor de la frontera* is an effective example of European writing about the south that extends beyond the default vision of the north-south gaze to interweave this specific Spanish-US-Mexican encounter with an effective critique of the effects of contemporary globalized mobility.

Alfredo Semprún's Viajes desaconsejables: *Producing Novelty and Consuming Violence*

In Alfredo Semprún's *Viajes desaconsejables* (2007), the interrelationship of instability and the encounter is even more structurally significant than in the work of Alfonso Armada. His stories did not arise from journeys directed to places as destinations in themselves, with the desire for experience and the opening out of the individual subject to difference that this supposes and that is so significant in more reflective and autobiographical modes of travel writing such as those discussed in the previous chapter. Semprún's trips were determined by the vagaries of instability, violence, and change; by *newsworthiness*. Reflections on the role of the traveler and explorations of the multiple historical circumstances contributing to the semi-enduring rather than circumstantial and provisional texture of place can only come *after* the exploration of the event or crisis demanding attention—if in fact they come at all.

For the narratives in *Viajes desaconsejables*, the motive was not a driving desire to visit places in the midst of transformation, at least not as a tourist; the places were chosen for Semprún, at least in part, since he traveled as a result of the nature of his profession. There is, however, a growing subgenre of contemporary travel writing that focuses explicitly on bad, ostensibly unappealing, or outright dangerous places, and works like Semprún's *Viajes desaconsejables* contend with some of the same problems and ambiguities seen in those texts. Within this framework, iconic tourism sites—the most hypertextualized places—are off the itinerary, and experiences are set up in active opposition to what Semprún himself calls "emblematic places" (17).[29] Semprún's work is one example of a type of travel writing that purports to offer something different from the information glut so readily accessible to the consumers of travel writing. However, the importance of novelty and difference in this strategy creates a potential exoticization of peril and violence. The constant production of new fantasies of authenticity has pushed the boundaries of what constitutes valuable transformative experience. A sense of menace is one way of distinguishing the apparently authentic from the prepackaged productions of mass tourism. As Huggan (2001, 33) writes, "the postcolonial exotic is, to some extent, a pathology of cultural representation under late capitalism—a result of the spiralling commodification of cultural difference, and of responses to it, that is characteristic of the (post) modern, market-driven societies in which many of us currently live."

Anti-tourism discourses in contemporary travel highlight global inequalities in access to both the representation of place, relating to the post-imperial roles of travel writing, and to travel conceived as leisure. The leisure definition of mobility reflects an extremely narrow view and is destabilized by actual patterns of global mobility, as already discussed throughout this book.

This book draws together the historical role of the genre of travel writing, the effects of globality, and the way the idea of transatlantic space inflects actual encounters between Spain and Mexico. The whole concept of representation, narrative authority, and the position of the traveling subject are themselves contingent and subject to change. Previous chapters also outlined something of the specific shape of these changes in relation to Spain and Spain's twentieth century, including shifts in the role of travel in Spanish literature. Given this understanding of the contingency of identity and the instability of ideas of place as well as the problems involved in *writing* place, this section therefore examines some of the travel writing of Alfredo Semprún through the intersection of two issues in contemporary travel writing: the representation of the exotic and writing of places, and the accessibility of information and knowledge in a globalized world.

The accessibility or indeed oversupply of information about distant locations is profoundly changing the conditions in which travel writing can be produced. Urry (2001, 3) describes "the mediatizing and circulating of images through print, TV, news, internet and so on" as part of what he calls the "economy of signs," a global circuit of place-related communications that inevitably influences the traveler/consumer's gaze, both in where it falls and how it operates. This same economy creates a new audience, aware of the structures of modernity and the global communications network to which they are attached. Travel writing in that context has become a bestselling genre of popular writing. Lindsay (2006, 76) identifies in this contemporary market (and more specifically in the readership of Bruce Chatwin's *Songlines*) some particular characteristics: "an audience which was created by and benefited itself from the radicalization of modernity: a readership which had the opportunity to travel, which was aware of mass communication structures and was sufficiently reflexive about the modernised context of their lives to sympathize with Chatwin's message." The conditions and meaning of travel have changed dramatically in the past century and with them, of course, travel stories and their readers too have changed. Belenguer Jané (2002, 94–95), in his exploration of the practices and generic limits of travel journalism, attached its rise to the twentieth century's "cultura del ocio" or leisure culture. Readers—the market—have access to myriad information and experiences unavailable to readers of yore, and consequently desire different stimuli.

In *Viajes desaconsejables* Semprún visits the badlands—*ciénagas* or quagmires—of the world. The book is framed as a by-product of years of international travel for media assignments. Foreign correspondents and local journalists working in unstable or corrupt nations inevitably confront a certain degree of danger as a feature of their jobs. Perils include accidents as well as deliberate repressions or reprisals. Dozens of journalists are killed around the world every year. (Mexican journalists are killed more often than most.) Semprún himself notes that he has "only" been shot at twice (21). Danger, therefore, becomes a condition of travel in a different way to the common experience of the leisure traveler. There is also a gendered dimension to the production of this type of travel narrative, both due to overrepresentation of men in that field of journalism and to ongoing stigma around women travelers, danger, and intrepidity as narrative persona. The other effect of this framework is, as mentioned above, that destinations are not selected for personal motives. Semprún is not responding deliberately to an image of place built up over time in his own mind, generating some desire, or even to chance changes of direction that can come to a traveler without a fixed itinerary. His destinations are determined by geopolitical turmoil and, according to the book's foreword, subject to the McLurg Law of newsworthiness wherein proximity increases news value to the audience.[30] Both factors create subjective as well as practical constraints specific to traveling journalists that influence their narrative production. Semprún does not engage in anti-touristic self-aggrandizement, and his travel writing owes more to the outwardly focused tradition of the *crónica* with its element of social commentary than to book-length journeys of personal discovery and self-exploration.

One way the conditions of his tales' production become apparent in *Viajes desaconsejables* is through Semprún's own reflections on newsworthiness and ephemerality. He questions the value of representations of places that contribute to information excess and analyses the limitations of news reporting. As a journalist, he also has a useful perspective on the mediation and targeting of global information flows and what they exclude.

> One asks oneself if the knowledge picked up about Paraguay, for example, in the middle of a coup and the fall of the dinosaur Stroessner, might not be completely wrong; mediated by the ambient noise of the moment. . . . I was only there five days and I filed four stories with the same aplomb of the author contributing the entry on Guaraní to the Espasa encyclopedia. (17)[31]

It is a concern echoed by Javier Reverte (2006, 72), who worked in the same kinds of conditions and the same period of foreign correspondence, in a style of reporting that global communications and globalized media flows have subsequently largely extinguished. In shifting from journalism to travel narrative, however, Semprún's writing comes up against a double genre reversal. First, the travel writing considered most literary is often that which is least journalistic in style (Mee 2009, 306). Second, travel writing reverses McLurg's Law: what is *least* known to readers and *furthest* away has the most value and impact as exotic and adventurous. Both journalists and literary travel writers have "a *liminoid* situation in society. They operate at the border between the foreign and the familiar" (Fürsich and Kavoori 2001, 163, original emphasis). Unlike news media, travel writing usually employs less an empathy/revulsion dialectic than a reliance on the fascination of difference. Unfortunately, difference, to create this value, is often narrated as an irreconcilable otherness, hence the remnant colonial flavor in a great deal of contemporary travel writing and the difficulties some of the other authors here discussed encounter in conveying a specificity of place without recourse to stereotype and generalization.

Semprún explicitly recognizes the effects of this othering and accounts for its eternal temptation. "Ever since man began to tell stories around the campfire, they have fed on fear. . . . Everything from outside was bad and dangerous. The *other* was always a proven enemy" (197; original emphasis).[32] The natural precursors of European travel writing are usually identified as the *Odyssey* and similar epics. Later adventurer-writers—male writers, that is—assumed the heroic role in their tales. What journalism offers against this tradition is a sense of currency—people encountered along the way are not frozen in timelessness but rather subject to immediate forces of change. The immediacy and contingency of the experience is what differentiates it from becoming only a posterior reflection of traditional forms of travel writing. The practice of journalism depends on movement, which is what allows the convergence with travel writing, but also on human contact, the development of networks, and information from local sources. When this point of view is expanded onto the broader canvas of a long feature or whole book, it also allows for examining the bigger picture behind those forces. These characteristics create what Catharine Mee (2009, 309) describes as a possible "antidote to the imperialist nostalgia." The stories conveyed in journalism depend on their geopolitical context and their human impact for their relevance and so resist privileging the traveler's gaze and a central heroic subject. However, they do put forward other truth claims that bring their own problems.

Similarly, a journalist has a potentially different source text for their understanding of place than the traditional literary traveler. Hui-Ching Chang and G. Richard Holt (1991, 103) point out that culture is "selectively manifested to the tourist." No traveler has a comprehensive understanding of their destination. The extent to which their specific circumstances and the limits of their gaze are recognized in their writings often determines the extent to which a travel writer produces an exoticist text rather than a more nuanced, self-reflexive account. Elfriede Fürsich and Anandam P. Kavoori (2001, 158) ask, "Is travel journalism a modernist text that reinforces rather than blurs traditional forms of authenticity or do postmodern travel texts blur the boundaries?" It can do either or both, destabilizing the identity and privilege of the traveler while still reproducing an authenticity myth defined through the primitive/exotic other.

The counterargument here is that through attention to actual material forces, a journalistic gaze has the potential to reinforce another face of difference, of otherness. As Lindsay (2009, 72) discusses, this alternate otherness may also connect to classic exoticism, since both confine a place to, as she puts it, the "literary ghetto of 'difference.'" Despite the often hyperbolic and sometimes speculative nature of journalism, journalistic discourse frequently still treats the world as an object of unproblematic descriptive narration, in tension with the reflective turn that has been suffusing travel writing. At its worst, this mode of narration plays into the naturalization of genocide critiqued by Huggan (2009), in which violence is produced for media audiences as the innate condition of the remote other. A fundamental question for considering the effects of journalistic discourse and resources in producing travel writing, then, is to what extent the focus on immediate material realities and the socially determined elevation of the truth value of journalism over literature simply creates another otherness.

The perils (and fascinations) off the beaten track are certainly a preoccupation of many writers apart from Semprún, including those who have no explicitly declared motive for their travels except producing a consumable description of their adventures. Semprún refuses adrenaline junkie adventure seeking for himself, even actively derides it, stating, "Certainly you don't see what normal people see on their travels and not all experiences are enriching as pretentious snobs claim" (22).[33] He plays down elements of personal danger, and rarely employs the hyperbole mentioned previously as a feature of certain kinds of journalism. As he commented in one interview, "I haven't ever had the sensation of danger because I have tried to be a living journalist and not a dead hero" (Blesa 2007, 4:00).[34] This statement does assert a level of control over his environment and circumstances that is perhaps false, but in effect he is claiming that as a journalist, extreme personal experiences are not and ought not to be the goal of his travels. A fundamental difference between Semprún's narrative and one dominant trend in current travel writing is that he, the traveler and narrator, is not at its center. He journeys not to be transformed by his experience, as has become standard in the travel writing of the global era, but to testify to transformations in the world. In this sense, *Viajes desaconsejables* relies even more on a globalized audience that recognizes interconnectedness and appreciates the presence of identifiable macro forces versus the alienness purveyed by pure exotica.

Journalistic travel narratives such as Semprún's, therefore, both take on something from a past era of travel writing, for journalists perforce describe something unknown to their readers, and embrace something essentially unique to contemporary travel writing: places as we encounter them today are subject to transformative global forces with an unprecedented level of interconnectedness and instantaneous communication. How does travel writing work in this environment? Holland and Huggan (1998, 38) suggest it "acts alternately as a repository for exoticist forms of cultural nostalgia and as a barometer for the recording and calibration of cultural change." There is a sense in which the yearning for bygone models of exploration and adventure is simultaneously reenacted and undone by the ways some contemporary travel writers perform novelty in their work by way of unpredictability and the constant transformation of place. Gone is even the illusion that what is described may endure, unchanging. For journalists, as Semprún acknowledges, "Current affairs control you" (Blesa 2007, 3:39).[35] Impermanence, alteration, emergences, and disappearances—these matter to reporters. Place cannot, by definition, be described statically; the encounter with place is subject to circumstance. Semprún accepts this in his own interpretation of his book's title, "It is not the destinations that are ill-advised so much as the circumstances in which the trip takes place" (in López Schlichting 2007, 4:30).[36] This active engagement with transience and change creates a very different sense of place for readers than that created by less journalistic travel writing. This is a reminder of the multiple functions of travel journalism and writing that, as Mee (2009, 306) points out, have "served purposes and played roles outside of literature, for example in their informative impulse." Literary style as unique criterion for assessing the interest of a text ignores the extent to which journalistic writing has value *because* of its connectedness to a time, not only a place.

Here also the style of chronicle exemplified by *Viajes desaconsejables* can be profitably compared to other arenas of journalistic endeavor. The so-called soft news forms of journalism are beginning to be more widely analyzed. Semprún's work is somewhere at the intersection between the forms, having experienced places under more traditional news-oriented conditions, eventually producing a text that is closer to travel literature traditions than the semicommercial tradition of travel journalism per se. The news impact that occasioned the original voyage has passed, but his pieces remain tied to the specific circumstances that allowed their production. "My stories are always about people, not landscapes . . . people who suffered" (in López Schlichting, 5:50).[37] The people of Semprún's stories are attached to particular places, but more importantly, attached to particular moments in time. Forneas Fernández (2004, 225) writes that "time, organizing element of the journalistic chronicle, in the travel chronicle moves to occupy a secondary place, in favor of space."[38] In work such as Semprún's, this is more complicated, with temporality privileged even to the point of a pervasive sense of unsettledness despite the focus on place.

The critique leveled at this type of journalistic writing, as opposed to other forms of travel writing, is that it is insufficiently self-reflexive and elides the journalist's privilege (Fowler and Kostova 2003; Muggli 1992). The issue becomes evaluating travel writing's balance between the actual, material conditions of peoples in a moment in time, and writing that indulges the traveler's sense of place and transformative personal encounters to the exclusion of temporal change and the host communities' realities. In the example of *Viajes desaconsejables* there is, as is so often the case, some slippage of genres, given the different structures framing the various journeys undertaken. However, the positioning of the narratives themselves via their publication and distribution—their discursive intervention—is as narratives of place in the travel writing mode rather than as reportage.

In the introduction I highlighted Fürsich and Kavoori's (2001, 161) questions about travel writing, to which they, in relation to writing conflict and inequality specifically, add the additional question of whether travel journalism can "be seen as an ongoing expression of cultural transgression and reinvention that reflects the current inequalities between the First and Third worlds?" In writing about Cuba, about the Sudan, about Melilla and the passage into Spain, Semprún confronts the reality of mobility in the world today; a reality defined by migration, exile, the search for refuge. This is precisely the understanding of all forms of human mobility as functions of globality disregarded in most literary travel writing. As Lindsay (2006, 66) writes, "the experience of displacement is . . . a widespread symptom of processes of modernization and globalization." Semprún's work certainly engages with the displacement of peoples as a defining feature of the modern world, including the extremities suffered by those attempting entry into Spain, a country that, like Mexico, clearly shows the extent two conflicting concepts of mobility are geographically and economically intertwined. He makes rare references to his own relative position in the places he visits, though these often seem like limited gestures toward expressing his position as writer/traveler. "One has a passport, a return ticket and, most of the time, a hotel protected by police in which to shower and rest. You go and write about it, but they, who are just like us, remain" (Semprún 2007, 21).[39] This does not reveal the fundamental inequities of the situation wherein dangerous and off-the-beaten-track destinations gain cachet partly through circulating media content. The residents of those places are most disadvantaged in the global hierarchy of mobility, constraint, and the power to interpret places and experiences.

The narratives collected in *Viajes desaconsejables* are not the reports Semprún might have filed with his editors at the time. (Although we do see over the course of the book his professional activities gradually evolving as chronicles and travel stories become more and more a part of his primary paid work.) Stylistically, they permit more of a sense of the narrator to emerge in the text than is conventional in print reportage, although a writer from a journalistic tradition is still likely to retain a different approach to prose than a poet, for example. The most potent element of this intrusion of the subject is the possibility of transparency about the process of news making. Occasionally, however, Semprún also touches on the influence of his own cultural background and the circumstance of being an errant Spaniard out in the world. His tone is usually ironic, but he brings out a couple of the problematics specific to a sense of Spanish cultural identity and to the Spain-Latin America relationship. He signals, for example, the peculiar effect of immersion in a continent of widespread *castellano* in the company of Spaniards of non-*castellano* speaking background: "To travel with Joaquín Ibars through Iberoamerica is the most Spanish thing that can happen to you; he always speaks Catalan with the switch operator at his newspaper, and those voices can only come from one distant corner, which is your home, even though you might live in Madrid" (17).[40]

In a further mention of language and its connection to cultural and national identity, Semprún gives visitors to Puerto Rico who come up against the lively debates over language in that country a warning:

> The thing Spanish travelers must keep their distance from is the internal politics of the island. They already have enough Hispanic troubles at home. So the best thing is to accept the pleasures: rum, coffee, beaches, music, architecture, nature, and cockfighting. On the other hand, the *hispanidad* battle can obsess even the best, and we, Europeans all our lives, are no longer fit for these events. (171)[41]

This comment equates Europeanness with a certain level of disconnect from the present day Latin American critiques of *hispanidad*—and with something of a superior tone of being outside them—and Spanishness with the imperative to limit one's attention to the complexities of Spain and Europe. It is almost an exhortation to remain on the surface of different cultures, echoing the introductory suggestion of the book to visit places and get to know the people only in their most peaceful moments, the classic domain of tourism. In such passages, Semprún seems to be resisting that which gives his work its marketability in the present moment—that what he recounts is off-the-beaten-track, below the surface, a trifle dangerous. The moments of reflexivity cited here are not from Semprún's passages on Mexico, but the same dynamics are at play, even though the explicit focus of his representations of Mexico is on politics, violence, and change.

As with *El rumor de la frontera*, implicit within Semprún's book is the understanding that the flipside of travel is migration, and that mobility does not equal freedom. Danger and crime are linked to movements—especially forced movements—of people. Semprún's piece on Mexico explores the transformation of Chiapas following the Zapatista uprising. This narrative is a very suggestive example of the volatility of not only textures but also ideas of place. Both are radically revised by power shifts affecting the control of physical space and control over representation. A polarizing event like the uprising has the potential to uproot inhabitants who find themselves caught between two extreme positions.

> Those who lived in areas under the control of the Mexican army keep their houses, but with fear of reprisals. The others wander the roads and the fields in search of somewhere to put up their shack. These days it is not only *indios* that carry their belongings on their backs. Hundreds of *mestizos* and *indios aladinados*, that is those who tried for better or worse to integrate into the white world, also had to abandon their villages in the war zone. (188)[42]

This forced mobility had as its counterpoint the insurgents' control over spaces and thoroughfares. As Semprún writes, "From [San Miguel] where the Red Cross has its field hospital to the Guatemalan border not a soul moves without the express authorization of the guerrillas" (187).[43] Mobility is defined also through immobilization, and the possibility to change the conditions of territorial control.

For its inhabitants, but also in the minds of visitors and distant readers, Zapatista Mexico becomes just that: adjectivally reconceived as a place defined by events. As Babb (2010) has described, this linkage of place to conflict has important implications for the idea of place as it is enacted in tourism encounters. The redefinition of place and the consolidation of that redefinition through tourism has important effects not just locally but also nationally and even regionally (Babb 2010). The style in which travel writers present place as defined through conflict is linked to regimes of power. The sensory environment that Semprún evokes suggests that the *olor a pólvora*, or scent of gunpowder, the Zapatistas ascribed to their newly seized stretch of jungle has come to suffuse the entire region. The predominant flavor and feeling of place arise not from some essentialist exoticism attributed to its people nor from the temporal yawn of geological features, but from the volatility of human action. Semprún's allusions to changeable and hostile nature reinforce this volatility rather than countermanding it as was the case in Armada's narrative. The landscape of Chiapas—the site of the displacements and immobilizing control previously mentioned—transforms around people as they are suffering these changes: "the dirt road becomes a muddy hell as soon as four drops of rain fall" (187).[44] These transformations reinforce a widening conceptual gap between European, democratic Spain and the turmoil of the Latin American badlands, a conceptual gap that contrasts with Fermín Heredero's alternative representation of Chiapas discussed in the next chapter.

Despite the focus on convulsive change arising from Semprún's motives for and mode of travel, the narratives he produced for the collection *Viajes desaconsejables* do not detach present volatility from its much more enduring historical causes and context. Changes may be abrupt, including violent displacement, but memories are long, and at times Semprún explores this dynamic in ways that would not be possible within traditional pieces of short-form news journalism. In one passage, Semprún evokes violence's potential to disrupt and remake connections to place, while noting that the origins of such connections and disconnections are more difficult to erase. "Thus, another town, Sitalá, simply becomes no man's land. In the nearby hills, the Tzeltal await reprisals. And although for now they are the landowners, they know by historical experience that vengeance will come" (190).[45] People move, but the memory of violence lingers, flavoring with hatred the relationships between different peoples and the lands in which they collectively dwell. Semprún comments that "The hatred *indios* expressed for the *mestizo* and the assimilated is shocking" (188),[46] noting the various mechanisms of exclusion within indigenous communities. These are mechanisms for maintaining control over their culture and community in order to resist the influence of laws, religions, and innovations coming from a source of which they have cause to be wary.

In the other direction, in a disquieting continuation of interrelated colonialist race/class hierarchies, *criollos* have an ongoing influence in decisions made around civil conflict, even where it affects them very little or not at all. Simultaneously, those *mestizo* and white landowners who have benefited most from displacements and the exploitation of labor "applaud when one of them calls out that 'those who spend their lives reclining in hammocks and not working have no right to eat'" (190).[47] Semprún quotes the interpretation of the lingering rancor over historical conflict and explanation of contemporary racism offered by then Bishop of San Cristóbal de las Casas Samuel Ruiz García: "there are those who project outward their own historical responsibility in order to feel free" (190).[48] The persistence of discord and resentment is just one area in which historical events have lasting repercussions within places. As discussed in Chapter 1, these kinds of transformative events also have enduring consequences for the idea of those places that is built up elsewhere. In moments of change, it becomes urgent to understand *who* can inscribe their version of events on the popular imagination, first in the short term while decisions made may influence their outcome, and ultimately into history.

In this struggle over representation, we see once again the tensions around the revision of popular truths that make the study of purportedly nonfictional accounts of personal experience so valuable. The Ejército Zapatista de Liberación Nacional (EZLN) and its spokesperson, by engaging with the media alongside their direct action, demonstrated in Mexico what has become a fundamental of modern territorial and civil conflict: first, convince the watching world of your righteousness—or at least try your hardest to do so. This dynamic has played out more recently through the numerous other conflicts, such as the Sidi Bouzid revolt in Tunisia and its sequelae in Egypt, Libya, and elsewhere, in which different state and rebel groups scrambled to control the message both inside their countries and in international media projections. Recent Mexican protest movements, like #Yosoy132 and the outpouring of responses to the Ayotzinapa disappeared, have further demonstrated the depths of complicity within media appropriation strategies that frame much public discourse about injustice and inequality and resistance in Mexico. Semprún references the potential disconnections between the experience of Zapatista zones of Mexico and the stories of the place, which themselves of course contribute to the broader imaginary of contemporary Mexico. He notes, for example, the paradoxes of propaganda: "Between the 20th and the 26th of May 1993, the EZLN made it through its first battle against the Mexican army troops. They resisted six days while moving their arms cache to a different safe place. Two soldiers died and another five were injured. But the Mexican government was categorical: 'Ladies and Gentlemen, there is no guerrilla in Chiapas'" (193).[49]

Attempted nullifications feed into the discourse alongside violent images. Official denials can, through sheer repetition and strategic reinforcement, shift the center of debate. The twenty-four-hour news cycle and the function of the information economy compound these tensions. Developments in distant crises are transmitted instantaneously, and misinformation is repeated, reinterpreted, and ingrained in the popular imagination before it has time to be countered or corrected, a dynamic that is having greater political consequences every day in all our nations. Storytelling, including the retransmission of partial or partially understood information, remains an enormously powerful force for the making of myths—myths that have not only symbolic but also material consequences. Semprún mentions as an example the story of bands of organ-trafficking kidnappers roaming impoverished regions of the world to service the Methuselan fantasies of the wealthy. According to Semprún (198), there had been at the time of writing not a single proven case anywhere in the world. Nevertheless, once again, pure repetition increases the apparent plausibility of the story and reinforces collective hysteria in poor communities that recognize the congruence between this myth of exploitation and the manifold mechanisms by which the hunger of the mysterious global consumer is in fact fed by their own deprivation. Stories, once told, are very slow to pass completely from memory. As Semprún puts it, "These urban legends, myths of the big city, or simply rumors, run through the world, jump continents, disappear and return with the passage of time, change protagonists and settings, but are always there. If anyone thought television would manage to extinguish oral storytelling, the facts could not be more decisive" (204).[50] Semprún's selected example is of a myth that had consequences for a stranger who was understood to be a threat and assaulted by a group of Guatemalans paranoid about organ trafficking. The same kind of beliefs lurk beneath the behaviors and choices of strangers and travelers too.

In the case of the stories of a perilous Mexico of the kind explored in this chapter, readers seeking adventure or extremes of experience as markers of authenticity are likely to be attracted to the sense of danger. Where Mexicans themselves buy into the romanticization of violence, as has been the case with some narco subcultures, fantasy combines with reality to shape an idea of place in which crime is rampant and therefore any kind of crime seems possible. Such is the power of storytelling, and stories are now not only repeated locally, person to person, but flash across the world in an instant. More considered or complete understanding, which may come weeks, months, and even years after the events to which the stories refer, cannot aspire to the impact of an explosive global news story in the first days after it breaks.

In the brief retrospective update with which Semprún frames his own narratives for this much later publication of collected stories, he picks up on the evanescence of public and media attention: "Today Chiapas has been relegated to the deepest corner of the closet of international journalism, but its problems persist with the same freshness as when the *indios* rose up, at the order of a descendent of Spaniards, that New Year's of 1994" (185).[51] The alighting and flitting away of global media attention is one of the processes that determines the production and consolidation of ideas of place at the turn of the millennium and into the new century. The transformative event then becomes part of the backstory of a place, which is vaguely held in association with it in the limited capacity of popular memory.

Despite a writer's own stated rejection of exoticizing danger, it is often the case that contemporary travel writing gains its readers through the promise of extreme scenarios. There is a whole subgenre in the vein of woman or man against nature or extreme circumstances. Travelers who venture into the no-go zones of war, social collapse, regime change, and so forth, as Semprún sometimes does, are also selling a story based on the rarity of their experience for the comfortable readers at home. *Viajes desaconsejables* is framed in the opening editorial note as competing for our attention in the information glut of contemporary media precisely by virtue of its representation of places transformed by "misery and pain, war and ideological violence" (11).[52] This note also acknowledges, however, that attention is a limited commodity; the fantasy of fame via reality programs and the artificial worlds of lifestyle programs is the new dream. Novelty rules, and the novelty of anything, from a civil crisis to a new celebrity, does not last very long. "Ambrose Bierce already said it: God created war to teach Westerners Geography. And in that situation, Mozambique does not exist nor is there a cachexic black kid that can compete with the kitsch and sordid world of celebrity culture and reality TV" (12).[53]

The media environment itself is changing, and information no longer flows to the interested (or the uninterested) in the way it might have in the heyday of broadsheet newspapers, or even in the early days of television. At least in the context of communications, there is now a single global city made up of those people who have access to almost unlimited quantities of information—though that is not the same thing as unlimited access. The greater the disgraces and disasters that overtake an otherwise distant people, the more attention, for a fleeting moment, their stories can command. The price of that attention, though, is the restricted nature of the kinds of stories permitted, and their subsequent enduring influence over the idea of place. The prefatory note to *Viajes desaconsejables* also suggests that "In the papers of the West there is no place for the disadvantaged beyond *costumbrismo* and tsunami (it seems human beings like the muck more than the context" (11).[54] If subalterns figure in the global imagination mostly for exotic color or disaster porn, it is little wonder that the predominant images of them and of their homes continue to be drawn within those two frames.

Within contemporary Spanish travel writing, *Viajes desaconsejables* offers one model that, via its journalistic origins and preoccupation with change, destabilizes some of the persistent tropes of a problematic, exoticizing, ex-imperial genre. The absence of sustained reflection on uncertainty in the traveling subject, however, mean that *Viajes desaconsejables* still sets the experiences of others at a distance, disconnected from the activities of both writer and reader. While this example does invoke the instabilities wrought by global forces, Semprún's inadvisable destinations remain a remote consumable for the readers who share what Phillips (1999, 64) would term the author's "cultural frame." *Viajes desaconsejables* does not fetishize danger like some of its more self-indulgent brethren; however, the attention to circumstance and transience in this work does not go very far in disrupting the dominant images in the global economy of travel. Contact with peoples in extremis, with few options, is something Semprún has undergone for the information and edification of those suffering the ennui of excessive choice. At times, however, his reflections on the function of news media and on the power of stories do, by implication, bring into question the reliability and limitations of the narration of places and encounters. While his own position of privilege is rarely the direct subject of his text, Semprún regularly alludes to global inequalities and the function of power in moments of change. In this sense, the focus on crisis conditions in travels through and near Mexico, for Armada as for Semprún, highlights the tensions commonly elided in that travel writing with a more static view of place and an overly authoritative narrator. The danger of travel writing about upheaval and trauma, however, is that danger itself can emerge as another exotic fantasy conflating interest with suffering, poverty, and violence.

CHAPTER 4

Describing Selves in Worlds

This chapter discusses the intersection of ethnographic, reflexive, and anecdotal styles in Suso Mourelo's *Donde mueren los dioses* (2011; Where the gods die) and Fermín Heredero's *Chiapas: Cuaderno de viaje* (2009; Chiapas: Travel journal). These different styles present different possibilities for understanding the historical and material conditions of cross-cultural transatlantic space and how these inform diverse modes of representation of self and other in a strongly constituted first person narration, and the kind of world created through sensory perception of the environment. It also presents the final example, Eloísa Gómez Lucena's *Del Atlántico al Pacífico: Tras los pasos de Cabeza de Vaca* (2018), which has a similarly personal voice, being the most diaristic of all works discussed in this volume, but with sensory perception focused internally, upon the traveler's body, and attention to the natural environment limited in comparison to historiographic reflection and anecdote. Suso Mourelo, author of *Donde mueren los dioses*, is an example of a professional travel writer. Mourelo has published travel narratives about several destinations, writing in a mix of the referential and anecdotal styles common in the genre, also relevant for the additional comparative analysis referencing sections of Paco Nadal's *Pedro Páramo ya no vive aquí* (2010; Pedro Páramo no longer lives here). Mourelo's book on Mexico is here compared to Fermín Heredero's less commercial *Chiapas*, simultaneously a more ethnographic and more sensory work. Gómez Lucena is discussed also in relation to quotidian detail and anecdotal style, though flavored with a historiographic rather than ethnographic orientation, which greatly alters the focus of representation of American people (including indigenous peoples), present and past. Comparison of these works allows a further engagement with the political implications of characterizing cultural and linguistic otherness and indigeneity in Mexico. The examples are also discussed in terms of global and historical responsibility and the authors' own interpretations of their individual and community relationships to the initiation and ongoing function of the world system that underpins contemporary global power, and Latin American decolonial frameworks in relation to worlds, destruction of worlds, and the representation of nature in travel writing. This chapter emphasizes the importance of the active constitution of cross-cultural transatlantic histories in relation to ideas of indigeneity in the Americas as well as symbolic and physical violence against indigenous peoples and their relationship to their environment. It describes how contemporary travel narratives function as performances of the forms of historical understanding that have ongoing implications under global capitalist worlding practices, in the Spivakian sense. The comparative analysis touches on broader questions of subjectivity and authority in writing, the recounting of quotidian experience, and transparency, contrasting the accumulation of detail against the extensive digressions, abstractions, and temporal and geographical leaps that characterized some of the works analyzed in previous chapters.

Chiapas in Heredero's Chiapas: Colonialities of Perception, Sensory Nature, and Indigenous Subjects

Chiapas: Cuaderno de viaje has, like other texts discussed in this chapter, a diaristic quality, dwelling attentively on the details of quotidian experiences and narrating sensory perceptions of varied places in the southern state of Chiapas. A book-length travel narrative taking Chiapas as its exclusive subject provides an opportunity to go into further detail about Mexico's cultural diversity and the politics of representation of indigeneity. This is because Chiapas is among those southern states whose population includes a very high percentage of indigenous people. While not as high in percentage terms as the more sparsely populated states of the Yucatán peninsula, in terms of absolute numbers of indigenous people, especially those who speak indigenous languages, Chiapas is near the top. In addition, it is near or at the bottom of the list of Mexican states for indicators like life expectancy, education, and income. Chiapas therefore highlights the historically determined racial component of economic injustice. It occupies a central place in narrating the histories and contemporary experiences of indigenous Mesoamerican people, in contrast to more homogenizing Mexican national narratives of *mestizaje*.

Chiapas's position as the site of the famous EZLN rebellion and ongoing resistance to Mexican state power in defense of self-determination and in the face of centuries of degradation and abandonment by central powers compounds the complexity of the projection of *chiapaneco* distinctiveness in relation to narratives of Mexicanness.[1] The Zapatista uprising focused global attention on Chiapas as a site of ideological struggle, and simultaneously created a new myth and instantaneous transformation of place-image of the kind that only arises through the outbreak of war or similarly extreme events. Since the focus of this book is tourist encounter through travel narrative, the discussion of Chiapas in relation to Zapatista resistance is presented primarily in relation to this transformation in the idea of place and the subsequent reinscription and redefinition of Chiapas for tourism. Indigenous resistance to state control, and the construction of the Selva Lacandona as a site of struggle, is partly reincorporated into capitalist spatial control through tourism, both of the political and ecological variety. In addition, therefore, to conflict-zone tourism as a potential form of exoticization of danger as discussed in the previous chapter, the image of the Zapatistas becomes a site of symbolic struggle within economies of ethnotourism and ecotourism and their associated production of indigeneity. Zapatistas, like other rebels in/against global capitalism, confront negation by biopower and governmentality as supposedly problematic subjects of the Mexican state in opposition to so-called authorized *indígenas* who collaborate with projects based on developmentalist logics (Cañas Cuevas 2016, 26). Patricia Viera-Bravo and Álvaro López López (2020) argue that ecotourism development, given the history of state-directed tourism policy in Mexico, constitutes a major form of governmentality enacted upon indigenous peoples in Chiapas. This enactment constitutes rebellious subjects as traitors to a development agenda that would supposedly elevate the life chances of their people (regardless of the state of evidence of uneven community benefits of ecotourism projects and rent capture in the tourism industry referenced in Chapter 1).

The representation of encounter with indigenous people and the interpretation of indigenous histories and cultures is one of the most heightened tensions in the dynamic between Spanish traveler and Mexican host (in as much as those national categories even apply to the complex systems of belonging of citizens of the two multipolar and heterogeneous nations). This, like other tensions, is partly attributable to the intensified juxtaposition of voluntary and involuntary mobility and immobilization. It also owes much to the persistent strength of colonial discursive modes in circulating imaginaries of indigeneity in Europe and the world. Indigeneity as a category has been heavily inscribed on one side of the binary of modern versus primitive/premodern. This same thinking forms the foundation for developmentalist economic theories and practices and contributes to forms of violence and genocide that are not confined to the past but continue into the present and project into the future. In many of the examples of contemporary Spanish travel writing discussed earlier in this book, the powerful convergence of travel writing genre conventions regarding generalization in the interpretation of cultures and the lingering colonialist visions of otherness infused aspects of the travel narrative of even the most reflective and progressive writers.

Heredero's detained gaze on this specific region of Mexico, then, creates space to explore the politics of representation of indigeneity by European travelers in more adequate detail in relation to these broader themes of mobility/immobilization, cultural binaries and alterity, and the subject position and gaze of the traveler. Writing about Chiapas requires some introduction to race and history. Heredero observes the presence of indigenous and ladino, *mestizo*, and *criollo* people, however his choice of the passive verb *reparar* to recount this presence tends to decenter his act of interpretation in categorizing this diversity as an outside observer (32–33). We can return briefly to the flippancy of a comment like Solano's (2001, 179) earlier cited "it is fake Aztec craftwork and fake Maya craftwork, and I suspect that they are also fake Lacandones."[2] Indigenous mobile and street vendors are often positioned in relation to tired tropes of authentic ethnicity within a tourist economy of souvenirs and spectacle. Heredero, going against this tendency, mentions vendors frequently and in a range of contexts and range of relations, both economic and historical. In the closest situational parallel to Solano, he simply notes the presence of vendors at archaeological sites (Palenque, in both cases) without any value judgement about industrial production of pseudo-artisanal goods nor assumptions about the vendors themselves (53). In another example, describing the less tourist-oriented ambulant sellers in San Cristóbal de las Casas, there is a productive though not labored juxtaposition within a single paragraph of the women selling articles of clothing and jewelry and a nearby statue of Fray Bartolomé de las Casas, namesake of the city and famous early defender of indigenous rights (34). On the next page, a similar passing mention of the presence of indigenous vendors wearing their babies, accompanied by a very typical description of their insistent sales tactics, is interrupted by a comment on Tzeltal beliefs about the concept of the *ch'ulel*, which among other things connects ancestral knowledge with futurity through shaping the individual destiny of unborn children. An experience that often features in touristic accounts of Chiapas as irksome persistence is recast in relation to familial hopes embedded in a system of spiritual beliefs. Heredero enters into unusual levels of detail regarding pre-Columbian as well as later history and the experiences of individual peoples of the region, and combines this precision with reference to specific aspects of the Conquest and historical actions of

Spaniards in the Americas, citing primary and secondary sources (20). Intertextuality and historical thinking are presented as intrinsically intercultural and multilingual. The consequences of these histories are also embodied in contemporary encounters and materialized in contemporary spaces, and the onus is on travelers to encounter peoples and read spaces differently, outside of their own histories and outside of their own beliefs.

Linking this historicized perspective to contemporary encounters, Heredero thus reverses the gaze as much as he is able, though this operation is inevitably incomplete. Although Heredero's direct critiques of tourism per se are limited, we glimpse the complexity of cultural commodification in the divide between the famous prohibition on photography in the church at San Juan Chamula and the circulation of photos of other parts of the town as pro-tourist propaganda (15). There are also some explicit critiques of the self-deception of travelers who project their desires onto seemingly idyllic places as potential cures for decadent ennui: "We tourists are that idiotic. The placidity and repose of a moment make us incapable of distinguishing a few days, from a month, from a year, from a lifetime. . . . We couldn't withstand the necessities of isolation, we would miss our little cravings and the consumption to which our civilization has accustomed us" (128).[3] Even the fleeting desire transforms the half-understood life of local inhabitants and their relationship to place into a touristic commodity. Heredero's critique is aimed directly at the vacuity underlying the circulation of touristic desires for a supposedly simpler life more connected to the environment, given the fact that tourism is defined by transience and an imminent return to privilege and, indeed, quite controlled insulation from the environment.

There is a fairly regular unsettlement of the touristic gaze through Heredero's employment of what verges on an ethnographic discourse in his travel writing, which allows readers to glimpse the way ethnographic desires to know of and learn from indigenous subjects—duplicated in ethnotourism discourse—can become a form of commodification. These moments of unsettlement and touristic reflection suggest spaces of reversal. Those who are most the objects of capitalism, including the knowledge extraction associated with ethnographic desire, come to know its practices and occupy a critical stance with decolonial potential (Burman 2018). As well as this self-alienating mode, Heredero incorporates heavy use of dialogue, foregrounding the voices of others, both travel companions and hosts. This moves in the direction of communicating what Macarena Gómez-Barris (2017, 11) calls "submerged perspectives" and voices of possibility against the obliterative power of neocolonial capitalism. In one extended interlude, a local man presents aspects of the more-than-human and human life in this place (near Maravilla Tenejapa), but not as a neutral representative of cultural difference from which visitors may draw their own conclusions and reflect upon their own culture. It is rather through a dialogue that makes explicit demands and judgements the man renders about his interlocutor:

> Don't hurry because of the time, around here it doesn't matter. The sun rises and sets, it brings us light to live, it happens gently, nothing else. . . . You know a lot, even though you've been educated in a Europe that has lost its soul from losing nature. . . . You have an excess of much that we need, you have excessive money, which we need for schools and healthcare. . . . But don't turn peace into a postcard, which is what happens to most tourists. The spirit is carried deep inside, in secret, it's of each person and cannot be given out, and if lost it can only be recovered by going deep into the guts of where it is found, here where I'm telling you, where all beings are free and in harmony with others. (128–29)[4]

This extended passage in the voice of a local informant centers responsibility in the individual, but an individuality that must account for connectedness and harmony. It is no picturesque flourish from which readers may feel momentarily transported from their busy and insipid lives, but a direct address: traveler (and by implication, reader) have money that is sorely lacking in this community. Furthermore, lack must be addressed by those who feel it. The culture of others is no medicinal corrective to be lightly consumed.

Through these kinds of narrative maneuvers Heredero brings the ethnographic aspects of his style together with the vulnerable authorial presence more characteristic of reflective modes of travel writing, approaching something that resembles an intersubjective mode of critically engaged contemporary encounter. This mode of encounter resists the social ordering that imagines a marginal "other" space that can be categorized according to utopian ideals (Lisle 2006, 92). Heredero does not position himself outside of what he describes, in the way Lisle critiques as occluding one's imperial heritage. I argue that he writes from the position of "ethical and political responsibility to the other," in a way that acknowledges the complicity of tourism and travel narrative in the manufacturing of cultural alterity (Lisle 2006, 265). This helps disrupt certain features of the prevailing territorialization of Chiapas in relation to conflict, authorized and rebellious indigeneity, and resource extraction.

The demands this particular host makes on him are not inscribed as a kind of transcendent magical wisdom pertaining to his ethnicity, but a form of knowledge located in concrete twentieth-century histories of liberation theology and priest activism, as well as Maoist engagement in the Unión de Uniones. The encounters of those times are also framed as multidirectional and productive, suggesting both cultural continuity in terms of relationship with place and the natural world and, importantly, change, which resists the preterization of indigenous subjects that would freeze them in an imagined premodern state.

> I'm not sure now whether what I heard that good man learned from those who had arrived decades before to support them or if he had acquired it through the roots of his ancestors and taught it to the newcomers or if the learning was mutual. Nature and humanity formed a unity here throughout centuries and millennia, until the civilized world came to these lands bearing its own economic interests. (129)[5]

This interpenetration of historical reflection, contemporary encounter with place, and self-reflection as a European traveler characterizes other passages of the book, so that descriptions of highly textualized and mythologized places like Palenque are not reinscribed purely through cliché. The historical Maya are not imagined as ineffably other, but as a diverse and internally stratified people, coping with conflict and experiencing and creating change. They, through sustained effort, science, and co-existence in the more-than-human world arrived at one of their accomplished points of difference with the culture of the author: "greater knowledge of nature, to the point of respecting it, deifying it" (54).[6] This is not essentialism, attributing an innate spiritual relationship with nature to their being, but achievement built out of concrete historical processes and circumstances. His reflection and historical imagination about this diversity and old Maya epistemologies are triggered by their occurrence in the place where he is (54). However, he recognizes that his and all contemporary visitors' knowledge has limits. Past inhabitants' secrets had not been and could not be revealed, and now are known only to their more-than-human cohabitants: "The watching sun, moon, firmament, the nature they venerated are the only witnesses and neither man nor his technology can approach them" (59).[7] This is no mere fanciful flourish but attributes observational agency to the environment and situates the forms of knowledge that may have been partly lost as belonging to place as well as to a now bygone era. Sexist language aside, by explicitly citing technology as failing to facilitate a recuperation of this knowledge, Heredero gestures to the failures of rationalism and the limits of scientific domination over either the past or the natural world.

In the encounter with nature, travel writing confronts an additional legacy of colonial discourse and neocolonial global capitalism's ongoing stake in subordinating all else to human industry. The natural world was first detached from its inhabitants and custodians to represent paradise, while being paradoxically positioned as the object of intervention and perfectibility, or something that could be rendered productive using science and technology. The genealogy leading to contemporary developmental extractivism is direct. One element of the framing of Heredero's Chiapas diary is a desire for a reformed relationship to nature, and the book does not avoid all the pitfalls of writing travel through the desire for transformation and idealizing other cultural relationships to the natural world. He writes that he comes "from a world that treats nature with disdain, and the desire for it made me seek out signs of harmony where it currently could not be found" (11).[8] This echoes the more problematic aspects of an authenticity myth that creates a modern/material versus primitive/spiritual binary. He also edges into fraught territory by explicitly linking indigeneity to nature, citing "the unity indigenous people maintain with nature" (23).[9] However, this romantic impulse is tempered somewhat by the degree of detail into which he enters. *Chiapas* is replete with details of the logistics of travel, for example, the cost, the documents and procedures, and even, on the very same page as the lament cited above, the difficulty of locating a Europcar employee to manage his car rental (18, 11). The problematic aspect of this linkage is also countered by the text's forceful resistance of any representation of landscape as uninhabited, and a sustained engagement with historical change that acts against essentialism (24).

A narrative that links histories of domination and exploitation to the past and present conceptualization of nature begins to suggest the ways the depredations associated with contemporary global power—and the ways we now live with ongoing extinctions and genocides—have a historically produced vocabulary. Gómez-Barris (2017, 4) analyzes the function through which "colonial capitalism" produces "the planet as a corporate bio-territory." Travel writing that works with both historical narrative and the representation of the more-than-human world, unless it is merely to reinforce the consumerist aspects of ecotourism and ethnotourism, must grapple with the mechanisms by which "the Global South has long been constructed as a region of plunder, discovery, raw resources, taming, classification, and racist adventure" (Gómez-Barris 2017, 3). This kind of perspective, when imbued with the historical critiques associated with decolonial thought, allows us to understand the ways the dual evocation of indigeneity and the natural world has been implicated in colonization and, subsequently and indeed consequently, in neoliberal capitalist extractivism, the logics of which accord both the human and the more-than-human value only as resources within a global economy. It also creates space for the recognition of the life potential implied by the resurgence and endorsement of perspectives that have been long submerged.

Heredero's narrative, as already suggested above, is far from free of traces of colonialist discourse about indigeneity and nature—it is probably barely possible for European travel writing relating encounters with indigenous hosts to attempt it. There are peculiar moments like an observational description of the physical characteristics of indigenous residents of San Cristóbal, "dark complexioned, black haired, round bodied" (32).[10] Another host, a tour guide on the Grijalva river, brings out some of the contradictions of ecotourism endeavors, state power, and the devastation brought by plastic waste: "All day speaking to tourists of the beauty of our land . . . to later find all this trash, because of the abandonment of the authorities" (23).[11] Heredero himself does not quite arrive at a critique of the underlying contradictions of ecotourism here; he is cheered to learn that the riverbanks were cleaned up shortly afterward, without interrogating whether the space is primarily cleansed to an illusory virginity for the tourist gaze, or with respect for the daily lives, river connections, and large-scale ecosystems of local human and nonhuman inhabitants.

However, the semi-ethnographic qualities (the details of *chiapaneco* people's histories, beliefs, economic practices, political actions, and so forth) of his text combined with a strong attention to the environment resist an unmediated myth of premodern indigeneity and Edenic nature. Local informants confirm aspects of his representation of how indigenous people have lived and continue to live relationally with their more-than-human environment. One, for example, recounts the intervention of "our" Namandiyuguá to heal the son of María de Ángulo (though Heredero cites the name as María de Alonso), with a strong emphasis on place and its varied inhabitants: "In the baths of Cumbujujú, the place the boar runs," and the continuity with this through the syncretic celebrations of Chiapa de Corzo (27).[12] In a similar reconfiguration so that place is understood in less anthropocentric terms, another local advises the travelers not to get lost "in the jungle, even though the eyes of the mountains see everything, nothing passes unperceived for them and those who live in them" (130).[13] This mountain being is not necessarily beneficent to humans.

Overall, the desire for relation with nature that Heredero expressed early in his book is not a mere stereotype of European decadence and American utopia, but a starting point for attempting a different poetics of place in the travel encounter with the natural world. The opening pages themselves, even before the expression of personal desire and critique of materialism, recount an extended version of the legend of the Laguna Bélgica, a version in which trees feel, resist, cohabit with beings, and defend themselves in the face of human torture and assassination (10). This vocabulary evokes a subjectivity that does not subordinate nature to the human (or the traveler's) gaze. That said, there is certainly some slippage into personification and the privileging of vision as the foremost instrument of (European) human knowing. However, even where personification shapes descriptive metaphors and nature is seen by the traveler, the natural world is still always in movement, and agential in its activity, as in the following example:

> The rock fell vertically to our feet, hidden by the vegetation. The wall leans gently before reaching the river, sheltered beneath leaves of fresh green. But sweetly and docilely it lets itself be wholly seen, opens in arms that extend their calm through the valley, covering the islands that lie between them. . . . The waters display their white petticoats, then immediately cover them again with their emerald dress. (131)[14]

The movement that marks this description throughout also suggests possibilities of resistance and what refuses seeing. Even where the sensory perception of the travelers is explicitly foregrounded, as in the verbs "observe" and "listen" in the following passage, there is a strong suggestion of the relationality of more-than-human beings that continues whether seen and heard by humans or not:

We observe the trees, tall and leafy, the parasitic plants up to several meters that grow on the trunks of some of them, the strangler and *matapalos* ficus that embrace and choke them, the lianas or *palos de agua* (dracaena) that fall and can be cut to drink the liquid inside. We listened to the birds between murmurs of the waters, trying to locate them, and when we saw one, joy grew in our hearts. All beautiful, some delicate and soft, others larger; of vibrant or muted colors, depending whether evolution had called them to exhibition or camouflage. (151)[15]

These examples demonstrate an approximation to nature that departs from the classic colonialist discourse of nature as perfectly comprehensible, as perfectible, as object of human action, as resource to be capitalized. To redefine the human in relation to the more-than-human, to look without dominating, Heredero proposes "it is necessary to forget domesticated reason, and become tree or grass, rock or sand, contemplate them for as much time as we are called to, like them, simply from the stillness of the mind, allowing oneself to be carried along in the original role that nature gave us" (179).[16] Heredero is echoing the exhortation that the solution is not to appropriate another culture's spiritual framework for interacting with the world, but to encounter and be part of the world ourselves, and understand our interdependence as well as the limits of our understanding.

Mourelo Following Turner Following the Yaqui in Donde mueren los dioses

The narrative voice in Suso Mourelo's *Donde mueren los dioses* is much more impersonal than Heredero's, and therefore its approach to the representation of indigenous cultures skirts closer to some of the problems of the traditional ethnography. However, its framing focus on the story of the Yaqui people creates a concrete historical and intertextual landscape that juxtaposes contemporary tourism—and spaces of potential ethno- and ecotourism development—with the intermingled histories of violent displacement of indigenous peoples and neocolonialist capitalism. The analysis of this text therefore addresses the effects of three diverse aspects of the text: intertextuality and historical thinking; the reporting of Yaqui beliefs and inclusion of Yaqui voices as popular ethnography; and explicit mentions of tourism practices in tension with the limitations of the impersonal mode of travel narration.

Although *Donde mueren los dioses* is a travel narrative that covers a fair bit of literal ground, unlike Heredero's more geographically contained *Chiapas*, its main intertext is John Kenneth Turner's *Barbarous Mexico* (1909; in its Spanish-language edition, *México bárbaro*) and the travel route of reference is the route of the forcibly displaced and enslaved Yaqui, from Sonora to Yucatán.[17] As Mourelo himself characterizes this displacement, "A hundred years ago thousands of *indios* were yanked from their villages and sold to the hacienda owners of the Yucatan, who were burning and needed a supply of fresh labor. The goods were the Yaquis, rebel nation, famous for rebelling against everybody" (17).[18] He calls those who eventually returned *henequén* survivors (49). The central emphasis on histories of displacement is linked to attempts to recognize their significance through cosmologies that suppose being-in-place as a form of history, memory, geography, and ecological relation: "all uprooted from that place that for them meant much more than a region since it encompassed their genesis, the meaning of their experience and interpretation of the world" (20).[19] This orients historical events that produced humans as labor resource within a broader project of exploitation of American resources in general; labor that could be reallocated for political and economic ends. The example gives us an initial sense of how the intertextuality in *Donde mueren los dioses* is applied to an alternative mode of historical thinking that relocates historical texts into conversation with the forms of memory attached to human being within a territorialized mode of existence, connected to place, to plant, to creature.

Having noted that the narrative voice is generally impersonal, narration in *Donde mueren los dioses* is not totally devoid of individual detail and reflection. The minimalist authorial presence is most notable in recounting historical events and in reporting encounters with and observations in Yaqui territory. However, some of the parameters of Mourelo's trip are made clear in other passages, such as the peculiar situation of teaching selections from the European literary and artistic canon in invited classes in Guadalajara, when Mourelo himself is preoccupied with—and in class is actually discussing—Mexico (136). He finds a bridge in Max Aub's *La verdadera historia de la muerte de Francisco Franco* (1960; The true story of the death of Francisco Franco), an ironic text about exile highlighting the connections as well as the distance between Spain and Mexico.[20] These moments of transparency and personal story provide a transatlantic bridging and shorten the distance it is possible to impose between reader and writer and the subject, though in this particular context the Yaqui still seem remote.

Encounters with other travelers as well as with hosts also provoke small moments of self-reflection. One arises when he contemplates his long-standing interest in the true locations associated with the places identified in the work of Juan Rulfo: "Twenty years after looking for that name on a map, I asked myself why some dreams are fulfilled and if it's us or the gods who decide which to grant" (165).[21] This moment opens up a space between the individual agency that defines the concept of voluntary mobility and the conditioned choices to which we are all subject, some more than others—here through the evocation of divine will. After a discussion with another traveler, a young Japanese man whose family story linked to the region he finds much more extraordinary than Mourelo's own, he reflects that their presence in the region, and implicitly that of other people, are interconnected, part of the same story (166). It is very different to the way Paco Nadal follows in the footsteps of Juan Rulfo, in his *Pedro Páramo ya no vive aquí*, embarking on a much more detailed recitation of the text of Rulfo's *Pedro Páramo* itself, the degree of convergence and divergence between the imagined literary Comala, Rulfo's memory of Apulco, and the real town that shares its name. This includes enumerating various posthumous truths and myths about the author himself, and the incipient literary tourism development in the area in response to the passage of Rulfo fans.

This region that, through primarily intertextual readings, constitutes a literary geography from Rulfo, is for others part of histories of family displacement and disconnection, or more drastically of relegation to precarity through corruption and macroeconomic change. Mourelo reports the impression of one local, Alejandro, who describes the region as "unjust. The houses are nice ... but inside there is need, it is no longer possible to live from the land. My friends are all in California, only I stayed. ... Working here for what, to acquire debts, so politicians can get fat" (172).[22] Alejandro explicitly links the precarity and suffering of his neighbors to the ways businesses shift in response to (similarly corrupt) economic impulses, such as those who manipulate schemes designed to foment and retain local industry rather than lose it to, for example, Poland: "They say they go so they can get money. With Poland in Europe, I don't think the salaries would be lower than Mexico and the controls would be greater, I don't think they can go there to do dumping" (173).[23] The imagined terrain of Rulfo is converted into a literal wasteland, with the forces of global capitalism creating pressure against environmental controls on industry; Mexico's competitive advantage against Poland becomes its willingness to be defiled and allow its human and more-than-human life to be exploited and endangered. Mourelo is further confronted by these distinct experiences of place when Alejandro decides to abandon his increasingly unviable business and make for the US, a passage Mourelo evokes with a direct quote from Rulfo: "There is hunger *padre*, you have no idea because you live well" (173).[24]

Here we see the disjunction between forms of intertextuality that shape privileged desire around leisure travel and the nature of encounter between traveler and host. In the case of *Donde mueren los dioses*, Mourelo decenters the traveling subject from his travel narrative in favor of the multiplication of experiences of place, which can be filtered through textual representations as well as materialities. Rulfo is brought into the present and returned to place in the context of new manifestations of exploitation and inequality. It is quite different to Nadal, whose local informant denies that there is any deprivation to the point of hunger but notes the presence of drug abuse, alcoholism, and despair at the lack of opportunity (83). While Nadal writes that Pedro Páramo doesn't live there anymore, his interest in the place remains literary and the novel shapes his gaze; he doesn't go beyond intertextual interrogation in analyzing why this region of Mexico is the way it is, nor does he interrogate his own expectations and their literary precursors. In contrast, Mourelo does at least briefly acknowledge the travel narrative project through the traveling subject's gaze to be an artifice, with the potential to obscure the actual suffering associated with histories of forced displacement: "I wanted to enter San Blas by sea to take in a vision similar to that which filled the eyes of the Yaqui; I knew it was a fraud, for even if the place had not changed at all in a hundred years, our sensations could never resemble each other because they were opposed: theirs, marked by disgrace; mine, by the satisfaction of arrival" (118).[25] This satisfaction is the mode by which we allow history to become a consumable pleasure akin to fiction. The literary intertextuality and the moments of reversal with extensive inclusion of dialogue with hosts, including his students—as well as the literal spaces of teaching and of traveling—open reflection and mutual encounter. These are relatively few, however, in a text with a prevailingly historical or, as we shall see below, ethnographic voice.

The asides recounting Yaqui stories provide a counterpoint to intertextual references the author cites to frame his historical thinking as a traveler. They recount the ways Yaqui stories constitute an enmeshment of history, geography, spirituality, and beliefs, framing of resistance and processing of ongoing colonial violence. This is the aspect of *Donde mueren los dioses* that places the kind of frequent intertextual references explored in the memoir-like travel writing of Chapter 2 instead at the service of a historicized encounter with place through the place-meaning reported by hosts. Mourelo avoids hierarchical relationships between his historical documentary sources (from mostly white outsider voices) and the histories of place and displacement as remembered by the Yaqui. The myth of *los sures* speaks of becoming animal/more-than-human in answer to a prophecy that suggested the future devastation of the arrival of the Spanish (38). How important this reorientation of historical thinking is to Mourelo is clear from the very title of the book, which echoes in the phrase with which he concludes his recounting of this myth: "The descendants of those *sures* lost their tree-prophets and buried their gods" (39).[26] This drive to encounter the *ongoing* relationship of humans with the more-than-human world informs Mourelo's practice as a travel writer in general. He describes this practice in relation to both *Tiempo de Hiroshima* (2018), his book about Japan with its reflections on Shintoism, and his general traveling orientation, which is partly inspired by Thoreau's *Walden*.

> Everything, however small, was life. . . . Losing this knowledge, this feeling, as has happened in the West and, generally, everywhere, impoverishes us, not only humanity, each people, but each person. . . . We are still adapting to change, to a world for sale, to a relationship with oneself of exploitation, to this liquid life that leaves no trace but generates depression and sickness, but human beings are, in the end, animals, which is to say part of nature, and nature always reacts to imbalance. (Mourelo, qtd. in Reguero 2018)[27]

This interview expresses Mourelo's own inclination toward a relational world with capacities for resistance to the apocalyptic force of accelerating extraction and over-production in the service of a logic of infinite capital-oriented and anthropocentric development.

In counter to the textualized framing of the history of the forced displacement of Yaqui people to the south of Mexico during their long wars in defense of independence, the relational narration of place-meaning shows a mode of representing nature in which geographies and more-than-human inhabitants play active parts in the direction of histories as well as their remembering. Myths about the formation of landscape are linked closely to human histories, such as a serpent-become-rock that coincides with a Yaqui community dwelling place, alongside a brief recounting of the political conditions and reorganization of communities under the influence of the Jesuits (40). In this way, the relationship between Yaqui and place/world is not restricted to a premodern temporality, remote from colonial domination and neocolonial extractivism, but a living, adaptive, and political belief system. The intensity of the pressures to which this system must respond is encapsulated in Mourelo's summary of the effects of economic change: "trees that have ceased being prophets in order to fill furnaces" (44).[28] His local informant on this particular aspect of economic change, Juan María Molina, describes the way ongoing displacements of water and of people (a town that moved from one site to another) are interconnected, the direct result of a government dam project. "When they built the dam we could no longer live from what the river gave us. Half the water was supposed to be for us and isn't. Now? There are nearly no crops, now we live from felling trees" (44).[29] These examples of ongoing displacement include indirect impacts dividing the community, as Juan María Molina also notes: "We don't want our children to go but because there's no work they go to the cities to seek a life, this is what divides humanity" (44).[30] Another later informant also mentions the penetration of drug abuse among younger Yaqui (49). At Guaymas, the Sonoran port through which many Yaqui were shipped away into slavery, a local man, Rafael, describes a similar atomizing process of economic change: "Before, there used to be fisheries, one lived from the sea. Not anymore. It finished. So we found a way to live, wherever it might be" (26).[31] The very port itself, at the time of Mourelo's visit, was in a state of partial transformation away from an industrial and fishing port toward tourism and the reception of cruise ships.

It is at these moments, when questions about economic change and its impact on local communities in Mexico turn toward tourism, that the ambiguous role of Mourelo as a travel writer may return to reader's minds. As has been a central focus throughout this book, Mourelo's books, like all travel narratives, are objects that intervene in an economy of consumption of cultural difference. Mourelo is never explicit about his own role in this cultural economy; however, *Donde mueren los dioses* includes frequent references to potential and actual conflicts of aspects of tourism development. Mourelo cites the Yaqui's past firm resistance to commercial tourism, including declining controlled visits from cruise passengers and the like (42). He connects this to a broader question about the economic options available to the community, asking whether they would open their doors to outside investment of some type. Colombo Romero Flores answers, "If an agreement could be reached, but the land is sacred, like the body. If we tried to impose ourselves there, they wouldn't like it either" (46).[32] This answer, in addition to reinforcing the oneness of humans and world, actively inverts the justifications of domination that consistently position indigenous peoples as objects of intervention. In other sections of the book about other points along his itinerary, Mourelo makes similar inquiries about tourism and finds its promises elusive, such as when don Enrique describes the minimal efforts toward a literary tourism route in Comala: "They've attempted a few things, but so far, nothing. Most people are still in agriculture though there are a few with businesses; for the rest it goes badly" (169).[33] The conversion via domestic and international leisure mobility markets of cultural patrimony into currency to buy food for families to eat is a much more complicated business than simply growing that food. The caprice of a Paco Nadal or even a Suso Mourelo in following a literary route is hard to scale up to a sustainable local economy—and much more so in Colima than in Paris, for example, given the mechanisms by which place-images circulate and the cultural value and consumption potentials attached to different countries.

As changes beyond Yaqui control, like the dam, transform their ways of living, the insidiousness of so-called development as economic default emerges in the complex relationships that Mourelo reports. His mediator Alfredo Montiel hints around an ecotourism/ethnotourism project: "With no hotel infrastructure or anything like that, nothing that breaks with tradition, but with for example a hiking route that doesn't pass too close to the houses" (51).[34] Juan Gregorio, a councillor in Guaymas, seems unconvinced and resistant, but proposals to capitalize on cultural tourism and supposedly sustainable forms of ecotourism have weight in Yaqui communities as in other indigenous communities in Mexico. Traditional modes of living and other economic alternatives are rendered less and less viable by displacement, state intervention, and the active reshaping of the landscape around them to extractivist ends. Mourelo, in writing this and other travel books, is contributing to an international economy of consumption of cultural difference that is tightly linked to ethnotourism development, and the insidious potential of tourism discourse is just glimpsed at times through his explicit description of the reluctance of many Yaqui people.

Along highly touristic routes, travel writing offers opportunities for direct comparison of travel writers' encounters with places that are written and rewritten in travel books and circulate in tourism discourse about Mexico. While the history of the Yaqui frames *Donde mueren los dioses*, Mourelo is, as already indicated in the above example of his Rulfo-inspired visit to Colima, traveling for a range of motives to varied sites and mobilizing distinct secondary interpretive schema in addition to this historicized encounter with one concrete people. To take one example of this textualization of tourist routes, we can productively compare the modes of narrative and touristic encounter within a travel story with one overarching intertextual framing device in *Donde mueren los dioses* with Eloísa Gómez Lucena's *Del Atlántico al Pacífico*, discussed in further detail in the following section. Vastly divergent texts that cover overlapping geographies, like Turner and Cabeza de Vaca, also overlap with the production of experiences and contemporary management of routes and spaces for touristic consumption. Both Mourelo and Gómez Lucena took the famous Chihuahua-Pacífico train known as el Chepe through Rarámuri territory, as have many other travel writers, and the effects of their differing approaches to the same mythologized and hyper-textualized route are analyzed below. Mourelo places the initial emphasis on the recent historical contingencies that allowed the construction of the railroad itself. Gómez Lucena reflects on pre-Colombian relations in the region and the characteristics—and misinterpretations—of American languages. Her focus is local, centering the nation state via its neglect, as "a complacent country that, in exchange for granting them autonomy and promoting them as an exotic group, abandons its indigenous people" (279).[35] The abandonment is via ongoing inequality and unconstitutional lack of support for education. On balance, however, Gómez Lucena's description, as it is throughout *Del Atlántico al*

Pacífico, is preoccupied with quotidian detail and personal encounters juxtaposed with cultural and linguistic histories over centuries. As described in Chapter 2, Francisco Solano remains primarily in a poetic and intertextual narrative mode throughout his *Bajo las nubes de México*. We can see the effect in Solano's (2001, 77) reference to the same people, "the Tarahumaras, the true masters of these lands, today imposed on the landscape like melancholic signs for the remorse of the cultural conscience."[36] The Rarámuri are literally merged with the landscape and reduced to signs, in one of the most stereotypical neocolonial modes of representation of indigeneity. Nadal, in *Pedro Páramo ya no vive aquí*, devotes a whole chapter to this hyper-textualized route, and uses the voice of his local informant Emilio mainly to distinguish himself from the tourists who take el Chepe and who are characterized by their ignorance and fear—believing Pancho Villa might still live, dressing like Rambo, vaccinating themselves in preparation for the "third world," and, Nadal claims, isolating themselves from the actual sensory life of Mexico while imagining themselves in a magical exotic land (2010, 87–88). Nadal himself, traveling second-class with locals, is by implication supposedly quite different to these tourists, and his focus throughout the rest of the chapter remains on interactions with other tourists and demonstrations of his own knowledge about the history and existing texts about the region as well as his anecdotes reinforcing his adventurous approach to travel. The connection between the contemporary tourist economy, the histories of conflict to which he refers by way of other texts, and the contemporary experience of Rarámuri people barely features. To briefly trace the different modes of representation, Solano's is a well-meaning but loaded metaphorization of indigeneity, Nadal's reinscribes myths of authentic travel experience, and Gómez Lucena's long-view historical thinking foregrounds the cultural and linguistic. In contrast, Mourelo's nineteenth- and twentieth-century history is explicitly transnational. He uses the figure of Albert Kimsey Owen, whose utopian project initiated construction, and references subsequent private infrastructure efforts. Mourelo also communicates the interventionist powers of the Mexican state in bringing it to completion some eighty years later. (Albert Kimsey Owen also appears in Nadal's book as a colorful eccentric, not particularly connected to other economic and military forces reshaping the region.) Mourelo's narrative approach produces a transnational and multi-actor historicism that writes the touristic gaze on the spectacular copper canyons and on the Rarámuri into a genealogy of imposed presences and projected power. This comparative analysis is not intended to impose a value-laden hierarchy of modes of travel narrative, but to articulate how the orientations and frames of reference of travelers shape the image of place—and the value judgements they themselves make about experiences, spaces, hosts, and fellow travelers.

It is productive to extend the comparison of Mourelo and Gómez Lucena, both because of the chronological coincidence in their travels, the structural coincidence of taking a single primary intertextual reference to frame their narrative, and some key convergences in their mode of narration through the accumulation of quotidian detail. They observe similar characteristics of the journey itself, such as train travel's facilitation of new acquaintance and conversation, as well as the presence of mobile vendors, a frequent characteristic of travel writing about Mexico already mentioned elsewhere. Given the similar timing of their trips, the two writers could very well be describing the same individual people at locations they visit, so that we can observe their different modalities of narrating place and other. Gómez Lucena connects geography to trade, describing, "the temperature contrast is so pronounced that Tarahumaras cultivate tropical fruit like mango and papaya by the river and in the valley, while their wives and daughters sell fruit and handicrafts in the heights, defenseless against cold or downpour" (278).[37] This initial framework of the relational background of mobile vending precedes a more stereotypical evocation of the care and sorrow of an indigenous woman, perceived in a moment in which "we watched each other in silence,"[38] that is, without the woman's individual voice defining her own experience (279). Mourelo's briefer description again foregrounds the directionality of gazes and, through the evocation of what is human-made (including human beings themselves, and the impulse to human contact) in the face of what is literally beyond human perception: "The Rarámuri serve enchiladas and souvenirs. A woman, her goods spread out on the stone, glances round at her offspring: the children play beside the railing that slices through the air in front of an incomprehensible gorge. Some tourists hold on and cover their mouths" (66).[39] Here we see an interplay of gaze and economics; the product is the view of the gorge, but the host community has been converted into a tourist economy from which they have to garner secondary profits as best they can. The presence of familial relationships along with commerce shows the multiple forms of (female) labor, and the local environment as familiar. Consuming a vista, on the other hand, is a luxury of sensation.

In this episode too, as in encounters with Yaqui people (and with mediators of Yaqui culture like Alfredo Montiel), Mourelo recounts situated narratives showing convergences of history, geography, and relational thinking in place and experiences and potentialities for resistance. In the key example here he tells a story, reported to him by an el Chepe acquaintance named Rafael, of how Rarámuri and other people were made by different gods: "The Rarámuri became peace-loving being, adapted to nature. . . . Others abandoned the land and became used to money and warfare. . . . The Rarámuri must stay at the margin, at the end of the world, and not mix with the *chabochi* [non-Rarámuri], to remain out of that evil cycle, but the other is involving and using the Rarámuri more all the time" (67).[40] The obvious critique of the colonial structures and violences of global capitalism, and the threat implied in the final sentence is made immediately explicit. The story is followed by Rafael's personal anecdote about having been stopped from passing through an area of the Sierra Tarahumara by a Rarámuri man guarding an opium plantation. There is little in *Donde mueren los dioses* as devastatingly understated in its critique of the violence of profit as Rafael's statement, "a shame, a race like that at the service of killers" (67).[41] Mourelo takes as read the problematic relationship between Rarámuri and the Mexican state that Gómez Lucena summarizes in brief (and Solano and Nadal virtually ignore). Similarly implied is the complexity of sustaining self-determination and resistance in the face of centuries—and evolving forms—of domination, only to arrive at the tragedy of subordinating all spaces of human experience to markets and the desire for licit and illicit consumption.

As a final point of comparison with Gómez Lucena, before moving into a detailed discussion of her work's own distinctive features, *Donde mueren los dioses* also cites Alvar Núñez Cabeza de Vaca's *Naufragios* (1542) as one of its sources. Hence we return to the ways the first Spaniards in the Americas imagined and attempted to explain their encounter with places and peoples, and the ways contemporary travelers consciously or unconsciously depart from colonialist language in their descriptions of the same, or from the ideas of America that have evolved over the intervening centuries. Mourelo passes over *Naufragios* with a pithy critique of such documentary sources that summarizes in one line the evolving understandings of travelers as subjects and as narrators: "as well as being a *crónica*, a travel book, and an adventure novel, *Naufragios* inaugurates a model of marketing in which the protagonist presents their worthiness for a position in the New Continent" (104).[42] The travel stories we read are not documents of what is—what happens, what is said, or how things are in a place. They are constructions of a self within a concrete economic and political situation, and often implicitly, a particular more-than-human world that constitutes the object—the objective—of exploitation.

In the section describing his trip on el Chepe, Mourelo also quotes a long passage from Robert Zingg, an anthropologist who visited the region in the 1930s. Zingg's work was put aside for its racist, colonialist, and misogynist tone—and here Mourelo explicitly engages with critical trends in anthropology (71). As Mourelo describes, "Nobody would have written it that way today, but its composition reflects not only the life of an indigenous people barely contaminated by the dominant culture, but a form of thinking, that of the narrator, that itself forms a part of History" (72).[43] Mourelo writes very much as travel writers write today, with more direct attention to race, power, and capital than was evident even ninety years ago in Robert Zingg, let alone five hundred years ago in Cabeza de Vaca. Nevertheless, Mourelo reads Zingg—and Cabeza de Vaca, propagandist though he considers him—as a source for understanding aspects of life in Mexico for indigenous peoples at a moment when that life was changing, as well as the way of thinking that characterized those who took it upon themselves to narrate places and describe peoples, and the ideologies and systems of domination to which they were linked. What is unwritten but clear in this statement is that Mourelo himself, in writing *Donde mueren los dioses*, is documenting people in another moment in time, while simultaneously documenting himself and his own way of thinking. Both traveler-writer-origin and host-subject-destination are connected to their temporal and spatial context, and also to the large-scale social and economic structures that not only shape the moment of encounter but also connect them, however great the prior and subsequent distance.

Historiography in Motion: In the Footsteps of Cabeza de Vaca

The closing remarks of the previous section reemphasized how tourism encounters are acts of spatial and temporal bridging. Encounters can show the interconnectedness of all the world with all its peoples, and how we act upon each other through invisible systems of desire. They can also show how those systems have come to be. Unique histories of places and peoples converge but are always told partially, by storytellers who feel one convergence more than another. To explore transatlantic convergence in the past and present, and extend the preceding discussion of how the narration of encounter evolves in relation to changing conceptualizations of subjectivity, history, and power, this section interrogates additional features of the unusual work of travel writing *Del Atlántico al Pacífico: Tras los pasos de Cabeza de Vaca*, by Eloísa Gómez Lucena. *Del Atlántico al Pacífico* is not unusual in its style, and covers similar destinations to some of the works analyzed previously in this book, like the much-written trip on el Chepe above. It is not, as we have also seen, even particularly unusual in taking one specific intertextual exploration as its premise. What is unusual is the referential text selected (Cabeza de Vaca's *Naufragios*) and Gómez Lucena's perspective on it, writing as a novelist-historian who had already invested many years and published several historical essays and one novel on the early presence of Spaniards in America, including essays on Cabeza de Vaca in particular. She nevertheless embarks on the writing of travel narrative in a highly personal, quotidian, and diaristic style. The historiographical reflections and the long-view sense of how places, peoples, and possibilities for communication change over time are peppered into a work that is the most transparent of all those discussed in articulating the daily exigencies and small indignities of the practice of tourism.

A major component of the ways places become invested with cultural identity is through names. We use names to signify our shared understanding of some bounded space as a place connected to human experience. In everyday speech, however, names are often imbued with an implication of permanence that obscures their invention as a historically loaded act. Naming, therefore, can serve as one approach to understanding the potential of historiographical thinking as a framework for interpreting travel. Throughout the earlier part of the book, Gómez Lucena situates her historiographical knowledge through an interest in naming, starting with the inappropriateness of naming the continent America for Amerigo Vespucci, proposing the alternative Colombia among various other whimsical reflections. Though she is doubtless familiar with it, she does not mention Las Casas's proposal along the same lines, nor Columbus's specific imperial associations both at the time and since, as ably traced by Elise Bartosik-Vélez (2014, 11). In another passage Gómez Lucena and husband Rubén correct a Floridian regarding the cultural significance of their state's name (47). The focus of her correction is the attitude and experiences of the Spanish expeditionaries who, in her view, were in no condition for poetic flourishes but named with expedience, by day of arrival (the case for Florida) or perhaps for their own home town. While this historical anecdote highlights the circumstantial contingency of naming, it does not touch the contradictions inherent in such an incidental detail as a date shaping centuries of sense of territory, identity, and investiture of meaning in places. Florida was nothing then, and has become something now, through processes that have little to do with the lack of poetic engagement or postjourney fatigue that Gómez-Lucena comically attributes to those arrivals.

This demonstrates Gómez-Lucena's relatively tight focus on the details of sixteenth-century and subsequent historical incidents, the peculiar contingencies of language, and the historical circumstances of inhabited places, rather than the broader implications of language and place in the ways we imagine the world. Galveston is a recurrent mention, with the link to Bernardo de Gálvez and hence Spanish imperial administration. As a figure—described in the book as *quijotesco*—Bernardo de Gálvez himself with his colonizing efforts, documentation and naming of territory, according to Gómez Lucena's recreated dialogue quoting Rubén, "put territory to what had been imagined" (137).[44] This characterization of Bernardo de Gálvez and an ensuing exploration of the possible chivalric romance origins of California introduce something of a contradiction with the pragmatic naming schema outlined previously for Florida. The literary language rather obscures the violent dispute over that territory, and what is involved in projecting place-concepts from medieval and early modern literature onto the physical landscape of the American continent. It is not that Bernardo de Gálvez's role in actual colonial governance and in military conflict over territory passes completely unremarked. In addition to the whimsical and comic tone that the author frequently takes, the authority on which she draws is documentary, vesting truth in archive, and focused on detail. A problem arises in taking this form of authority as overriding the ways places become invested with meanings through the living in them. These first examples indicate the particularity of historiography as a framework for travel, with the frequency of her asides on names and their relationship to places buttressing a history-inflected account of place that suggests the mutability of how it has been and is coming to be known to its changing inhabitants, but not necessarily how that knowing links to overarching histories of power. Recounting the nature of the evidence available to us about how certain names came to be is instructive, but in a didactic rather than interpretive mode.

Names and associated peculiar local histories also provide readers a window into more recent history, and there is a recurrence of the unromantic intercession of commerce in creating our geographies, though again more archival or anecdotal than analytical. For example, the exotic architecture of the University of Tampa is the result of a hotel constructed with minarets as a kind of Moorish revival folly (32), and Saint Petersburg was named following a coin flip between the dominant nineteenth-century retail entrepreneurs (44). In several cases, these toponymical asides dwell on the indeterminate nature of some names' origins and evolution, as well as the ways names can be temporary or disputed. Gómez Lucena mentions, for example, the various name changes of Chihuahua (246) and the disputed etymologies of Culiacán and of Tamaulipas, with different versions lending themselves to different interpretations of both history and the character of place (225). With these examples we also see the way Gómez Lucena's historiographical engagement does sometimes include exploration of the movements and fates of indigenous peoples, and the ways these can be partially glimpsed in changes to language. Traces of Náhuatl are present in many languages today, but through Náhuatl-inflected insect names—*chapulines, jumiles, escamoles, chilocuiles, chicatanas*—in Mexican Spanish we glimpse intimacies of life in relation to specific environments (232). In the intersection between the names Rarámuri and Tarahumara, Gómez Lucena touches not only on histories of Spanish colonial interpretation of names (Tarahumara being a Castilianized version of Rarámuri) but also pre-Colombian relations between indigenous peoples and their names for each other, since the name is one they were supposedly called by others, not what they called themselves (269).

On the other hand, the word Seminole, derived from *cimarrón*, records the influence of Spanish—and the displacements and regroupings of diverse indigenous tribes as a result of both Spanish and English colonialism—though histories of violence are only sometimes brought into the etymological discussions in *Del Atlántico al Pacífico* (55). More explicitly than in the mention of the Seminole, in exploring the example of the Muskogee she cites the confluence of Creek, Hitchiti, and other groups in concrete historical conditions (127). The historical emergence of a name may mirror aspects of the emergence of a new mixed culture. Gómez Lucena is more specific in referring to discrete indigenous American peoples and connecting their histories to current places than most nonexpert travelers, although her engagement with present-day representatives of the diverse First Nations mentioned is limited. These are a few of the aspects of the way historiographical thinking creates a productive preoccupation with language and with naming that supports a more mutable conceptualization of human relationship to place. Its strength is also its limitation. Etymological and historical evidence do potentially disrupt mythmaking around place and identity, which creates a false sense of permanence and inevitability. However, potential connections between past and present remain embedded in historical detail, rather than articulated and observed through lived experience.

In Gómez Lucena's own itinerary we also see the intermingling of the names of places and histories of mobility, but this observation of the present does not appear to achieve the same level of explicatory possibility as the archive. "The nearby Mexican border was noticeable in the names of the towns and streams, gas station and store employees, men turning over the fields and women doing shopping" (198).[45] What defines the initial sensory perception of Mexico, having crossed the border, however, is heat, something not related to objective temperature but to "dust ... drivers ... sidewalks ... people ... indigent indigenous people" (202).[46] Despite the oppressive heat already experienced north of the border, Mexico's daily life and urban experience is somehow hotter. Gómez Lucena's observation of the present is also steeped in detail, but the detail tends to briefly alight on some scene, sketch some person, or reproduce some colorful dialogue, with few conclusions. Names, in the quote above, mark the increasing proximity of Mexico as well as the changing demographics of the US as one moves through its current territory, but any such understanding of the broader significance of this contemporary texture of place is usually left for the readers to achieve.

However, *Del Atlántico al Pacífico*'s juxtaposition of this kind of contemporary touristic experience with Cabeza de Vaca's relating of his experience of mobility, and the hardship, hunger, confusion, loss, and mix of voluntary and involuntary displacements can provoke readers to productive reflections on the present nature of mobility. Rather than adopting an impersonal voice, focusing the prose on descriptive passages surrounding the evidence and commemoration of Cabeza de Vaca's passage, Gómez Lucena gives enormous amounts of personal and quotidian detail, as well as some gentle self-parody recognizing the absurdity of the comparison: "we blushed to compare the comforts of our movements with the fatigues of the explorers" (59).[47] Sometimes this comparison edges toward mythologizing the past: "Because they broke the mold with those long-suffering Spaniards of past centuries, the oppressive heat undid Rubén and me" (191).[48] The lightness of her personal voice as well as the intimacy of description of Cabeza de Vaca and companions tends to counter this occasional tendency, however. In a similar ironic tone, when mentioning plans to travel by coach to appalled Mexican acquaintances, she reports saying, "we want to imitate don Álvar Núñez's sufferings in some way" (215).[49] In addition to regularly referring to the sixteenth-century travelers' unshod and denuded state, Gómez Lucena occasionally gives specific details to evoke the extremity of Cabeza de Vaca and companions' experience, for example launching a conquest of Appalachia with a little unleavened bread and bacon (53). This might seem mythologizing also, but the specificity and the comedy of the contrast undo any overly heroic construction.

Despite lighthearted acknowledgments of these qualitative differences in the experience of mobility, Gómez Lucena's investment in the historical events and figures creates intimacy with the earlier travelers, especially the earlier author himself, often affectionately dubbed *nuestro amigo Álvar Núñez*. The act of being in the same locations gives the experiences recounted in *Naufragios* embodied life. One of the benefits of a comic tone is its reliance on specificity and relatability. This makes historical figures more human, linking them to the frailties of the contemporary traveler and hence further undermining the quality of myth—and inevitability—that can otherwise accumulate around well-known events. The eternal threat of mosquitos hovers around both authors, and Gómez Lucena writes, "I had a well-matched impression of the fierce struggle Cabeza de Vaca maintained with the three species he mentions" (62).[50] She subtly highlights the contemporary conditions of the border region, joking the mosquitos were fewer in Mexico as they didn't have a visa to follow her south, while elsewhere remarking on Cabeza de Vaca's crossings of what was not yet a border but a space inhabited in other ways. The way space—geography—escapes place-making is described by Gómez Lucena in her derision of the "intellectual pygmies" who try to bound mountains, seas, and forests with waving colored cloths. The evocation of material geographies weaves into the intimacy of the author's perspective on her historical counterpart. For example, she remarks that because he complains only of the cold, not the unbearable heat that Eloísa and Rubén experience, she began to consider Cabeza de Vaca over sensitive to cold (79). However, the intimate comparison of reported sensory perception in different times is brought into dialogue with historical evidence of the mini–ice age of the sixteenth century and hence opens up a kind of embodied doubling in the experience of place to the expansiveness of geological time—though this is far from being the recurrent feature it is in the work of Alfonso Armada.

However, when historical knowledge is deployed as a form of distinguishing authority—as it sometimes was in the example around naming above—it creates limitations to the anti-mythologizing potential of Gómez Lucena's mode of time-traveling historiographical travel writing. As with the example of Florida, the statements that go furthest in this direction are often put in the mouth of Rubén, not Eloísa, with a possible gendered dimension in terms of the author's assumption of an often self-deprecating narrative persona. For example, Rubén claims that their mission to "observe, wander, and imagine what Cabeza de Vaca and friends were able to see" separates them from tourists (259).[51] This authorizing framework (and reinscription of traveler/tourist opposition) incorporates the latent Eurocentrism of foregrounding the written record and European-style material manifestations of civilization. Gómez Lucena is aware of and sympathetic to the diversity and complexity of pre-Colombian American civilizations, and that the European perspective on history is a specific not a universal one, evident in comments like "five centuries of history, according to our European understanding" (166–67).[52] Nevertheless, there is an evident derision in her description of a touristic description by a trolley diver who "explained the Historic District buildings with such unction about the supposed antiquities that it triggered a sarcastic grin in us, globetrotters from the Old Continent" (158).[53] This attitude does not acknowledge that both trolley driver and travelers are equating history with material traces of civilizations, and the production of European antiquity for touristic consumption that creates. The written record is also emphasized as a source for "atrocities committed against American indigenous peoples that we know about through books written by members of religious orders, chroniclers, interpreters, captains, and even simple Spanish soldiers" (300).[54] Historical violence is given additional weight through European written testimony as an authoritative and reliable source. The divergent effects of the examples from the previous paragraph and those explored here show the contradictions possible within a generally historiographic orientation. Different approaches to recounting histories of place within the same travel narrative can demythologize the past while reinscribing the principles that have underpinned Eurocentric disciplinary practices. The other problem with the representation of violence is the textual distance from violence in the sixteenth century that emphasizes the survival of those like Cabeza de Vaca who left a written record, alongside the reproduction of tropes of contemporary Mexico as a killing zone (to be fair, often quoted from Gómez Lucena's local informants) (283). This extends rather than shortens the temporal distance between events and peoples in the same location at different times, and therefore shores up the past as finished rather than continuous with the present.

The stance of historian also complicates her understanding of herself as a textualized figure, both in her own narrative and in others. She objects to how she is misrepresented by a journalist in an interview. There is also discomfort in becoming the object of the reversed gaze and being perceived as a representative of Spanishness by Mexicans. We see this in their response to a use of *gachupines*—an often-pejorative term for Spaniards in America—after which Rubén suggests "Let him ask his grandparents for an accounting. None of yours nor mine ever left the Peninsula. . . . I'm sick of hearing the same old story from the uneducated" (258).[55] This is a common defensive reaction to charges of historical culpability. It fails to account for the practice of tourism itself within contemporary global capitalism, to take merely one example of practices of mobility and consumption that continue to bolster inequality.

Gómez Lucena's form of historiographical orientation to travel creates intimacy with the past, as well as a sustained intertextuality that at times suggests the divergence between popularly held cultural and historical myths and the evidence suggested by archival/documentary sources. There is, however, a very limited connection of past to present in terms of its continuities and ongoing consequences. For example, the "environmental horror" of petroleum enterprises in the Gulf of Mexico is linked to an apocalyptic aesthetic of science fiction, and to ecological disaster, but not to the historical roots of global capitalism (187). And though Gómez Lucena's style is transparent about the practices of travel in a quotidian sense (restaurants, transport, accommodation) it is not reflective about tourism as an industry and her participation in it.

CONCLUSION

On Writing a Twenty-First-Century Hispanic Transatlantic

Travel writing remains a popular genre. As a practice, it cannot and should not be separated from the global economics of tourism and the broader context of the representation of place and of cultural difference. The shifts in the nature of travel and the meaning of travel writing between Spain and Mexico, framed by the history of discourses of Mexicanness and of transatlantic mobility in Europe, establish the limits for performances of travel and travel writing for contemporary Spaniards in Mexico. My goal here has been to explore the evolution of ideas of Mexico and Spanish-Mexican encounters and locate specific examples of travel narrative as interventions within these discourses. I have argued for a historicized understanding of the Hispanic transatlantic that does not separate that history from the present. Similarly, the contemporary travel narratives are studied from two different angles—Spain and Europe as point of origin, and Mexico and America as destination concept and as site of representation.

Travel writing still tells, most often, stories of tourism, and mainly still in European languages from and for Western markets. To reiterate, we return then to where we started; what value does travel writing have in the twenty-first century? What does it help us to understand? Writing and reading can still open imagined worlds and extend our horizons of understanding. In accepting that both tourism and the writing of otherness are compromised practices, however, effective twenty-first century travel writing should endeavor to communicate both traces of worlds as they are threatened and resist and change, and the vocabulary and instruments of domination to which tourism itself is connected. Peñate Rivero (2012, 324) identifies one of the modes by which travel writing may now achieve this, by implicating the reader (alongside the writer, I suggest) as agents of what is occurring rather than articulating it as distant. Throughout this book, I have tried to identify the complicities and silences but also the strengths and possibilities of different narrative modes.

Engaging with the theme of travel necessarily foregrounds the continued significance of physical location and the specificity of place despite what at times seem like the totalizing effects of global forces. Travel, as a form of mobility, carries very different meanings in different spaces and times. Travel as leisure—especially international travel—is largely the province of privileged elites, while such transnational trajectories have a totally different significance in the context of conquest, migration, exile, and other forms of permanent or coercive mobilities. Place, time, and movement produce radically differentiated experiences. These differentiations do not correspond cleanly with nationally bounded communities but are more individually contingent and potentially transnational than is suggested by traditional ideas of coherent cultural belonging. I have employed Spain and Mexico as grouping terms throughout; nevertheless, I have endeavored to underline the limits of the national as a concept for thinking about place, both in terms of a sense of origin and a perception or concept of destination.

Alongside the differentiation in the experience of place and mobility, this book emphasizes the interconnectedness of mobility, representation, and power both historically and in the present day, which is why it is valuable to look at particular routes (like Spain-Mexico) that have distinctive historical, spatial, and cultural dimensions. Travel and tourism, from origins in trade, religion, and imperial projects, have evolved through the nineteenth and twentieth centuries as industrial-scale practices that are still closely implicated in the function of global capitalism. Contemporary travel writers reflect to different degrees on the nature of their own activity and on the production of Mexican spaces as objects of tourist consumption, thus rendering this production more or less transparent within the space of their representation of Mexico. This reflexivity sometimes extends to the way travel narratives themselves engage with existing images of place, and sometimes only gesture toward the constructedness of narrative through their own intertextual references and the ways they reiterate and revise prior travelers' descriptions. These existing images can come from deliberate image management, as is the case with the recent reinscriptions of the alternative figurations of Mexico as coastal paradise or as distinctive exotic culture, or as unintended effects brought about by social rupture, natural disaster, crime, and so on. In that sense, my project here has been to investigate the constitution of an individually variegated sense of place that responds to the popular imaginary, draws on literary precursors and intertextual reference, is performed through encounter, and that is ultimately expressed and thus rendered accessible to remote audiences through narration. The narration of experience brings that sense of place into a space of legible contact and contagion with the history of encounter as a site for the enactment of ideas of self, cultural identity, and otherness.

In terms of the historical significance of the encounter between Europe and America, the focus here has not been on the significant material consequences for both continents so much as the way the idea of America in general and Mexico in particular has been coopted into particular discourses of European, Mexican, and Anglo-American identities and territorializations as well as cross-cultural commonalities and differences. Narratives of transatlantic travel highlight aspects of the significance of Mexico in Spain, long after empire, independence, and Revolution, and through Spain's own processes of national redefinition and internal change. The idea of Mexico in Spain has been shaped by both more remote and more recent histories, through events on both continents, from the post-imperial crisis through the Mexican Revolution and Spain's

Civil War and subsequent diaspora. Democratic late twentieth- and early twenty-first-century Spain navigates rethinkings of history and social justice, the touristification of Spain itself, and the manifestations of late capitalist mass-migration and displacement, turbulence, and terror. Other parts of the Spanish-speaking world offer new forms of encounter and moments of critique and reflection on these realities.

Independence, along with the severance of Spain's direct political action in Mexico (though not the end of Spanish soft power or investment, including in tourism), meant the severance of the obvious link between narratives of Mexico and political utility. Other kinds of connections between travel narratives and political utility and power therefore came forward. Alongside the specifics of Spanish-Mexican ties, such as pan-Hispanism (and its inverse of Latin-chic in which the Spanish-speaking world is acted upon rather than actor) and the fraternity of the exchange of exiles, the changing conditions for travel in each country have also revised the political subtext of travel narratives. Both nations have, in the late twentieth century, undergone major changes in relation to tourism and simultaneously experienced an upheaval in the experience of mobility more generally via migration. Some of these changes have disrupted old concepts of global centers and peripheries, underscoring the emergence of multiple allegiances, diverse transnational networks, and multidirectional flows of power. Others, however, reinforce the consumption of place and reproduce long-familiar exoticist tropes of alterity. What this book argues is that the two functions are not mutually exclusive within the space of a single transatlantic encounter and narrative.

Even contemporary texts inevitably respond in some way to the lingering influences of colonialist structures of thought and forms of language, which are not separable from current day questions of mobility, power, and exploitation. Through much of the twentieth century, the dominance of nationalist interpretations of Spain's history acted against the generation of significant new narratives and new ways of thinking about history and responsibility, as well as influencing the intellectual climate in Spain more generally. However, during the postdictatorship and in struggles to redefine Spain's identity and redirect its future, different critical stances against nationalism, alternative forms of belonging, and changing ethics of transnational engagement have emerged. Simultaneously, the concept of travel as an activity of personal development available to all those who can afford it has become more and more important, including the flourishing of all kinds of niche tourism experiences promising transformative or supposedly more authentic experience. The ascendance of pleasure and the journey of self-discovery produced a model for the experience of difference and the disruption of routine as an opportunity for reflecting on and reinventing the self. Travel narratives can reveal the constructedness of narratives of transformation, as well as communicating the ways leisure travel converges with other forms of mobility.

Within this prevailing idea of voluntary travel, the interrelationship between past experience and expectation and the traveler's frame of reference for dealing with the strange and the new becomes more important. The idiosyncratic intertexts and the urgencies and silences of memory contribute to the creation of a historical and geospatial consciousness. This can undercut the authority of the narrative voice and gesture toward competing interpretations of place and limits of perception. What is more debatable—and variable from case to case—is the extent that historical and geospatial consciousness constitutes a meaningful engagement with the textures of place and the historical, political, economic, and natural forces that bring them into being. David Dickens and Andrea Fontana (2002, 393) draw on Jameson to suggest today's cultural dynamics generate only layers of pastiche and random eclecticism rather than a "genuine sense of historical time." Given one of the themes of this book has been memory, history, and existing representations of place defining conditions of encounter, this proposition is useful for thinking about the use of the past in storytelling as a mode of appropriation. In addition to appropriation of the past to a partial accounting, however, the form of historical consciousness articulated in a particular travel narrative shapes the orientation to the concrete experience and encounter. In some of the examples of travel writing analyzed, we see instead the inability of the traveling subject to marshal a wholly adequate interpretive schema (with its capacity to produce totalizing—if false—narratives) for present experience while drawing only on memory, expectation, and past experience. Eduardo Jordá's explicit recognition of the disconnection between his own imagination and expectation about Mexico, founded as it is more on personal memory and literature, and his material encounter with place acts against the reliability of his own narrative as a representation of Mexico and speaks rather to the incommensurability of description and reality, as well as the impossibility of arresting places in time and hence the inevitable failures of static characterizations. Francisco Solano, meanwhile, with his preoccupation with the inheritance of history and its penetration into the present, and his acknowledgment of his own process of narrativization, recognizes that what appears and what is said may alternatively draw from and conceal histories of violence.

These disjunctions support the interpretation that there are elements of contemporary globality and its flow of information that act against people's ability to "unify the past, present, and future of their own biographical experience" (Dickens and Fontana 2002, 393). The vacillation between reliance on existing knowledges and beliefs about places and the acknowledgment of their limits in the traveler's ability to interpret experience is something that complicates the dynamics of representation in contemporary travel narrative. Clearly, writers' own cultures affect their perception of and ability to describe the complexities of their subjects. What varies much more is the level of transparency within the text about the writer's concept of the responsibilities implicit in the act of writing places. Different travel writers acknowledge themselves as travelers and writers, with responsibility for their own participation in both tourism and in discursive production of place-image, to different degrees.

The predominantly external focus of Alfonso Armada and Alfredo Semprún—on politics, violence, and social change—reinforces the authority of the narrator. This reduces the sense of the instability of subject displayed in more memory and text-oriented narratives, where the traveler's sense of self was seen to be evolving and their voice and the shape of their recounted experiences transparently subject to the artifice of narrative construction. What the analysis of Armada and Semprún suggests, however, is the testimonial possibility of a more externally oriented engagement with place. These texts, which focus outward on change and interpretation of present conditions, perhaps better reflect the nature of mobility in a world ever more compressed, with millions of involuntarily displaced people, hundreds of millions of migrants responding to global-level disruptions that shift patterns of migration, post-terror security paranoia, and a jump in the virtualization of place and communication.

The examples explored in the final chapter, given their critical narration of histories and experiences of concrete encounters with indigenous American peoples, foreground the urgency of questions of representation in the context of the original colonialist configuration of America as economic resource, alongside ongoing domination and violence against the more-than-human world. Fermín Heredero, through intensive sensory immersion and quotidian description, as well as inclusion of diverse voices of indigenous hosts and their knowledge, decenters the authority of the more journalistic travel narrative. Suso Mourelo foregrounds intertextuality, but of a kind rarely seen, by framing his narrative through a specific history of violent displacement and enslavement of a sovereign people, with the implicit provocation to the reader regarding what voluntary and involuntary mobility mean and what kinds of histories become invisible through economic logics of territorialization or the illusion of permanence that sometimes attaches to the present. Eloísa Gómez Lucena does not focus consistently or explicitly on indigenous people in the present day. However, by taking the foundational text *Naufragios* as her framing device and narrating each place she visits through a historiographical as well as detailed quotidian descriptive approach, the circumstances of the foundation of those economic logics and the impermanence and contingency of the present are implied, though *Del Atlántico al Pacífico* is never particularly reflective about their continuities. She also makes the most direct critiques of nationalism of any text, and offers an unusual juxtaposition of a journey to Mexico with reflection on post-Francoist Spain, though readers are left to draw their own conclusions about how conquest and colonization, nationalism, democratization, transnationalism, and travel and tourism connect to each other.

Even the intertextual reference and evocation of memory in the travel narratives here discussed support a sense of instability, at least inasmuch as the space of memory and interpretive framework of expectation they create are manifestly insufficient to the task of coming to terms with the moveable present. While the intertextuality, exploration of the space of expectation, and personal memory in dialogue with historical and geospatial consciousness speak to the instability of the traveling subject, the narration of trauma, violence, and unrest speaks more to the instability of place. However, as some of the examples in this book suggest, the two modes can intersect at times, more effectively evoking the contingency of encounter and the ways different kinds of mobility are implicated in power and inequality.

In Chapter 3 I highlighted the problem of conflating danger with novelty as a romantic trope in contemporary travel writing, but encounters with trauma and instability can have other effects instead—or even at the same time. In the discussion of border zones and in Spanish travel writers' treatment of actual passage and confrontation with others' experiences of place this contingency is most evident. Armada's evocation of some of the variable—and historically unstable—ways of being in, thinking about, and passing through the border was not wholly free of romance but also suggested the significant differentiation in the experience of place. Semprún evoked both tourist landscapes and insurgent landscapes, and though he unrepentantly promotes the former over the latter without much consideration for the internal traumas and transformative consequences of industrial tourism itself, the nature of his travel, with its original journalistic imperative, foregrounds the presence of local actors and the nonstatic character of place. Even Solano, in his references to indigenous people and to the different cultures and civilizations in Mexico hazards some recognition of the way the tourist production of archaeological sites, in narratives of history for museums and similar spaces has produced simulations around cultural and ethnic identity that individuals find themselves inhabiting and performing. This is to argue that the experience of mobility, which is, as I have reiterated, a differentiated one according to privilege and other factors, may nevertheless destabilize the very factors that determine that differentiation, or at the very least destabilize the preexisting framework that the traveler-writer brings to the interpretation of the meaning of movement and place.

Just as each moment of a journey is a crossroads, so too are the choices taken in its narration. The crossroads marks a decision between two paths. Travel writing in particular, with its exoticizing conventions and tropes of otherness—specifically in this case Mexican otherness (or, occasionally, sameness, through the perpetuation of a discourse of pan-Hispanic continuity)—has the potential to recreate or reinforce compromised cartographies and partial histories. Indeed, in its very nature travel narrative is inevitably in dialogue with histories and practices of power and oppression, if not directly recreating them. However, such accounts can have other functions at the same time, demonstrating horizontal and individual rather than national and hierarchical affiliations. In the fluctuation between reflexivity or self-exploration and witnessing, contemporary travel narratives simultaneously encompass multiple functions—even some that seem contradictory. Complacency may be interrupted by self-doubt. Exoticizing descriptions may run up against the limits of the traveler's perception and the reversal of the gaze. Nonfiction narrative, with its claim to completeness and authority, may reveal its own constructedness. Merrill (2009) argues for interpreting travel as one dimension of soft power, but not for individual travelers as straightforward conduits for transmitting imperialist ideas. Tourist encounters are individual negotiations of unequal relations that can nevertheless produce contestation and suggest potential avenues of resistance.

While sequencing and telling remain important parts of the narration of experience, some contemporary narratives also privilege the process of accumulation, of fragmentary and overtly unreliable telling, such that the narration of subjective experience may be represented in partial, and indeed contradictory, moments of revelation and in images and be molded around fundamentally contingent identities. Given the nature of representation of place under globalized communications and information excess, narratives of experience contend with what is within the text, its explicit subject, but also what is outside—competing versions of same object of representation, be it place, event, or people. Contemporary travel writers contend with the fluidity and contradictions that occur as broader understandings of their subject matter change around them. Pure contingency and the sheer accretion of images plastered into the consciousness carries another kind of danger. Augé (1999) warns that with the dissolution of reference accumulation can replace meaning. Where reference is hyper-individualized and detached from a collective sense of history, the material elements of encounter and the presence of realities beyond the interpretive framework of the author become abstracted, almost fictive. Within that acceleration of image, all the problems of conceiving place as a pure object of consumption, of conflating difference with novelty—that is, its value for individual stimulation—overwhelm any possibility of encounter with place and with difference as a space for humanizing the effects of global power.

The traditional travel book, particularly the travel diary, is a disappearing genre, and in its most recognizable form fundamentally a product of the nineteenth and twentieth centuries. This book has therefore addressed itself to the ways a medium that has a degree of inbuilt nostalgia and a clearly compromised heritage can, by those who take it up, transform itself to try to articulate the present conditions of travel encounter. Travel narration will continue to evolve in both style and medium to reflect the flows of information and the flows of people now in the twenty-first century. Younger travelers than those discussed here have come of age in the twenty-first century, and shared in 2020 a mass experience of immobilization. It is reasonable to expect changes in the way they communicate their experiences, and also in their demonstrated historical and geospatial consciousness based on the evolving situation of both Spain and Mexico and the space in between in the new millennium. The frameworks for thinking about the natural world in the face of the threat of extinction and the catastrophes approaching as a result of human-triggered climate change also add urgency to questions of who travels and who is displaced and questions of justice in the disparity between those two rarely overlapping categories. Rapid transformations in the possibilities for movement and the use of territorial control (witness the closure of borders and abrupt immobilization of privileged elites in the wake of pandemic) reshape people's relationship to leisure, mobility, and choice. Future research on the kinds of stories we tell about mobility, and the specifics of concrete transnational routes and their histories, will need to account much more for the instantaneity of communications, visual storytelling in various media (travel stories told in documentaries, nonfiction comic books, or even in social media feeds), and new causes of mass displacements, along with new mechanisms of unequal immobilization.

This book analyzed the implications of different dynamics of encounter and representation in response to existing discourses of place and conditions of mobility along contemporary transatlantic routes from Spain to Mexico. It should not, however, convey the impression that the case studies here have a completely generalizable value. Their value is in their particularity and the way they suggest not the whole nature of Spain-to-Mexico travel narration but rather the shape of those discourses and collective ideas that new narratives about Mexico by Spaniards intervene in or respond to. Throughout this investigation I have drawn together the historical role of the genre of travel writing, the effects of globality, and the way the discourses around transatlantic histories and American spaces inflect actual encounters between travelers from Spain and Mexican hosts and worlds. Cross-cultural narratives in this formulation become possible sites for understanding the tensions in different concepts of transatlantic mobility and in experiences of place. I have tried to show how different orientations to place and different narrative modes create different critical possibilities for engaging with the world. Contemporary travel writing often reproduces stereotypes and naturalizes widely circulated myths about the world order. At its best, however, it can foreground global-scale inequality, the dangers attached to the commodification of cultural difference, and their concrete historical and economic causes and consequences. It is one space to understand how narrating place and encounter transmits an ethics of what we owe to the past, to others human and not, and to the future.

NOTES

INTRODUCTION

1. When I use the word *Spanish* in this work, unless there is a specific reference to language, I intend it to signify Spanish national origin. Thea Pitman, among others, has also wrestled with this problem of terminology. She discusses the way *Mexican* is assumed to refer to destination rather than authorship. This assumption is given as an example of the extent to which a "colonialist mentality" still underpins discussions of travel writing (Pitman 2007).
2. In using *imaginary* here I am following Walter Mignolo's (2000, 23) interpretation of it as a term describing a collectively constructed sociocultural perception of the world.
3. As Pere Gifra Adroher (2006, 159) writes, "the heterogeneity that travel literature and its critical practice so conspicuously display certainly indicates . . . that this is a complex field of study in a constant state of transition." This heterogeneity makes selecting critical tools and determining interdisciplinary dynamics difficult. Joan-Pau Rubiés (2000, 6) describes travel literature as a "genre of genres." One of the problems this creates is limiting the area of study, with a slippery tradition and elusive definitions. The research in Spanish assumes more flexible thematic definitions of narrative. An example is the collection *El viaje en la literatura hispanoamericana* (Mattalía, Celma, and Alonso 2008), which brings together essays that specifically engage with tourism, with travel memoir, with the major periods of migration between Europe and Latin America (in both directions), and also with fiction that deals conceptually with travel. The voyage's cultural meaning is the unifier, rather than its materiality. Similarly, Monteleone's *El relato de viaje* (1998) marks the nonlinear nature of the composition of a narrative, and echoes that in the nonlinearity of its critical framing. These two, like other similar examples, resist categorical summations or strict genre definitions.

4. "Los viajeros viajan con los ojos puestos en los libros que han leído, esperando su confirmación en la experiencia o incluso adaptando ésta a sus lecturas previas." [All translations my own unless otherwise noted.]
5. Global travel is a US$1.7 trillion industry representing, prior to the 2020 contraction, 7 percent of the world's exports in 2018, according to the United Nations World Tourism Organization (2019).
6. While this is a deliberate process, it is also a difficult and contested one, which in Latin America also contends with histories of the formation of national identity and sovereignty around Latin American difference. See for example Dunja Fehimović and Rebecca Ogden's volume *Branding Latin America* (2018).
7. For a discussion of the political implications of regimes of otherness in late twentieth century European politics and international relations, see Neumann's 1998 *Uses of the Other*.
8. While Pratt's work is the most influential in travel writing studies of Latin America, there many excellent histories of European travel and the emergence of travel writing genres. Among these, Campbell's *The Witness and the Other World* (1988) and Stagl's *A History of Curiosity* (1995) provide context for understanding changes in travel practices in Europe and associated European epistemologies from the Middle Ages through to the eighteenth century—corresponding to Spain's imperial expansion in the Americas. Buzard's *The Beaten Track* (1993) continues with the nineteenth and early twentieth centuries, with a specific eye to the role travel and literature in those times played in the emergence of notions of authenticity and the accessibility of cultural experiences. Korte's *English Travel Writing from Pilgrimages to Postcolonial Explorations* (2000) traces the progression of the genre in English, relevant here for documenting tendencies in travel writing like shifts between objectivity and subjective experience, transcultural hybridity, and the importance of the postcolonial. Imperialist modes of description they identify clearly persist in the genre.
9. With the term *globalization* I am referring to the creation of a single world system as a product of global imperialism and its ongoing consequences and influence in every aspect of local experience following its detachment from imperialism as a system of government.
10. See, for example, a selection of some relatively recent studies among the plethora in existence focusing specifically on Mexico: Berger and Wood (2009); Everitt et al. (2008); Goertzen (2010); Hellier-Tinoco (2010); Manuel-Navarrete (2016); Monterrubio, Osorio, and Benítez (2017); Papanicolaou (2009; 2012); Wilson (2008; 2012).
11. These include influential works by MacCannell (1976, 1992); V. Smith (1989); Chambers (1999); and Clifford (1997). *Hosts and Guests*, edited by Smith, was a significant early text in tourism studies examining the impact of tourism on sites and communities, the role of leisure and imperialism, historical context, new modes of tourism, and tourism in non-Western societies. Subsequent works by MacCannell and others such

as Urry (1990) are significant for their contributions to tracing the rise of industrial-scale tourism, its use in definitions of travel versus tourist behaviors, and its significance for the traveler's idea of self and representation of place and experience. Chambers surveys historic, economic, social, environmental, and cultural dimensions of tourism in anthropological research, and evolving concepts of "hosts" and "visitors" under globalization. Clifford has turned to travel and the travel narrative as a means of exploring power and representation, the politics of location, divergent identities, and moving histories. Clifford and Marcus (1986) and other contributors to the rethinking of ethnography critiqued various aspects of the ethnographic project that are relevant also for thinking through travel writing, including the authority of the researcher, the exclusion of "objects" of study—human beings—from their representation, the use of an ahistorical present, and the elision of the researcher's motives, position and beliefs in the assumption of an objective narrative. These theories have since been revised in terms of broader social preoccupation with globalization, shifting the emphasis from textual negotiations to a dual ethical process where the politics of the cultural encounter are as important as its description.

12. Existing studies in both languages focus more on the nineteenth century or early twentieth at the latest, as in the work of Lily Litvak (1987) or Chantal Roussel-Zuazu (2005).

13. See Stephanie Lawson, *Culture and Context in World Politics* (2006), a comprehensive exploration of the abuse of the word *culture* and artificial difference at the expense of understanding systemic inequalities and political power.

CHAPTER 1

Epigraph. "Nada penetra en nosotros sin desplazar algo: la imagen nueva se disputa con la que estaba adentro, moviéndose con desahogo de medusa en el agua; después la cubre como una alga suavemente, sin tragedia."

1. Influential works from the seventeenth and into the eighteenth century include the memoirs of Mme d'Aulnoy, the letters of Alexander Jardine, and some of those anthologized in García Mercadal's monumental *Viajes de extranjeros por España y Portugal* and in Guerrero's *Viajeros británicos en la España del siglo XVIII*. Later famous chroniclers of Spain included writers like George Sand and others from further afield such as Ernest Hemingway and Richard Ford. Soldiers passing through Spain made a major contribution in their memoirs of Napoleonic wars and later the Spanish Civil War. Mitchell traces some of the more recent history in *Viajeros por España: De Borrow a Hemingway* (1989), and as Burns (in Mitchell 1989, 9) writes in the prologue to the study, 'Lo español llegó a ser una

mezcla de picaresca, orgullo, coraje, indolencia, sensualidad y fanatismo religioso' (Spanishness became a mix of picaresque, pride, courage, indolence, sensuality and religious fanaticism.)

2. "Entiende que a partir de 1492, la imagen de España estuvo alterada por las crónicas de Indias con su brutal proyección de edénica bondad y maldad sin cuento."

3. The most relevant precursors to contemporary travel writing are from the last century or so. In the nineteenth century, Spain was undergoing the first juddering awakenings from the long fantasy of sustainable empire. Roussel-Zuazu's (2005) useful work summarizes and classifies different travel and travel narratives in Spain through this period, and Nunley (2007) explores a number of key examples of individual texts that also reflect cultural preoccupations and ideological dynamics of the time. Pérez Mejía (2004) partly covers the same period with reference to examples of European travel writing about South America, suggesting some of the first consequences of collapsing empire for the idea of America. Quite a few writers of the late nineteenth century, including iconic figures like Emilia Pardo Bazán, Pedro Antonio de Alarcón, Benito Pérez Galdós, and Emilia Serrano (Baroness Wilson), produced texts that in various ways are ancestors of contemporary Spanish travel writing. Twentieth century improvements in literacy and developing popular publishing industries accelerated some travel writing production, however, all artistic and literary endeavors were warped inside Spain by Francoist constraints. A few iconic works of Spanish travel writing were produced in this period, such as Camilo José Cela's *Viaje a la Alcarria* (1948), which in certain respects reflects the insularity and nationalism of the period, or works produced effectively from exile, such as the travel writing of Juan Goytisolo, which have a more ambivalent relationship to Spain as origin.

4. Any discussion of the trajectory of travel writing in Spain owes a debt to the bibliographic labors of Peñate Rivero, and for my purposes particularly volume 2 of his *Introducción al relato de viaje hispánico del siglo XX* (2012), covering roughly the same period as that which is my focus in this book and constituting an instructive and inclusive survey (though of course any such project will remain inevitably incomplete in contemporary conditions of constantly fracturing small presses and novel modes of distribution.)

5. Jorge Luengo and Pol Dalmau (2018) summarize some ways Spain has been marginalized in thinking—and writing—global history.

6. We can see for example the simple indicator of flights per week shows exponentially greater constant mobility through Buenos Aires, for example, serving as one hub into South America in a way that Mexico cannot for North America.

7. Padilla and Cuberos-Gallardo (2016) have outlined the ways contemporary Spanish immigration policy and migration sentiment are explicitly linked to neocolonialism, and how the idea of Iberoamerican continuity in Spain serves a colonialist spirit of dominance.

8. Peñate Rivero (2012, 428–30) provides numerous examples showing that this tourist/traveller distinction is as prevalent in contemporary Spanish contemporary travel writing as it is elsewhere.
9. Or who would aspire to be and remain culturally connected to a middle-class identity, however precarious their actual economic circumstances, especially into the 2010s/post-crisis.
10. "México es percibido como un país *amigo*, algo *ecológico*, con cierta *estabilidad política*, con *futuro*, pero *pobre*. Lo sitúan con cierto equilibrio en lo que se refiere a *la seguridad, el desarrollo, su parecido con España* y al *desarrollo cultural*."
11. "sol y playa, cultura, ecoturismo y aventura, buceo, cruceros, negocios y convenciones."
12. Luzón (2010) gives one pointed example of the ways Spanish support of events commemorating centenaries of independence 1910–1911 was imbued with Spain's own ambitions and nationalist project.
13. Relations between the two countries have varied through the early twentieth century (see Meyer 2014).
14. Though this was nothing in comparison the global convulsion of COVID-19, the sequelae of which impact tourism perhaps most of all industries.
15. The first television adaptation of *La reina del sur* was Spanish and primarily for the Spanish market, although a popular *telenovela* was produced in the US. It would be valuable to compare the various versions of the same story to explore the nuanced valences in the image of Mexico and transnational drug crime presented to different markets and via different distribution mechanisms.
16. Art house and festival circuit films as well as films with primarily domestic audiences negotiate different aesthetics and narrative exigencies—as well as different audience frameworks of reference. On the tensions between transnational art cinema and national cinema in Mexico, see Shaw (2011).
17. "una necesidad para resignificar a las culturas que habían sido excluidas de la historia y del diálogo intercultural"
18. Useful starting points for historical foreign travel narratives about Mexico are anthologies like Glantz's *Viajes en México: Crónicas extranjeras* ([1964] 1982) or Iturriaga de la Fuente's *Anecdotario de viajeros extranjeros en México, siglos XVI–XIX* (1989–92) and *Anecdotario de forasteros en México, siglos XVI–XXI* (2009), which include a range of texts by authors of less prominence than Alexander von Humboldt whose shorter or minor works are consequently less likely to be available in print.
19. "el escudriñamiento de 'lo primitivo' como intento de reencuentro con unos supuestos valores perdidos en las sociedades desarrolladas"
20. "negar la humanidad del Otro creyendo encontrar en esa actitud la seguridad de un sistema que en realidad conduce hacia el abandono de su propia humanidad"
21. Not that Spanish colonialism was free of interweaving scientific knowledge and political power—for example the Malaspina Expedition,

recently reenacted in a new context of global knowledge production. This scientific exploration was, however, less characteristic of early periods of Spanish Empire than it became by the eighteenth and nineteenth centuries in the expansion of other European empires.

22. "no considerar a los refugiados como tales ni mantenerlos a base de pensiones, sino asimilarlos efectivamente a la vida cultural del país anfitrión, aprovechando así todas sus virtudes. . . . se buscaba rescatar la calidad humana de los desterrados, con todas sus características profesionales y morales."
23. Clifford (1997) articulated this in broad terms, and Lindsay (2009, 3) defined it in relation to Latin America in particular.
24. "la particularidad de darse desde zonas no centrales, de iniciarse desde la periferia. El punto de partida, entonces, es una precariedad. El punto de llegada puede ser otra precariedad o una zona más estable, cargada de historia, conocida de antemano por el aura de prestigio que confieren la historia, el arte y la literatura."
25. "he sentido en Europa, como el rasgo dominante, la presencia de la historia, que confiere sentido y perspectiva al presente, por mediocre que éste pueda ser. Como tal cosa nos es en América totalmente desconocida, ella provoca en el ánimo del americano la más violenta y definitiva experiencia."
26. "Efectivamente, para un europeo que llega a América, la sensación de liberación de un pasado histórico es enorme."
27. "'América' es un producto del relato histórico europeo que trató de asimilarse los nuevos territorios en detrimento de las poblaciones aborígenes, lo que traducido en términos prácticos viene a configurar a América como una inmensa superficie de tierras ricas en recursos naturales y con abundante mano de obra barata."
28. "Nuestra América debe vivir como si se preparase siempre a realizar el sueño que su descubrimiento provocó entre los pensadores de Europa: el sueño de la utopía, de la república feliz."
29. It should be noted that mythmaking around narcoculture is also strong inside Mexico itself. It becomes, in literature for example, a point of inflection in the production of marketable narrative, often reinforcing the discourse of lawlessness—though, as Zavala (2014) describes, with more critical alternatives that link *narco* violence to capitalism and state power still possible.
30. There are too many studies and reports touching on, for example, transformations of specific communities of Mayan people on the peripheries of the touristic development of the Yucatán, or sex or drug tourism to detail here. A few indicative examples of the secondary economies around tourism include Conde Olivares (2006) on drug commerce; Azaola Garrido and Estes (2003) on interconnections between tourism and paedophilia networks in North America; Robertson et al. (2014) or Yolocuauhtli Vargas and Alcalá (2015), among many others, on prostitution; Arriaga Rodríguez (2000) on informal economies; Bianet

Castellanos (2010) on displacement of Maya people and economic change in historical context.

31. NAFTA is widely recognized as having brought significant structural changes to the Mexican economy, notably via shifts in the viability of agricultural production regions versus foreign-owned industrial and manufacturing areas.

32. Despite the common denial of a popular travel genre in Mexico—related to the negative associations the genre carries—Pitman (2008, 26–27) notes the existence of publishers' series devoted to travel, conferences on the subject, and travel writing competitions.

CHAPTER 2

1. See for example Alonso Álvarez de Toledo, *Un tranvía naranja y polvoriento: México, Alemania, el muro, la OTAN, el 92* (Madrid: Compañía Literaria, 1996); or Alfonso de la Serna, *Las fronteras sensibles de España* (Burgos: Dossoles, 2004).
2. "se quiere parecer a Europa, pero Europa le muestra un espejo vacío, un marco sin cristal donde se refleja el rostro de la dominación."
3. "de las Américas al Mediterráneo, y del Mediterráneo a las Américas."
4. "Muy bien, cuando acabemos con esto empecemos con el genocidio en hispanoamérica, creo que también habrá que pedir el certificado de defunción de Hernán Cortés." Gonzalo, October 16, comment 559 on José Yoldi, "Garzón investigará la represión franquista y abrirá la fosa de Lorca," *El país*, October 16, 2008, https://elpais.com/elpais/2008/10/16/actualidad/1224145022_850215.html.
5. "las repúblicas socialistas bananeras tercermundistas en que la Justicia está al servicio de la política." jordi lopez, October 16, comment 588 on Yoldi, "Garzón investigará."
6. "una limpieza urgente de las principales instituciones de la nación." Castro Urdiales, October 16, comment 552 on Yoldi, "Garzón investigará."
7. "Estamos preparados para otra vez volver a plantar cara a los herederos del terror." Arturo, October 16, comment 571 on Yoldi, "Garzón investigará."
8. "la imaginación proyecta espacios más luminosos, una vida más justa, una riqueza mejor repartida, un modo de reír que no sea sarcástico."
9. "la caída de una hegemonía"
10. "melodía del español de los siglos de oro"
11. Johannes Fabian's *Time and the Other* (1983) traces European temporality and historical thinking and how they have been and continue to be used to distance others temporally as well as spatially, excluding them from modernity, a significant trope in the representation of Mexico.
12. "Un estado de conciencia de lo que fue México antes de los españoles . . . de la época colonial . . . y del tiempo presente."

13. "Las flechas son iguales que las que venden a los turistas de D.F. en la Calzada de los Muertos de Teotihuacán, a 700 kilómetros; así que es falsa artesanía azteca y falsa artesanía maya, y sospecho que también ellos son falsos lacandones."
14. "la plata que se admiraba . . . en los salones de Europa"; "los niños de seis años se extenuaban o caían muertos a unas pozas de reflejos cobrizos"
15. "la comprensión general de que ha sido el sufrimiento de los indígenas. . . . Eso, y la vergüenza de no mostrarnos indignos de su memoria."
16. "A journey that flies from cliché" (A description of *Bajo las nubes* in a review at *Clubcultura.com* 9, 2001).
17. "reflexivo y austero"; "geometría caótica"
18. "tiende al sedentarismo . . . a la repetición"
19. "paseante en firmes aceras . . . usuario del metro y de autobuses . . . peatón"
20. For example, at one stage Solano mentions the professional roles, status, and power of some Mexicans he stays with as well as their personal choices and lifestyles, thus giving space within the text for their own dually personal and analytical or textualized relationship to Mexican culture (35).
21. "un país que se multiplica"; "una entonación de palabras, según se ponga el acento sobre la fábula o sobre la trama que rige el espejo que nos contempla."
22. "asombra de ellas no lo que se conoce . . . sino todo lo que ignoramos"
23. "tan abrumada por la realidad histórica que, para soportar su peso, la combinación de su suelo, rico en minerales, es capaz de momificar un cadáver en cinco años. . . . Se apelmazan, se solidifican, se convierten en momias de un gore *avant-la-lettre* hollywoodense."
24. "sufrimiento mitológico que ocasionó la llegada de los españoles."
25. "Convertido en héroe, en símbolo, en objeto de preservación histórica, de Villa se recuerda ahora menos su tozudez y sus estrepitosas derrotas en Celaya y Aguascalientes, que al victorioso revolucionario, jefe de la División del Norte, que se sentó en el sillón presidencial. La memoria estiliza las figuras controvertidas."
26. "Sólo es real lo que está escrito. Pero lo que no está escrito está igualmente vivo, y se agita en los posos de la memoria como peces inasibles."
27. "a quienes las palabras nos crean el mundo, nuestra línea de flotación es siempre un rumor de sílabas, y el resto es silencio, o una devoción de labios cerrados frente a ese espacio en blanco que hay entre dos palabras."
28. "Escribir, sobre todo, es una continua toma de decisiones . . . hay palabras que se atraen, por simpatía o costumbre, y hay que aceptar sus adherencias, que a veces también son infecciones; el orden del discurso no puede desviarse, impone su corriente, excluye una ciudad si queda lejos; la narración de un viaje es como un culto maniático a una actriz, un enamoramiento público."
29. "mirar es también interpretar, y a veces inventar."

30. "la última línea y al golpe final sobre las teclas."
31. "'¿Qué significa decir bien, decir interesante? . . . Cualquier palabra es inferior a la experiencia que designa."
32. "Todo depende, claro está, del espiritú del viajero."
33. "personajes extravagantes, con necias pulsiones sociales, con un yo inflamado de necesidad de redimir"; "pareja vestida de exploradores, a la moda de *Memorias de África*, tan cinematográficos y atildados que aguardo, con toda convicción, que me ofrezcan un trago de whisky en una petaca de plata."
34. "Creíamos que estábamos solos, pero un indio, con un perro mudo, ha contemplado toda nuestra fantasía."
35. "Neutralizados por la indistinción turística, todos somos gregarios o estúpidos, y hasta que entramos en el coche, también ridículos."
36. "Estas mujeres indias hacen resaltar un falso color local, son arqueología viva para turistas. . . . Toleran su presencia, que colorea el ambiente, son el vínculo con el México profundo, pero no deben excederse con los blancos."
37. "También México está hecho de palabras, ha sido construido con palabras. . . . México se hace más transparente en la medida en que, con su lectura, se atenúa el aturdimiento que provoca una actualidad que se transforma y, a la vez, se perpetúa en su presente."
38. "Un país lo conforma su geografía, su historia y los textos memorables que intentan abarcar su mundo de profecías, de fracasos y de pasiones secretas."
39. "dentro de un sueño incumplido, de un sueño que se está soñando"; "Sobre qué México escriben esos libros?"
40. "Como a los borrachos y a las mujeres resignadas a un matrimonio de atropello, también a los mexicanos les importa más el melodrama de su vida, que siempre es una narración, que la propia vida."
41. "Una niña tzeltal cruzando la carretera, tres campesinos bebiendo pulque a los pies de un maguey, una serpiente de piedra, el lagarto que asoma la cabeza en la columna caída, una cara de ámbar, el huipil en la acera para no oír las monedas, todo lo visto, registrado en un momento, refulgía otra vez en la luz del sueño."
42. "los indios tarahumaras, los verdaderos señores de estas tierras, hoy superpuestos al paisaje como signos melancólicos para remordimiento de la consciencia cultural."
43. "Como todos los descubridores, él debía sacarlos de la oscuridad, y al mismo tiempo contribuir a su aniquilamiento."
44. Some of the simultaneous advantages and problems of the public location and media representation of Amazonian groups, to take one example, are summarized in Collins Rudolf (2011), Vidal (2011), and Perivolaris (2011). The much more manifestly tragic sequel, in which drug traffickers are suspected to have forced the tribe to flee, followed in August 2011 (Castillo 2011).

45. Jordá makes reference at different moments to writers as diverse as Gustave Flaubert, Eamonn McThomas, William Butler Yeats, Vladimir Nabokov, Jorge Luis Borges, Samuel Beckett, William S. Burroughs, Bram Stoker, Federico García Lorca, Luis Cernuda, Witold Gombrowicz, and José Donoso, as well as constantly expressing his interest in the history of places as imagined through their famous visitors such as actors and directors.
46. I am drawing here on the work of theorists of memory like Avishai Margalit and Aleida Assman.
47. "flotando en una tierra de nadie, que no pertenecía a ningún continente, a ninguna civilización"
48. "Más allá de esa casa, más allá del triángulo de calles que reaparecen en un sueño, más allá de algunos amigos y de algunas calles, la ciudad es una simple entidad administrativa que figura en los mapas, nada más."
49. "tour por Europa y otras tierras."
50. "Vista desde dentro, con los ojos de la memoria, Palma era una ciudad habitable y simpática, aunque supongo que cualquier ciudad en la que uno ha nacido y crecido acaba convirtiéndose, con el paso del tiempo, en el espejismo de una ciudad habitable y simpática."
51. "la única patria que el autor considera suya."
52. "Lo que pasa es que el tiempo desaparecido hace que hasta lo menos memorable se vea envuelto en una aureola que lo ennoblece."
53. "Mis personajes suelen vivir en otra parte, lejos de su lugar de origen"; "las únicas patrias que valen la pena son las que uno puede elegir."
54. "edificios heridos por las bombas, las casamatas, pequeños fortines y nidos de ametralladora en los desmontes . . . aquel Madrid cutre de la posguerra era un universo emocionante, pues nos dejaba ver las trazas de terribles batallas."
55. "sociedad española que comenzaba a demandar una información veraz."
56. "'nace una buena parte de mi nostalgia de lo que no conozco."
57. "Hay que procurar darle a la propia biografía un cierto sabor épico"; "'En algún momento tuve la impresión de que, a pesar de tanto vuelo, tanto hotel, tanto palacio, tanto mundo recorrido y tantos desplazamientos con reyes y presidentes, yo no había viajado."
58. "Reina burguesa" for "King Burger."
59. "género fronterizo que incorpore autobiografía, ficción, ensayo y crónica." The source of this description is presumably Jordá or his publishers, since it appears in the standard biographical note that accompanies his public appearances and professional activities.
60. "contrastar sus lecturas con la aprehensión directa de los escenarios que las generaron." *Vanguardia*, "Otras lecturas," May 5, 2004, 13.
61. "Si regreso alguna vez, Puerto Escondido será una variante perfeccionada de cualquier lugar de la costa mallorquina."
62. "Nunca podemos volver al mismo sitio. Incluso en el caso de que ese lugar no se haya vuelto irreconocible—cosa cada vez más difícil—, el paso del tiempo nos ha hecho irreconocibles a nosotros."

63. "qué quedaba ahora de todo aquello que había leído muchos años antes."

CHAPTER 3

1. The failure of community and belonging to place to adequately counterbalance the traumas of migration have also been illustrated in another text that also takes Lampedusa as its primary example: the award-winning documentary *Fuocammare* (2016; *Fire at Sea*).
2. "el contenido crítico o incluso de denuncia aparece de forma bastante clara."
3. One exception is the direct sphere of influence of the Mexican government in, for example, tourism policy and development, worth mentioning as part of a broader attempt to avoid obscuring the role of economic and political forces in the production of ideas of place. However, even this national strategy is designed to reach beyond Mexico's borders, and the northern border region is hardly the most successful example of the centralized tourism development projects of the last several decades.
4. "la herencia no caducada de exploradores, aventureros y frailes españoles"; "un país que parece aplastado por el peso de su impresionante historia."
5. "No tuvo la suerte de los hermanos que se quedaron en España . . . ha hecho de todo, y los últimos cinco años de peón agrícola."
6. "las misiones españolas que surgieron como apariciones en tierras del todo ignotas para los europeos que, siglos después, siguen sin acabar de entender muy bien qué carajo es Estados Unidos."
7. "dos mundos que no se parecen en nada."
8. "todos son mexicanos, hayan nacido en este o en el otro lado."
9. "son los hispanos mayoría abrumadora y el español la lengua que empapa como limo todo el trazo de este a oeste, como si callandito estuvieran reconquistando un territorio arrebatado."
10. "Ciudad Juárez, donde todos los horrores se consuman. Aquí se concentran todas las opulencias, las que sangran y las que olvidan, las que nunca se sacian y las que ponen a prueba a quienes no tienen más remedio que vivir aquí o se niegan a rendirse. Junto a El Paso, una de las ciudades que año tras año se sitúa a la cabeza de las más seguras de Norteamérica."
11. "La frontera es, también, un impulso a ir más allá, a modificar lo que es fruto de la lógica de la historia, una máscara de colmillos de hierro viejo. Como la pared que el mar carcome en Tijuana. La carcasa de un *Titanic* político."
12. "capaz de burlarse de todos los episodios históricos en los que interviene la memoria humana, nuestros legajos fronterizos, nuestros títulos de propiedad"
13. "menos que escoria para el reloj geológico, que nos contempla sin conciencia, y por lo tanto sin desdén ni compasión."
14. "El antiguo océano de la era glacial es hoy texto inconcebible, deslumbrante blancura. Tanta pureza resulta inhumana."

15. "La austera belleza del desierto de Sonora nada entiende de política: dos terceras partes son de México, pero se prolonga por el sur de California y Arizona."
16. "rejilla de seguridad entre la parte delantera y la trasera."
17. These three intertextual references have the greatest poetic resonance throughout the book, however he also mentions in passing writers like Fyodor Dostoyevsky, Albert Camus, and Jack Kerouac and noted earlier travelers through the region like Alvar Núñez Cabeza de Vaca, and regularly refers to a broad selection of nonfiction accounts of the problems and history of the border region, notably González Rodríguez's *Huesos en el desierto* (2002) and Bassett's *Organ Pipe: Life on the Edge* (2004), as well as a smattering of articles from the *New York Times*, *El país semanal*, the *New Yorker*, and other publications.
18. "como metáfora del horror y el mal en el siglo XX."
19. "en sintonía con las leyendas del viejo Oeste y la mística de la carretera."
20. "A Texas le gusta presumir, hasta la obscenidad infantil, de hacerlo todo a lo grande. Incluso las matanzas."
21. "A pesar de que la literatura permite muchas licencias que la realidad no se toma, hace tiempo que la vida en México ha adquirido tintes extraordinarios."
22. "las lavadoras del Pentágono son tan eficientes, tan higiénicas, que el último rastro de vida ha sido bienintencionadamente borrado."
23. "El núcleo del viaje, su epicentro, está en una escombrera: calcinada y habitada. El corazón desollado de la frontera está en su mayor metrópoli, Ciudad Juárez . . . sinónimo de deshuesadero, en el ejemplo en carne viva del impulso de la sociedad contemporánea por 'normalizar la barbarie,' como anota Sergio González Rodríguez . . . donde el narcotráfico y el poder político se han machihembrado hasta parir un mutante que devora carne humana."
24. "un pasado que compagina lo texano con un orgullo que parece intrínsecamente gringo y es al tiempo de raíz mexicana e índole española."
25. "conviven la tecnología punta de las cadenas de montaje multinacionales (maquilas), la pobreza más extrema, el paso constante de emigrantes que buscan una vida mejor al norte de la línea, el crimen organizado, el narcotráfico y todas sus ramificaciones, y donde los que resisten lo hacen organizándose al margen de un Estado que no sólo no les ampara sino que aparece como cómplice del mal. El rumor de la frontera se hace aquí odioso, insoportable."
26. "un eco de los subsaharianos deportados por el Gobierno español a Marruecos, que a su vez los abandona en el desierto, sin agua, sin comida, sin amparo."
27. "Cortada la frontera en los dos puntos por un efecto colateral y desmesurado del 11 de septiembre de 2001, vendedores de Boquillas del Carmen salvan aquí [cerca de Big Bend] la casi siempre vadeable corriente del río (Bravo para ellos, Grande para esta orilla), dejan en las sendas piedras

pintadas, escorpiones de cobre y garrotas historiadas junto a un bidón lastrado con una piedra para que el viajero pague lo que estime."
28. "para que los emigrantes ilegales puedan rendirse antes de que les cace la muerte."
29. "lugares emblemáticos"
30. Classically formulated as merit for reporting determined by relative death toll based on race/country of origin.
31. "uno se pregunta si los conocimientos adquiridos sobre, por ejemplo, Paraguay, en pleno golpe de estado y caída del dinosaurio Stroessner, no estarán absolutamente errados, mediatizados por el ruido ambiental del momento. . . . Apenas estuve cinco días y envié cuatro crónicas con el mismo aplomo que el redactor al que debemos la entrada guaraní de la enciclopedia Espasa."
32. "Desde que el hombre, alrededor del fuego, comenzó a contar historias, los relatos se han nutrido de los miedos . . . todo lo que venía de fuera era malo y peligroso. El *otro* era siempre un enemigo probado."
33. "Ciertamente, no sueles ver lo que la gente normal ve en los viajes y no todas las experiencias humanas son enriquecedoras, como pretenden los cursis."
34. "Yo no he tenido nunca la sensación de peligro porque he procurado ser un periodista vivo no un héroe muerto."
35. "La actualidad es la que te manda."
36. "No es que los destinos sean desaconsejables sino las circunstancias en las que se produce el viaje."
37. "Mis historias son siempre historias de personas no son historias de paisajes . . . las personas que sufrían."
38. "El tiempo, elemento ordenador de la crónica periodística, en la crónica viajera pasa a ocupar un segundo plano, en beneficio del espacio."
39. "Uno tiene pasaporte, billete de vuelta y, la mayor parte de las veces, un hotel protegido por la policía donde ducharse y descansar. Vas y lo cuentas, pero ellos, que son como nosotros, se quedan."
40. "viajar con [Joaquín] Ibars por Iberoamérica es lo más español que te puede ocurrir; siempre habla en Catalán con la telefonista de su periódico, y esas voces sólo pueden venir de un rincón, allá lejos, que es tu casa, aunque vivas en Madrid."
41. "Con lo que el viajero español debe mostrar una cierta distancia es con la política interna de la isla. Para líos hispánicos ya tiene bastante con los de casa. De modo que lo mejor es procurar atenerse a los placeres: ron, café, playas, música, arquitectura, naturaleza y gallos de pelea. Por otro lado, la batalla de la Hispanidad puede obsesionar al más pintado y nosotros, europeos de toda la vida, ya no estamos para esas fiestas."
42. "Los que vivían en zonas bajo control del Ejército mexicano conservan sus casas, pero tienen miedo a las represalias. Los otros deambulan por carreteras y predios en busca de un lugar donde levantar la choza. En estos días no son sólo los indios los que cargan con sus pertenencias a

cuestas. Cientos de mestizos y de indios aladinados, es decir, indios que intentaron mal que bien integrarse al mundo blanco, tuvieron también que abandonar sus pueblos en la zona de guerra."
43. "A partir de [San Miguel], donde la Cruz Roja Internacional tiene instalado su hospital de campaña y hasta la frontera guatemalteca no se mueve un alma sin la autorización expresa de los guerrilleros."
44. "la pista de tierra se convierte en un infierno de barro en cuanto caen cuatro gotas."
45. "Así, sencillamente, otro pueblo, Sitalá, pasa a la tierra de nadie. En las lomas próximas, los tzeltales esperan las represalias. Y aunque, por ahora, son los dueños del terreno, saben por experiencia histórica que la venganza llegará."
46. "El odio que profesaban los indios al mestizo y al asimilado llega a estremecer."
47. "aplauden cuando uno de ellos grita que 'los que se pasan la vida tumbados en la hamaca y sin trabajar no tienen derecho a comer.'"
48. "hay quien proyecta hacia el exterior su propia responsabilidad histórica para sentirse libre."
49. "entre el 20 y el 26 de mayo de 1993, el Ejército Zapatista de Liberación Nacional libró su primer combate contra las tropas del ejército mexicano. Resistieron seis días mientras trasladaban sus depósitos de armamento a otro lugar seguro. Murieron dos soldados y otros cinco resultaron heridos. Pero el Gobierno de México fue categórico: 'Señores, no existe guerrilla en Chiapas.'"
50. "Y es que estas leyendas urbanas, mitos de la gran ciudad o, más simplemente, rumores, recorren el mundo, saltan de continentes, desaparecen y resurgen con el paso del tiempo, cambian de protagonistas y de escenarios, pero siempre están ahí. Si alguien creía que la televisión iba a conseguir que se extinguiera la tradición del relato oral, los hechos no pueden ser más contundentes."
51. "Hoy, Chiapas ha sido enviada al último rincón en el armario de los periodistas internacionales, pero sus problemas se mantienen con la misma lozanía que cuando se sublevaron los indios, al mando de un descendiente de españoles, aquel Año Nuevo de 1994."
52. "la miseria y el dolor, la guerra y la violencia ideológica."
53. "Ya lo dijo Ambrose Bierce: Dios eligió la guerra para enseñarnos a los occidentales Geografía. Y en tales circunstancias, ni existe Mozambique, ni hay negrito caquéxico que compita en prime time con ese mundo kitsch y sórdido del famoseo y el reality."
54. "en los papeles del Occidente no hay lugar para el paria más allá del costumbrismo y el tsunami (parece ser que a los humanos nos gusta más el lodo que el contexto)."

CHAPTER 4

1. I am using *chiapaneco* in the general sense referring to the state of Chiapas.
2. "es falsa artesanía azteca y falsa artesanía maya, y sospecho que también ellos son falsos lacandones."
3. "Los turistas somos así de idiotas. La placidez y el descanso del momento nos hacen incapaces de diferenciar unos días, de un mes, de un año o de toda una vida ... no soportaríamos las necesidades del aislamiento, echaríamos de menos nuestros caprichos y el consumo a los que nos tiene acostumbrados nuestra civilización."
4. "No se apuren por el tiempo, que por estos lados no se cuenta. Sale y se pone el sol, nos trae la luz para vivir, quedito eso pasa, nada más. . . . Saben ustedes mucho, aunque hayan sido educados en una Europa que ha perdido su pura alma al perder la naturaleza ... les sobra a ustedes mucho que a nosotros nos falta, les sobra plata, a nosotros nos falta para escuelas y sanidad. . . . Pero no conviertan la paz en mera postal, que es lo que les sucede a la mayoría de los turistas. Su espíritu se lleva muy dentro en secreto, es de cada uno y no se presta, y si se ha perdido sólo se recupera acudiendo al vientre de donde se halla, acá donde les digo, donde todo ser es libre y en armonía con los demás."
5. "Dudo ahora si lo que escuché lo aprendió aquel buen hombre de quienes habían llegado décadas antes para apoyarlos o si él lo había adquirido de las raíces de sus antepasados y se lo enseñó a los advenedizos o si el aprendizaje fue mutuo. Naturaleza y hombre formaban aquí una unidad durante siglos y milenios, hasta que le mundo civilizado llegó a estas tierras portando sus propios intereses económicos."
6. "un mayor conocimiento de la naturaleza, hasta el punto de respetarla, divinizarla."
7. "El sol, la luna, el firmamento que observaron, la naturaleza que veneraban son los únicos testigos y nunca el hombre ni su tecnología podrán acercarse a ellos."
8. "de un mundo en el que se trata con desdén la naturaleza y el deseo de ella me hizo buscar los indicios de la armonía donde de momento no se encontraba."
9. "la unidad que mantienen los indígenas con la naturaleza."
10. "de tez tostada, melena negra, cuerpo regordete."
11. "Todito el día platicando a los turistas la belleza de nuestra tierra ... para lueguito encontrarnos con esta porquería, no más por el abandono de las autoridades."
12. "en los baños de Cumbujujú, el lugar donde corre el jabalí."
13. "por la selva, aunque los ojos de las montañas todo lo ven; nada pasa desapercibido para ellas y quienes las habitan."
14. "Caía vertical a nuestros pies la roca, ocultada por la vegetación. Se inclina la pared suavemente antes de alcanzar el río, cobijado bajo las hojas de verde fresco. Pero con dulzura y mansedumbre luego se deja ver entero, se abre en brazos que extienden su sosiego por el valle, arropando

las isletas que entre ellos quedan. . . . las aguas presumen de sus blancas enaguas, pero al instante se cubren de nuevo con su vestido de esmeraldas."

15. "Observamos los árboles, altos y frondosos, las plantas parásitas, hasta de varios metros, que crecen en los troncos de algunos de ellos, las higueras ahorcadoras y matapalos que los abrazan y ahogan, las lianas o palos de agua, que caen y pueden cortarse para beber el líquido de su interior. Escuchamos el canto de las aves entre el rumor de las aguas, intentábamos localizarlas y, cuando veíamos alguna, el corazón aumentaba su alegría. Todas bellas, unas delicadas y suaves, otras más grandes; de vivos o apagados colores, según su evolución les hubiera pedido exhibirse o camuflarse."

16. "es necesario olvidarse de la razón domesticada, hacerse árbol o hierba, roca o arena, contemplarlo el tiempo que nos reclame, como ellos, simplemente desde la quietud de la mente, dejándose llevar sin más por el papel primero que la naturaleza nos designó."

17. *Barbarous Mexico* was also a major reference point for Lowry's *Under the Volcano*.

18. "Hace cien años miles de indios fueron arrancados de sus pueblos y vendidos a los hacendados del Yucatán, que quemaban y requerían mano de obra fresca. La mercancía eran los yaquis, la nación rebelde, famosa por sublevarse contra todos."

19. "arrancados todos de aquel lugar que para ellos significaba mucho más que una región pues recogía su génesis, el sentido de su experiencia y su interpretación del mundo."

20. Faber (2002) also identifies Max Aub as a key figure in understanding the experience of Spaniards in Mexico as well as the act of looking back to Spain from Mexico. In the work of Max Aub, Faber identifies the ambivalence between disillusionment and the sustained urge to active engagement with the cultural life of a nation, as well as ambivalence toward both Spain and Mexico as nations sustained under specific political realities that create categories for belonging and also for exclusion.

21. "Veinte años después de buscar aquel nombre en un mapa, me preguntaba por qué algunos sueños se cumplen y si somos nosotros o los dioses deciden cuáles conceder."

22. "injusta. Las casas están bonitas . . . pero dentro hay mucha necesidad, ya no se puede vivir de la tierra. Mis amigos andan todos en California, solo yo me quedé aquí . . . Trabajar aquí para qué, para hacer deudas, para que se engorden los políticos."

23. "dicen que se van para que les den la plata. Con Polonia en Europa, no creo que tenga salarios más baratos que México, y los controles serán mayores, no creo que puedan ir allí a hacer dumping."

24. "Hay hambre padre; *usté* ni se las huele porque vive bien."

25. "Quise entrar a San Blas por mar para aprehender una visión semejante a la que llenaba los ojos de los yaquis: sabía que era impostura, que por

más que este lugar no hubiera mutado en cien años, nuestras sensaciones nunca se asemejarían porque eran enemigas: la suya, marcada por la desgracia; la mía, por la satisfacción de la llegada."
26. "Los descendientes de aquellos sures perdieron a sus árboles profetas y enterraron a sus dioses."
27. "Todo, por pequeño que fuera, era vida. . . . Perder ese conocimiento, esa sensación, como ha sucedido en Occidente y, en general, en todas partes, nos empobrece, no solo a la humanidad, a cada pueblo, sino a cada persona. . . . Todavía estamos adaptándonos a un cambio, a este mundo en venta, a esa relación con uno mismo de autoexplotación, a esa vida líquida que no deja posos y genera depresiones y enfermedades, pero el ser humano es, a fin de cuentas, un animal, es decir, parte de la naturaleza, y la naturaleza siempre reacciona cuando se produce un desequilibrio."
28. "los árboles que han dejado de ser profetas para llenar calderas."
29. "Cuando hicieron la presa no pudimos ya vivir de lo que nos daba el río, el agua de riego ya no alcanzaba los cultivos. La mitad del agua debía ser para nosotros y no lo es. ¿Ahora? Casi no quedan cultivos, ahora vivimos del carbón."
30. "Nosotros queremos que los hijos no se vayan pero por falta de trabajo se van a las ciudades y se buscan allí la manera de vivir, eso es lo que separa la humanidad."
31. "Antes había mucha pesca, aquí, se vivía del mar. Luego ya no. Se acabó. Y nos pusimos a buscar la vida, donde estuviese."
32. "Si llega a un acuerdo pero la tierra es sagrada, como el cuerpo. Si nosotros fuéramos a mandar allá, tampoco les gustaría."
33. "Han pretendido algo pero hasta la fecha, nada. Todavía la mayor parte se dedica a la agricultura aunque hay algunos comerciantes; a los más les va mal."
34. "Sin infraestructura hotelera ni nada de eso, nada que quiebre la tradición, pero sí por ejemplo una ruta de senderismo que no pase junto a las casas."
35. "país comodón que, a cambio de permitirles un gobierno autónomo en su territorio y de publicitarlos como pueblo exótico, desasiste a muchos indígenas."
36. "los indios tarahumaras, los verdaderos señores de estas tierras, hoy superpuestos al paisaje como signos melancólicos para remordimiento de la consciencia cultural."
37. "El contraste de temperatura es tan acusado que los tarahumaras cultivan frutos tropicales como mangos y papayas en las laderas de los ríos y en los valles mientras sus mujeres e hijas venden frutas y artesanía en las alturas, indefensas ante el frío o la nubada."
38. "Nos miramos en silencio."
39. "Los rarámuri despachan enchiladas y recuerdos. Una mujer, con su mercancía extendida en la piedra, echa una mirada a su prole: los niños

juguetean junto a la barandilla que corta el aire ante una hoz inaprensible. Unos turistas se agarran y se tapan la boca."
40. "El rarámuri se convirtió en un ser amante de la paz y adecuado a la naturaleza . . . el otro abandonó la tierra y se acostumbró al dinero y a la guerra. . . . El rarámuri debe quedarse al margen, al cabo del mundo, sin mezclarse con el chabochi, para no entrarse en ese ciclo malvado pero, cada vez más, el otro lo envuelve y lo utiliza."
41. "Es una lástima, una raza así al servicio de los sicarios."
42. "además de crónica, libro de viajes y novela de aventuras, Naufragios inaugura un modelo de marketing, donde el protagonista se postula como merecedor de un puesto en el Nuevo Continente."
43. "Nadie lo habría escrito así hoy pero su redacción refleja no solo la vida de una población indígena apenas contaminada por la cultura dominante, sino una forma de pensar, la del narrador, que ya forma parte de la Historia."
44. "puso territorio a lo imaginado."
45. "Se notaba la cercana frontera mexicana en los nombres de los pueblos y de los arroyos, en los empleados de las gasolineras y de las tiendas, en los hombres que roturaban los campos y en las mujeres que iban a la compra."
46. "polvo . . . conductores . . . aceras . . . las gentes . . . las indigentes indígenas."
47. "nos sonrojamos al contrastar las comodidades de nuestros desplazamientos con las fatigas de los exploradores."
48. "Como el molde se rompió con aquellos españoles tan sufridos de siglos pasados, a Rubén y a mí la calorina nos desintegraba."
49. "Queremos emular en algo los sufrimientos de don Álvar Núñez."
50. "tuve una idea muy ajustada de la lucha encarnizada que Cabeza de Vaca mantuvo con las tres especies que menciona."
51. "observar, callejear, imaginar lo que Cabeza de Vaca y sus amigos pudieron ver."
52. "cinco siglos de historia, según nuestro entender europeo."
53. "explicaba los edificios del Historic District con tanta unción por las supuestas antiguallas que siempre provocaba un rictus sarcástico en nosotros, trotamundos del Viejo Continente."
54. "Atrocidades cometidas contra los indígenas americanos que conocemos a través de los libros escritores por religiosos, cronistas, intérpretes, capitanes y hasta por simples soldados españoles."
55. "Pues que pida cuentas a sus abuelos. Ninguno tuyo ni mío salieron de la Península . . . estoy harto de oír la misma cantinela en gente indocumentada."

REFERENCES

Abellán, José Luis. 2009. *La idea de América: Origen y evolución*, 2nd ed. Madrid: Iberoamericana.
Adams, Paul C., Steven Hoelscher, and Karen Till. 2001. "Place in Context." In *Textures of Place: Exploring Humanist Geography*, edited by Paul C. Adams, Steven Hoelscher, and Karen Till, xiii–xxxiv. Minneapolis: University of Minnesota Press.
Adn.es. 2008. "El poeta Eduardo Jordá asegura que 'la poesía incomprensible es un fraude.'" February 9, 2008.
Aguilar Fernández, Paloma. 1996. *Memoria y olvido de la Guerra Civil española*. Madrid: Alianza.
Alasuutari, Pertti. 2006. "Globalization, Sacred Principles, and Modernity." In *Questions of Method in Cultural Studies*, edited by Mimi White and James Schwoch, 221–40. Malden, MA: Blackwell.
Álvarez, María Inmaculada. 2006. *Usos de lo cubano en la transnación española: La revisión del deseo 1984–2004*. PhD thesis. Tulane University.
Anderson, Benedict. 1991. *Imagined Communities*. London: Verso.
Anthony, Jennifer. 2005. *Souvenirs of the Other*. PhD thesis. American University.
Armada, Alfonso, and Corina Arranz. 2006. *El rumor de la frontera*. Barcelona: Grup.
Aronczyk, Melissa. 2013. *Branding the Nation: The Global Business of National Identity*. Oxford, UK: Oxford University Press.
Arnold, Kathleen. 2007. "Enemy Invaders! Mexican Immigrants and U.S. Wars against Them." *borderlands* 6: 3.
Arreola, Daniel D. 1996. "Border-City Idée Fixe." *Geographical Review* 86, no. 3: 356–69.
Arriaga Rodríguez, Juan Carlos. 2000. "Sector informal y economía del turismo en Cancún." In *Tourism in the Caribbean*, edited by Ian Boxill and Johannes Maerk, 67–91. México, DF: Plaza y Valdés.

Assman, Aleida. 2006. "Memory, Individual and Collective." In *The Oxford Handbook of Contextual Political Analysis*, edited by Charles Tilly and Robert E. Goodin, 210–26. Oxford, UK: Oxford University Press.

Augé, Marc. 1995. *Non-Places: Introduction to an Anthropology of Supermodernity*. New York: Verso.

Augé, Marc. 1999. *The War of Dreams*, transl. Liz Heron. London: Pluto Press.

Azaola Garrido, Elena, and Richard Estes, eds. 2003. *La infancia como mercancía sexual*. México, DF: CIESAS, Siglo XXI.

Babb, Florence. 2010. *The Tourism Encounter: Fashioning Latin American Nations and Histories*. Stanford, CA: Stanford University Press.

Baker, Vicky. 2008. "The Rise of the Cocaine Tourist." *Guardian.co.uk*, April 1, 2008. http://www.guardian.co.uk/travel/2008/apr/01/colombia.southamerica.

Barthes, Roland. 1982. *Camera lucida*, trans. R. Howard. London: Jonathan Cape.

Bartosik-Vélez, Elise. 2014. *The Legacy of Christopher Columbus in the Americas: New Nations and a Transatlantic Discourse of Empire*. Nashville, TN: Vanderbilt University Press.

Bartra, Roger. 1992. *The Cage of Melancholy: Identity and Metamorphosis in the Mexican Character*, trans. Christopher J. Hall. New Brunswick, NJ: Rutgers University Press.

Bassett, Carol Ann. 2004. *Organ Pipe: Life on the Edge*. Tucson: University of Arizona Press.

Bauman, Zygmunt. 2000. *Liquid Modernity*. Cambridge, UK: Polity.

Belenguer Jané, Mariano. 2002. *Periodismo de viajes: Análisis de una especialización periodística*. Sevilla, Spain: Comunicación Social Ediciones y Publicaciones.

Berger, Dina, and Andrew Grant Wood. 2009. "Introduction: Tourism Studies and the Tourism Dilemma." In *Holiday in Mexico: Critical Reflections on Tourism and Tourist Encounters*, edited by Dina Berger and Andrew Grant Wood. Durham, NC: Duke University Press.

Beverley, John. 1999. *Subalternity and Representation: Arguments in Cultural Theory*. Durham, NC: Duke University Press.

Bianet Castellanos, María. 2010. *A Return to Servitude: Maya Migration and the Tourist Trade in Cancun*. Minneapolis: University of Minnesota Press.

Blasco, Roge. 2008. "Eduardo Jordá: *Pregúntale a la noche*, una novela inspirada en un viaje a Burundi." *El blog de Roge*, October 26, 2008. http://www.blogseitb.com/rogeblasco/2008/10/26/eduardo-jorda-preguntale-a-la-noche-una.

Blesa, Laura. 2007. "Entrevista a Alfredo Semprún." *Periodista Digital*, July 13, 2007. https://www.periodistadigital.com/periodismo/20070713/periodistadigital-alfredo-semprun-period-6744-noticia-689402986757. Video recording.

Bolaño, Roberto. 2004. *2666*. Barcelona: Anagrama.

Bowker, Paul. 2009. *Ibero-American Intersections: Constructing (Trans)national Imaginaries in Spain and Latin America, 1898–1938*. PhD thesis. University of Auckland.

Boyd, Carolyn P. 1997. *Historia Patria: Politics, History and National Identity in Spain, 1875–1975*. Princeton, NJ: Princeton University Press.

"Buenas cifras para el turismo mexicano." 2008. *Expreso*, September, 22, 2008. http://www.expreso.info/es/noticias/internacional/buenas_cifras_para_el_turismo_mexicano.

Burman, Anders. 2018. "Are Anthropologists Monsters? An Andean Dystopian Critique of Extractivist Ethnography and Anglophone-Centric Anthropology." *HAU: Journal of Ethnographic Theory* 8, no. 1/2: 48–64.

Buzard, James. 1993. *The Beaten Track: European Tourism, Literature, and the Ways to Culture, 1800–1918*. Oxford, UK: Clarendon Press.

Campbell, Mary Baine. 1988. *The Witness and the Other World: Exotic European Travel Writing 400–1600*. Ithaca, NY: Cornell University Press.

Cañas Cuevas, Sandra. 2016. "Pueblo trágico: Gubernamentalidad neoliberal y multicultural en el sureste mexicano." *Revista pueblos y fronteras digital* 11, no. 21: 3–30.

Cantú, Irma. 2006. *La escritura de viaje desde la perspectiva latinoamericana*. PhD thesis. University of Texas (Austin).

Castillo, Mariano. 2011. "Brazil Searches for Clues of Amazon Tribe Gone Missing." CNNWorld, August 11, 2011. http://edition.cnn.com/2011/WORLD/americas/08/11/brazil.uncontacted.tribe/index.html.

Chabram-Dernersesian, Angie. 1996. "The Spanish Colón-ialista Narrative: Their Prospectus for Us in 1992." In *Mapping Multiculturalism*, edited by Avery F. Gordon and Christopher Newfield. Minneapolis: University of Minnesota Press.

Chambers, Erve. 1999. *Native Tours: The Anthropology of Travel and Tourism*. Prospect Heights, IL: Waveland.

Chang, Hui-Ching, and G. Richard Holt. 1991. "Tourism as Consciousness of Struggle." *Critical Studies in Mass Communication* 8, no.1: 102–18.

Chasteen, John. 2001. *Born in Blood and Fire*. New York: W.W. Norton.

Chávez, Daniar. 2015. 'La literatura de viaje y su función en la representación del otro." In *Cartografía de la literatura de viaje en Hispanoamérica*, coord. by Daniar Chávez y Marco Urdapilleta. Toluca, Mexico: UAEM.

Clancy, Michael. 2001. *Exporting Paradise: Tourism and Development in Mexico*. Tourism Social Science Series. Bingley, UK: Emerald Group.

Clark, Steve. 1999a. Introduction to *Travel Writing and Empire: Postcolonial Theory in Transit*, edited by Steve Clark. New York: Zed Books.

―――. 1999b. "Transatlantic Crossings: Recent British Travel Writing on the United States." In *Travel Writing and Empire: Postcolonial Theory in Transit*, edited by Steve Clark, 212–30. New York: Zed Books.

Clifford, James. 1988. *The Predicament of Culture*. Cambridge: Harvard University Press.

———. 1997. *Routes: Travel and Translation in the Late Twentieth Century.* Cambridge, MA: Harvard University Press.

Clifford, James, and George Marcus. 1986. *Writing Culture.* Berkeley: University of California Press.

Clubcultura.com. 2001. "Itinerarios Clubcultura.com: América." *Clubcultura* 8 http://www.clubcultura.com/clubliteratura/airlines/airlines2.htm.

Collins Rudolf, John. 2011. "Isolated Amazon Tribes Threatened by Logging, Groups Say." *New York Times,* February 3, 2011. http://green.blogs.nytimes.com/2011/02/03/isolated-amazon-tribes-threatened-by-logging-groups-say.

Como agua para chocolate. 1992. Directed by Alfonso Arau. Film. Mexico: Arau Films/Aviacsa/Cinevista/Fonatur/Fondo de Fomento a la Calidad Cinematográfica/Gobierno del Estado de Coahuila/IMCINE/Secretaria de Turismo.

Conde Olivares, Mauricio. 2006. "La plaga del narcotráfico." *Contralínea,* year 1, August, http://www.quintanaroo.contralinea.com.mx/archivo/2006/agosto/htm/plaga_narcotrafico.htm.

Cooper Alarcón, Daniel. 1997. *The Aztec Palimpsest: Mexico in the Modern Imagination.* Tucson: University of Arizona Press.

de Certeau, Michel. 1984. *The Practice of Everyday Life,* trans. Steven Rendall. Berkeley: University of California Press.

Díaz del Castillo, Bernal. 2005. *Historia verdadera de la conquista de la Nueva España,* edición crítica de José Antonio Barbón Rodríguez. México, DF: El Colegio de México.

Dickens, David, and Andrea Fontana. 2002. "Time and Postmodernism." *Symbolic Interaction* 25, no. 3: 389–96.

Eagleton, Terry. (1976) 2006. *Criticism and Ideology.* New York: Verso.

Euromonitor. 2007. *Tourism Flows Inbound – Mexico.* London: Euromonitor PLC. http://www.euromonitor.com/travel-and-tourism.

———. 2007. *Tourism Flows Outbound – Spain.* London: Euromonitor PLC. http://www.euromonitor.com/travel-and-tourism.

———. 2007. *Tourist Attractions – Mexico.* London: Euromonitor PLC. http://www.euromonitor.com/travel-and-tourism.

———. 2007. *Travel and Tourism – Spain.* London: Euromonitor PLC. http://www.euromonitor.com/travel-and-tourism.

———. 2007. *Travel Retail – Spain.* London: Euromonitor PLC. http://www.euromonitor.com/travel-and-tourism.

Everitt, John, Bryan Massam, Rosa M. Chávez-Dagostino, Rodrigo Espinosa Sánchez, and Edmundo Andrade Romo. 2008. "The Imprints of Tourism on Puerto Vallarta, Jalisco, Mexico." *Canadian Geographer* 52, no. 1: 83–104.

Faber, Sebastiaan. 2002. *Exile and Cultural Hegemony: Spanish Intellectuals in Mexico, 1939–1975.* Nashville, TN: Vanderbilt University Press.

———. 2003. "Between Cernuda's Paradise and Buñuel's Hell: Mexico through Spanish Exiles' Eyes." *Bulletin of Spanish Studies* 80, no. 2: 219–51.

Fabian, Johannes. 1983. *Time and the Other.* New York: Columbia University Press.

Fehimović, Dunja, and Rebecca Ogden, eds. 2018. *Branding Latin America:*

Strategies, Aims, Resistance. Lanham, MD: Lexington.
Forneas Fernández, María Celia. 2004. "¿Periodismo o literatura de viajes?" *Estudios sobre el mensaje periodístico* 10: 221–40.
Fowler, Corinne, and Ludmilla Kostova. 2003. "Travel Writing and Cultural Terrae Incognitae." *Journeys* 4, no. 1: 1–5.
Fradera, Josep. 2018. *The Imperial Nation: Citizens and Subjects in the British, French, Spanish, and American Empires*, transl. Ruth McKay. Princeton, NJ: Princeton University Press.
Fuentes, Carlos. 1992. *El espejo enterrado*. México, DF: FCE Colección Tierra Firme.
Fürsich, Elfriede, and Anandam P. Kavoori. 2001. "Mapping a Critical Framework for the Study of Travel Journalism." *International Journal of Cultural Studies* 4, no.2: 149–71.
García Canclini, Nestor. 1995. *Hybrid Cultures*. Minneapolis: University of Minnesota Press.
García Jambrina, Luis. 2005. "De adioses y pérdidas." *Abc.es*, June 25, 2005. http://hemeroteca.abc.es/nav/Navigate.exe/hemeroteca/madrid/cultural/2005/06/25/022.html.
García Mercadal, José. 1952. *Viajes de extranjeros por España y Portugal*. Madrid: Aguilar.
García Pérez, Juan. 2000. "Entre el 'imperialismo pacífico' y la idea de 'fraternidad hispanoamericana': Algunas reflexiones sobre la imagen de América Latina en la España de fines del siglo XIX." In *1898 ¿desastre o reconciliación?*, edited by Leopoldo Zea and Mario Magallón, 101–20. México, DF: Fondo Cultura Económica.
Gifra Adroher, Pere. 2006. Review of *Perspectives on Travel Writing*, edited by Glenn Hooper and Tim Youngs. *Atlantis* 28, no. 2: 159–63. https://www.jstor.org/stable/41055256.
Glantz, Margo, ed. (1964) 1982. *Viajes en México: Crónicas extranjeras*. México, DF: Fondo de Cultura Económica.
Goertzen, Chris. 2010. *Made in Mexico: Tradition, Tourism, and Political Ferment in Oaxaca*. Jackson: University Press of Mississippi.
Gómez-Barris, Macarena. 2017. *The Extractive Zone: Social Ecologies and Decolonial Perspectives*. Durham, NC: Duke University Press.
Gómez-Lucena, Eloísa. 2018. *Del Atlántico al Pacífico: Tras los pasos de Cabeza de Vaca por Estados Unidos y México*. Córdoba: Almuzara.
González Rodríguez, Sergio. 2002. *Huesos en el desierto*. Barcelona: Anagrama.
Graham, Helen. 2004. "Coming to Terms with the Past: Spain's Memory Wars." *History Today* 54, no. 5: 29–31.
Grant, Michelle. 2009. "Mexico Tourism: Strong Decline." *Latin Business Chronicle*, October 5, 2009. http://www.latinbusinesschronicle.com/app/article.aspx?id=3695.
Gray, Ann. 2003. *Research Practice for Cultural Studies*. London: Sage.
Grosfoguel, Ramón. 2012. *Sujetos coloniales: Una perspectiva global de las migraciones caribeñas*. Quito, Ecuador: Editorial Abya Yala.

Guelke, Leonard, and Jeanne Kay Guelke. 2004. "Imperial Eyes on South Africa: Reassessing Travel Narratives." *Journal of Historical Geography* 30, no.1: 11–31.

Guerrero, Ana Clara. 1990. *Viajeros británicos en la España del siglo XVIII*. Madrid: Aguilar.

Hanley, Jane. 2019. "International Solidarity, Volunteer Tourism and Travel Writing: Mexico and Central America in Spanish and English." *Text*, no. 56. http://www.textjournal.com.au/speciss/issue56/Hanley.pdf.

Harvey, Sally. 1992. "Alejo Carpentier: Travel and Perspective." In *Travelers' Tales, Real and Imaginary, in the Hispanic World and Its Literature*, edited by Alun Kenwood, 75–90. Madrid: Voz Hispánica.

Hellier-Tinoco, Ruth. 2010. "Corpo-Reality, Voyeurs and the Responsibility of Seeing: Night of the Dead on the Island of Janitzio, Mexico." *Performance Research* 15, no. 1: 23–31.

Heredero Salinero, Fermín. 2009. *Chiapas: Cuaderno de viaje*, Burgos: Editorial Gran Vía.

Hicks, D. Emily. 1991. *Border Writing: The Multidimensional Text*. Minneapolis: University of Minnesota Press.

Hodge, Robert. 2002. "Monstrous Knowledge in a World without Borders." *borderlands* 1, no. 1. https://webarchive.nla.gov.au/awa/20020903191010/http://www.borderlandsejournal.adelaide.edu.au/vol1no1_2002/hodge_monstrous.html.

Holland, Patrick, and Graham Huggan. 1998 *Tourists with Typewriters: Critical Reflections on Contemporary Travel Writing*. Ann Arbor: University of Michigan Press.

Huggan, Graham. 2001. *The Postcolonial Exotic*. London: Routledge.

———. 2009. *Extreme Pursuits: Travel/Writing in an Age of Globalization*. Ann Arbor: University of Michigan Press.

Hughes, John. 2004. *The Idea of Home*, Artarmon, NSW, Australia: Giramondo.

Iturriaga de la Fuente, José. 1989–92. *Anecdotario de viajeros extranjeros en México, siglos XVI–XIX*, 4 volumes. México, DF: Fondo de Cultura Económica.

———. (2009), *Anecdotario de forasteros en México, Siglos XVI–XXI*, México, DF: Consejo Nacional para la Cultura y las Artes.

Jenkins Wood, Jennifer. 2014. *Spanish Women Travelers at Home and Abroad, 1850–1920: From Tierra del Fuego to the Land of the Midnight Sun*. Lewisburg, PA: Bucknell University Press.

Jiménez-Martínez, César. 2018. "Protests, News, and Nation Branding: The Role of Foreign Journalists in Constructing and Projecting the Image of Brazil during the June 2013 Demonstrations." In *Branding Latin America: Strategies, Aims, Resistance*, edited by Dunja Fehimović and Rebecca Ogden. Lanham, MD: Lexington.

Jordá, Eduardo. 2001. *La ciudad perdida*. Palma de Mallorca, Spain: La Foradada.

———. 2004. *Lugares que no cambian*. Barcelona: Alba.

Kaelber, Lutz. 2006. "Place and Pilgrimage, Real and Imagined." In *On the Road to Being There*, edited by William H. Swatos, 277–96. Boston, MA: Brill.

Kamen, Henry. 2003. *Empire: How Spain Became a World Power, 1492–1763*. New York: Penguin.

Kaplan, Robert D. 1998. *An Empire Wilderness: Travels into America's Future*. New York: Random House.

Kearney, Richard. 1995. *States of Mind: Dialogues with Contemporary Thinkers on the European Mind*. Manchester, UK: Manchester University Press.

Korte, Barbara. 2000. *English Travel Writing from Pilgrimages to Postcolonial Explorations*, translated by C. Matthias. New York: St Martin's.

Lawson, Stephanie. 2006. *Culture and Context in World Politics*. Basingstoke, UK: Palgrave Macmillan.

Lindsay, Claire. 2009. *Contemporary Travel Writing of Latin America*. London: Routledge.

———. 2006. "Luis Sepúlveda, Bruce Chatwin and the Global Travel Writing Circuit." *Comparative Literature Studies* 43, no. 1–2: 57–78.

Lisle, Debbie. 2006. *The Global Politics of Contemporary Travel Writing*. Cambridge, UK: Cambridge University Press.

Litvak, Lily. 1987. *El ajedrez de estrellas*. Barcelona: Laia.

López Santillán, Ángeles A., and Gustavo Marín Guardado. 2010. "Turismo, capitalismo y producción de lo exótico: Una perspectiva crítica para el estudio de la mercantilización del espacio y la cultura." *Relaciones: Estudios de historia y sociedad* 31, no. 123: 219–58

López Schlichting, Cristina. 2007. "Entrevista a Alfredo Semprún." *La tarde con Cristina* (radio show), Cadena COPE, July 12, 2007.

Louvel, Liliane. 2008. "Photography as Critical Idiom and Intermedial Criticism." *Poetics Today* 29, no. 1: 31–48.

Luengo, Jorge, and Pau Dalmau. 2018. "Writing Spanish History in the Global Age: Connections and Entanglements in the Nineteenth Century." *Journal of Global History* 13, no. 3: 425–45.

Luke, Timothy W. 2016. "Design as Defense: Broken Barriers and the Security Spectacle at the US-Mexico Border." In *Building Walls and Dissolving Borders: The Challenges of Alterity, Community and Securitizing Space*, edited by Max O. Stephenson and Laura Zanotti, 115–31. New York: Routledge.

Luzón, Javier Moreno. 2010. "Reconquistar América para regenerar España: Nacionalismo español y centenario de las independencias en 1910–1911." *Historia Mexicana* 60, no. 1 (237): 561–640.

MacCannell, Dean. 1992. *Empty Meeting Grounds: The Tourist Papers*. London: Routledge.

———. 1976. *The Tourist: A New Theory of the Leisure Class*. New York: Schocken Books.

Maestre, Agapito. 2003. *Viaje a los ínferos americanos*. Madrid: Tecnos.

Manuel-Navarrete, David. 2016. "Boundary-Work and Sustainability in Tourism Enclaves." *Journal of Sustainable Tourism* 24, no. 4: 507–26.

Margalit, Avishai. 2002. *The Ethics of Memory*. Cambridge, MA: Harvard University Press.

Martí Olivella, José. 2001. "Cuba and Spanish Cinema's Transatlantic Gaze." *Arizona Journal of Hispanic Cultural Studies*, no. 5: 161–76.

Martínez Zarracina, Pablo. 2006. "Ninguna vida es gris ni carece de importancia." *Diario vasco*, December 15, 2006. http://www.diariovasco.com/prensa/20061215/cultura/ninguna-vida-gris-carece_20061215.html.

Mattalía, Sonia, Pilar Celma, and Pilar Alonso, eds. 2008. *El viaje en la literatura hispanoamericana*. Madrid: Iberoamericana.

McCarthy, Cormac. 2010 (1985). *Blood Meridian*. London: Picador.

———. 1999. *The Border Trilogy: All the Pretty Horses, The Crossing, Cities of the Plain*. Knopf: New York.

Mee, Catharine. 2009. "Journalism and Travel Writing: From *Grands Reporters* to Global Tourism." *Studies in Travel Writing* 13, no. 4: 305–15.

Menéndez, Fernando. 2006. "Memorias y buenas intenciones." *Literaturas.com*, no. 10.

Mercille, Julien. 2014. "The Media-Entertainment Industry and the 'War on Drugs' in Mexico." *Latin American Perspectives* 41, no. 2: 110–29.

Merrill, Dennis. 2009. *Negotiating Paradise: U.S. Tourism and Empire in Twentieth-Century Latin America*. Chapel Hill: University of North Carolina Press.

Meyer, Lorenzo. 2014. *El cactus y el olivo: Las relaciones de México y España en el siglo XX*. México, DF: Océano.

Mignolo, Walter. 2000. *Local Histories / Global Designs*. Princeton: Princeton University Press.

———. 2003. "Globalization and the Geopolitics of Knowledge." *Nepantla* 4, no. 1: 97–119.

Mistral, Gabriela. 1978. *Gabriela anda por el mundo*. Santiago: Andrés Bello.

Mitchell, David. 1989. *Viajeros por España: De Borrow a Hemingway*. Madrid: Mondadori.

Monsiváis, Carlos. 1984. "Travelers in Mexico," transl. Jeanne Ferguson. *Diogenes* 32: 48–74.

Monteleone, Jorge. 1998. *El relato de viaje: De Sarmiento a Umberto Eco*. Buenos Aires: El Ateneo.

Monterrubio, Carlos, Maribel Osorio and Jazmín Benítez. 2017. "Comparing Enclave Tourism's Socioeconomic Impacts: A Dependency Theory Approach to Three State-Planned Resorts in Mexico." *Journal of Destination Marketing & Management* 8: 412–22. https://doi.org/10.1016/j.jdmm.2017.08.004.

Morgan, Tony. 2000. "1992: Memories and Modernities." In *Contemporary Spanish Cultural Studies*, edited by Barry Jordan and Rikki Morgan-Tamosunas, 58–67. London: Arnold.

Mourelo, Suso. 2011. *Donde mueren los dioses: Viaje por el alma y por la piel de México*. Madrid: Gadir.

———. 2018. *Tiempo de Hiroshima*. Madrid: La Línea del Horizonte.

Muggli, Mark. 1992. "Joan Didion and the Problem of Journalistic Travel Writing." In *Temperamental Journeys*, edited by Michael Kowalewski, 176–94. Athens: University of Georgia Press.

Musgrove, Brian. 1999. "Travel and Unsettlement: Freud on Vacation." In *Travel Writing and Empire: Postcolonial Theory in Transit*, edited by Steve

Clark, 31–44. New York: Zed Books.
Nadal, Paco. 2010. *Pedro Páramo ya no vive aquí*. Barcelona: RBA.
Neumann, Iver B. 1998. *Uses of the Other: "The East" in European Identity Formation*. Minneapolis: University of Minnesota Press.
Nunley, Gayle R. 2007. *Scripted Geographies: Travel Writings by Nineteenth-Century Spanish Authors*. Lewisburg, PA: Bucknell University Press.
Olins, Wally. 2002. "Branding the Nation—The Historical Context." *Brand Management* 9, no. 4-5: 241–48.
Padilla, Beatriz, and Francisco José Cuberos-Gallardo. 2016. "Deconstruyendo al inmigrante latinoamericano: Las políticas migratorias ibéricas como tecnologías neocoloniales." *Horizontes antropológicos* 22, no. 46: 189–218.
Papadopolous, Nico, and Louise Heslop. 2002. "Country Equity and Country Branding: Problems and Prospects." *Brand Management* 9, no. 4-5: 294–314.
Papanicolaou, Anna. 2009. "Representing Mexicans: Tourism, Immigration and the Myth of the Nation." *Journal of Policy Research in Tourism, Leisure and Events* 1, no. 2: 105–14.
———. 2012. "The Selling of Mayan Culture in Mexico's Mayan Riviera." In *Controversies in Tourism*, edited by Omar Moufakkir & Peter M. Burns. Wallingford, UK: CABI.
Paz Soldán, Edmundo. 2008. "Roberto Bolaño, literatura y apocalipsis." In *Entre lo local y lo global: La narrativa latinoamericana en el cambio de siglo*, edited by Jesús Montoya Juárez and Ángel Esteban, 217–28. Madrid: Iberoamericana.
Peñate Rivero, Julio, 2004. "Camino del viaje hacia la literatura." In *Relato de viaje y literaturas hispánicas*, edited by Julio Peñate Rivero, 13–29. Madrid: Visor.
———. 2012. *Introducción al relato de viaje hispánico del siglo XX: Textos, etapas, metodología II: 1981–2006*, Madrid: Visor.
Perea, Héctor. 1996. *La rueda del tiempo*. México, DF: Cal y Arena.
Pérez Mejía, Angela. 2004. *A Geography of Hard Times: Narratives about Travel to South America 1780–1849*, transl. Dick Cluster. Albany: State University of New York Press.
Pérez Reverte, Arturo. 2002. *La reina del sur*. Madrid: Alfaguara.
Pérez Villalón, Fernando. 2004. "Variaciones sobre el viaje." *Revista Chilena de Literatura* 64: 47–72.
Perivolaris, John. 2011. "Outside Looking In: The Amazon's Isolated Tribe." *Guardian*, February 2, 2011. http://www.guardian.co.uk/commentisfree/2011/feb/02/amazon-lost-tribe-aerial-photograph.
Phillips, John. 1999. "Lagging Behind: Bhabha, Post-Colonial Theory and the Future." In *Travel Writing and Empire: Postcolonial Theory in Transit*, edited by Steve Clark, 61–80. New York: Zed Books.
Pitman, Thea. 2003. "An Impossible Task? Hector Perea's *México, crónica en espiral* and the Problems of Writing a Travel-Chronicle of Contemporary Mexico City." *Studies in Travel Writing* 7, no. 1: 47–62.
———. 2007. "Mexican Travel Writing: The Legacy of Foreign Travel Writers in Mexico, or, Why Mexicans Say They Don't Write Travel Books." *Comparative Critical Studies* 4, no. 2: 209–23.

———. 2008. *Mexican Travel Writing*. Bern, Switzerland: Peter Lang.

Prado Fonts, Carles. 2018. "Writing China from the Rest of the West: Travels and Transculturation in 1920s Spain." *Journal of Spanish Cultural Studies* 19, no. 2: 175–89.

Pratt, Mary Louise. 1992. *Imperial Eyes: Travel Writing and Transculturation*. New York: Routledge.

Price, Patricia. 2004. *Dry Place: Landscapes of Belonging and Exclusion*. Minneapolis: University of Minnesota Press.

Pugliese, Joseph. 2009. "Crisis Heterotopias and Border Zones of the Dead." *Continuum* 23, no. 5: 663–79.

Quijano, Aníbal, and Immanuel Wallerstein. 1992. "Americanity as a Concept, or, the Americas in the Modern World System." *International Social Science Journal* 44, no. 4: 549–57.

Rabasa, José. 1993. *Inventing America*. Norman: University of Oklahoma Press.

Raducanu, Daniela. 2015. *Traveling for Spain: Modernity and Otherness in Spanish Travel and War Narratives (1860–1929)*. PhD diss. University of Illinois at Urbana-Champaign.

Reding, Sofía. 2009. *El buen salvaje y el caníbal*. México: Centro de Investigaciones sobre América Latina y el Caribe/ Universidad Nacional Autónoma de México.

Reguero, Luis. 2018. "Suso Mourelo, el escritor lento que salió a buscar el tiempo, la luz y la naturaleza." El Asombrario & Co., October 24, 2018. https://elasombrario.com/suso-mourelo-tiempo-luz-naturaleza.

Reverte, Javier. 2006. *La aventura de viajar*. Barcelona: Mondadori.

Riaño, Peio H. 2019. "Los hombres publican el doble de libros que las mujeres." *El país*, June 6, 2019, https://elpais.com/cultura/2019/06/06/actualidad/1559805239_962042.html.

Robertson, Angela M., Jennifer L. Syvertsen, Hortensia Amaro, Gustavo Martínez, M. Gudelia Rangel, Thomas L. Patterson, and Steffanie A. Strathdee. 2014. "Can't Buy My Love: A Typology of Female Sex Workers' Commercial Relationships in the Mexico–US Border Region." *Journal of Sex Research* 51, no. 6: 711–20.

Rodríguez, Richard. 1992. *Days of Obligation: An Argument with My Mexican Father*. New York: Viking Press.

Rodríguez Ducallín, Emira Josefina, Karen Elisa Requena Mago, José Francisco Muñoz Rengel, and María Cristina Olarte Pascual. 2006. "Imagen turística de los países latinoamericanos en el mercado español." *Cuadernos de turismo*, no. 17: 189–200.

Roussel-Zuazu, Chantal. 2005. *La literatura de viaje española del siglo XIX, una tipología*. MA thesis. Texas Tech University.

Rubiés, Joan-Pau. 2000. "Travel Writing as a Genre." *Journeys* 1, no. 1: 5–35.

Said, Edward. 1978. *Orientalism*. New York: Vintage.

Saldívar, José David. 1997. *Border Matters: Remapping American Cultural Studies*. Berkeley: University of California Press.

Saukko, Paula. 2003. *Doing Research in Cultural Studies*. London: Sage.

Schmidt-Nowara, Christopher. 2008. 'Spanish Origins of American Empire: Hispanism, History, and Commemoration, 1898–1915." *International History Review* 30, no. 1: 32–51.

_____. 2004. "'La España Ultramarina': Colonialism and Nation-Building in Nineteenth-Century Spain." *European History Quarterly* 34, no. 2: 191–214.
Scurrah, Martin J. 1992. "From Wandering Pariah to Union Organiser: The Influence of Flora Tristán's Voyage to Perú on Her Life and Work." In *Travelers' Tales, Real and Imaginary, in the Hispanic World and Its Literature*, edited by Alun Kenwood, 25–36. Madrid: Voz Hispánica.
SECTUR. 2014. "Programa Mundo Maya." http://www.sectur.gob.mx/programas/programas-regionales/programa-mundo-maya.
Selby, Jennifer. 2006. "The Politics of Pilgrimage: The Social Construction of Ground Zero." In *On the Road to Being There*, edited by William H. Swatos, 159–86. Boston, MA: Brill.
Semprún, Alfredo. 2007. *Viajes desaconsejables*. Huesca, Spain: Barrabes.
Sennett, Richard. 1999. "Growth and Failure: The New Political Economy and its Culture." In *Spaces of Culture*, edited by M. Featherstone and S. Lash, 14–26. London: Sage.
Shaw, Deborah. 2011. "(Trans)national Images and Cinematic Spaces: The Cases of Alfonso Cuarón's *Y tu mamá también* (2001) and Carlos Reygadas' *Japón* (2002)." *Iberoamericana* 11, no. 44: 117–31.
Siebenmann, Gustav. 2007. "Observaciones acerca de ciertas imágenes de la América Latina que se formaron los españoles a lo largo del siglo XX." In *America en España: Influencias, intereses, imágenes*, edited by Ingrid Simson, 173–95. Madrid: Iberoamericana.
Sirgy, M. Joseph, and Chenting Su. 2000. "Destination Image, Self-Congruity, and Travel Behavior: Toward an Integrative Model." *Journal of Travel Research* 38, no. 4: 340–52.
Smith, Paul Julian. 2003. "Transatlantic Traffic in Recent Mexican Films." *Journal of Latin American Cultural Studies* 12, no. 3: 389–400.
Smith, Valene, ed. 1989. *Hosts and Guests: The Anthropology of Tourism*. Pittsburgh: University of Pennsylvania Press.
Solano, Francisco. 2001. *Bajo las nubes de México*. Barcelona: Alba
_____. 2008. *Tambores de ejecución*. Barcelona: Bruguera.
Sólo quiero caminar. 2008. Directed by Agustín Díaz Yanes. Film. Mexico/Spain: Canana/Boomerang Cine.
Spurr, David. 1993. *The Rhetoric of Empire: Colonial Discourse in Journalism, Travel Writing, and Imperial Administration*. Durham, NC: Duke University Press.
Stagl, Joseph. 1995. *A History of Curiosity: The Theory of Travel 1550–1800*. Chur, Switzerland: Harwood Academic.
Staudt, Kathleen. 2014. "The Border, Performed in Films: Produced in both Mexico and the US to 'Bring Out the Worst in a Country.'" *Journal of Borderlands Studies* 29, no. 4: 465–79.
Strizzi, Nicolino, and Scott Meis. 2001. "Challenges Facing Tourism Markets in Latin America and the Caribbean Region in the New Millennium." *Journal of Travel Research* 40, no. 2: 183–92.
Tabuenca Córdoba, María Socorro. 1995. "Viewing the Border: Perspectives from 'the Open Wound.'" *Discourse* 18, no. 1/2: 146–168.
Todorov, Tzvetan. 1984. *The Conquest of America: The Question of the Other*, trans. R. Howard. New York: Harper & Row.
_____. 1991. *Les morales de l'histoire*. Paris: Grasset.

Turner, John Kenneth. 1910. *Barbarous Mexico*. Chicago: C. H. Kerr.
Unceta Satrústegui, María. 2005. "La escritura actual de los textos de viaje." In *Los libros de viaje: Realidad vivida y género literario*, coord. by Luis Romero Tobar and Patricia Almarcegui Elduayen, 196–205. Madrid: Akal.
United Nations World Tourism Organization. 2019. "Key Tourism Figures." https://webunwto.s3.eu-west-1.amazonaws.com/s3fs-public/2020-06/unwto_key_figures_barom_may2019_en.pdf.
Urry, John. 1990. *The Tourist Gaze*. London: Sage.
———. 2001 "Globalizing the Tourist Gaze." Cityscapes Conference, Graz, Austria, November 2001.
Valenzuela, Pedro M. 2008. "Eduardo Jordá." Comentarios de Libros, February 15, 2008. https://www.comentariosdelibros.com/entrevista-eduardo-jorda-137e993a.htm.
Vargas Rojas, Salvador Yolocuauhtli, and Brenda Alcalá. 2015. "Aspectos territoriales de la prostitución masculina vinculada al turismo sexual en Acapulco." *Estudios y perspectivas en turismo* 24, no. 4: 867–88.
Vidal, John. 2011. "Amazon's Uncontacted Tribe: How Media Coverage Can Trigger Action." *Guardian*, February 4, 2011. http://www.guardian.co.uk/environment/blog/2011/feb/04/amazon-uncontacted-tribe-media-coverage.
Viera-Brazo, Patricia, and Álvaro López López. 2020. "Centros ecoturísticos en la Selva Lacandona como mecanismo de control territorial del Estado mexicano en la zona de conflicto zapatista." *Journal of Iberian and Latin American Research* 26, no. 2: 159–80.
Villalonga, José Luis de. 1996. "Tánger, mon amour." *Vanguardia*, September 23, 1996, 17.
Virilio, Paul. 2005. *Negative Horizons*, translated by Michael Degener. New York: Continuum.
Walsh, Catherine. 2009. "Interculturalidad crítica y pedagogía de-colonial: In-surgir, re-existir y re-vivir." *Entre palabras* 3, no. 4: 129–56.
Wilson, Tamar Diana. 2008. "Economic and Social Impacts of Tourism in Mexico." *Latin American Perspectives* 35, no. 3: 37–52.
———. 2012. *Economic Life of Mexican Beach Vendors: Acapulco, Puerto Vallarta, and Cabo San Lucas*. Lanham, MD: Lexington Books.
Y tu mamá también. 2001. Directed by Alfonso Cuarón. Film. Mexico: Anhelo/Bésame Mucho Pictures.
Yépez, Heriberto. 2006. *Made in Tijuana*. Mexicali: ICBC.
Youngs, Tim. 2004. "Where Are We Going? Cross-Border Approaches to Travel Writing." In *Perspectives on Travel Writing*, edited by Glenn Hooper and Tim Youngs, 167–80. Aldershot, UK: Ashgate.
Zavala, Oswaldo. 2014. "Imagining the US-Mexico Drug War: The Critical Limits of Narconarratives." *Comparative Literature* 66, no. 3: 340–60.

INDEX

Abellán, Luis
  exotic as source of energy, 67
  La idea de América, 62–64, 68
Adams, Paul C., Steven Hoelscher, and Karen Till
  "Globalization, Sacred Principles, and Modernity," 11
  "Place in Context," 23, 35, 75, 112–35
  "textures of place," 75
Adroher, Pere Gifra, 199n3
agency, 167
Alasuutari, Pertti
  "Globalization, Sacred Principles, and Modernity," 11
  "textures of place," 75
"Alejo Carpentier" (Harvey), 36–53
Álvarez, María Immaculada, *Usos de lo cubano en la transnación española*, 39
Álvarez de Toledo, Alfonso, *Un tranvía naranja y polvoriento*, 205n1
America
  as future, 53, 64–65
  as history-less, 62–63
  idea of, 58–59, 63–64, 189
América Latina, 60
"Americanity as a Concept" (Quijano and Wallerstein), 3, 97–98, 178–86

Anderson, Benedict, *Imagined Communities*, 42
Anecdotario de viajeros extranjeros en México (Iturriaga), 203n18
Anglo-American hegemony, 2
anti-Francoism, 31–32. *See also* Franco, Francisco; Republican exiles; Spanish Civil War
anti-imperialist, 70, 136
anti-Latin American, 59
anti-tourist, 138
Armada, Alfonso, and Corina Arranz. *See rumor de la frontera, El* (Armada and Arranz)
Arreola, Daniel, "Border-City Idée Fixe," 8, 121
asylum seekers, 33. *See also* exiles
Aub, Max, *La verdadera historia de la muerte de Francisco Franco*, 167
Augé, Marc
  Non-Places, 113
  The War of Dreams, 196
authenticity
  fantasy of and globalization, 65
  markers of experience, 150
  myth, 56, 174
authorial presence, 166–67

230 INDEX

authority
  of border, 98
  to describe, 82
  of impersonal description, 3
  narrative, 137, 195
  of narrator, 20, 192
  provided by imperial dynamic, 98
  of researcher, 200n11
  written, 74
aventura de viajar, La (Reverte)
  childhood memories, 105–8
  post-Franco era, 106
  Puerto Escondido, 109
  See also Reverte, Javier
Aztec Empire, 9
Aztec Palimpsest, The (Cooper Alarcón), 56–58, 65

Babb, Florence, *The Tourism Encounter*, 146
Bajo las nubes de México (Solano), 19, 76–98, 100, 112, 157, 176, 192, 194
  autobiographical focus of, 73
  and "fall of hegemony," 83
  in historical context, 77–78
  historical imagination in, 79
  poetic and narrative mode in, 174
  Yucatan, 84
  See also Solano, Francisco
Barbarous Mexico (Turner), 166. *See also* Turner, John Kenneth
Barthes, Roland, *Camera lucida*, 132
Bartosik-Vélez, Elise, *The Legacy of Christopher Columbus in the Americas*, 179
Bartra, Roger, 9
Bassett, Carol Ann, *Organ Pipe*, 210n17
Belenguer Jané, Mariano, *Periodismo de viajes*, 137
Benjamin, Walter, 124, 128
Beverley, John, *Subalternity and Representation*, 40, 54–55
Blood Meridian (McCarthy), 124
Bolaño, Roberto, *2666*, 124, 126
"Border-City Idée Fixe" (Arreola), 8, 121
borders, Mexican-US, 2, 50, 68

Born in Blood and Fire (Chasteen), 60
Boyd, Carolyn P., *Historia Patria*, 52
branding, 34, 40–41. *See also* "Branding the Nation" (Olins)
Branding Latin America (Fehimović and Ogden), 200n6
"Branding the Nation" (Olins), 42, 46
buen salvaje y el caníbal, El (Reding), 56
Butler, Judith, 11
Buzard, James, *The Beaten Track*, 200n8

Caba, Rubén, 179–80, 183–84, 186
Cabeza de Vaca, Alvar Núñez, 173, 177–78, 182
Camera Lucida (Barthes), 132, 177–86
"Camino del viaje hacia la literatura" (Peñate Rivero), 5, 114, 123, 125, 130–31, 188, 202n3, 202n4, 203n8
Campbell, Mary Baine, *The Witness and the Other World*, 200n8
Cancún, 47, 49, 204n30
Cantú, Irma, *La escritura de viaje desde la perspectiva latinoamericana*, 9
capital, 56
  flows of, 34–35, 49, 130
  global, 42, 113–15, 123
capitalism, 16, 27, 41, 130–31, 155
  "colonial," 162
  late, 80, 129, 136, 190
  modern colonial world system, 24
  neocolonialist, 159, 165–66
  neoliberal, 163
  scrapyard of, 127
  transnational, 129
  world-economy, 3
  See also global capitalism
Caribbean, 3, 47
castellano, 39, 144–45
Castillo, Mariano, "Brazil Searches for Clues of Amazon Tribe Gone Missing," 207n44
Cela, Camilo José, *Viaje a la Alcarria*, 202n3
Chabram-Dernersesian, Angie, 177–78
  "The Spanish Colón-ialista Narrative," 32–33

"Challenges Facing Tourism Markets in Latin America" (Strizzi and Meis), 43
Chang, Hui-Ching, and G. Richard Holt, "Tourism as Consciousness of Struggle," 140
Chasteen, John, *Born in Blood and Fire*, 60
Chatwin, Bruce, *Songlines*, 137
Chávez, Daniar, "La literatura de viaje y su función en la representación del otro," 54
Chepe, el, 173–74. See also *Donde mueren los dioses* (Mourelo)
Chiapas, 154–65
  indigenous people of, 109–10
  landscape of, 147
  transformation of, 146
  See also *Chiapas* (Heredero Salinero); drugs
Chiapas (Heredero Salinero), 20, 153–66, 193. See also Mourelo, Suso
Chihuahua-Pacifico train. See Chepe, el
ciudad letrada, 54
ciudad perdida, La (Jordá), 19, 73, 76, 97–112, 104, 192. See also Jordá, Eduardo
Civil War. See Spanish Civil War
Clancy, Michael, *Exporting Paradise*, 43–44
Clark, Steve, 37, 98–99
Clifford, James, and George Marcus, *Writing Culture*, 200n11
Clifford, James, *The Predicament of Culture*, 200n11, 204n23
closure, 31, 52
cocaine tourism, 49. See also drugs; tourism
Colombia, 48–49. See also drugs
colonialisms, 9, 64
  power, 3–4
  Spain, 32
  See also colonialist
colonialist
  classic discourse of nature, 164
  discourses, 163–64
  language of, 177
  structure, 176
"Colón-ialista" narrative, 32–33

"Coming to Terms with the Past" (Graham), 52. See also memory
commerce, 181
commodity tour, 158
Como agua para chocolate (Arau), 50
conceptualization of subjectivity, history, and power, 178
Conquest, the, 9
Conquest of America, The (Todorov), 3, 9
consumption, 24
Contemporary Travel Writing of Latin America (Lindsay), 15, 67–69
  alternative otherness, 140–41
  characteristics of, 137
  displacement, 144
  Distrito Federal, 44
  hybridity, 63
  textuality, 65
  tourist paradise vs. human rights crisis, 57
  See also difference; Lindsay, Claire; otherness
contingencies, 19, 62, 95, 98, 196
  of encounter, 194
  of experience, 140
  historical, 53, 55, 135
  of identity, 137
  of language, 180
  of naming, 179
  of place, 105
  of present, 193
contingent, 16, 58, 188
conventions, 195. See also exoticism
convergence, 178
Cooper Alarcón, Daniel, *The Aztec Palimpsest*, 56–58
cosmopolitan gaze, 37. See also Lisle, Debbie
"Country Equity and Country Branding" (Papadopoulous and Heslop), 41–42
crime, 47–48, 77, 146, 189
  drugs, 50
  narco subcultures, 150
  narcotráfico, 128

crime (continued)
  touristic commodification of, 48
  See also danger
crimen del padre Amaro, El, 50
criollos, 147
crónica, 3, 26, 143
cross-cultural, 11, 35, 197
Cuarón, Alfonso, Y tu mamá también, 49–50
"Cuba and Spanish Cinema's Transatlantic Gaze" (Marti Olivella), 39
Cuban Revolution, 53
cultural
  allegiance, 34
  capital, 38
  difference, 42–43, 88, 187
  distinctiveness, 35
  histories, 61
  identity, 4, 25–26, 54–55, 145, 179
  images, 34
  inscriptions, 40
  networks, 49–50, 61
  nostalgia, 34, 142
  transgression, 143
  See also exoticism
cultures
  Central American, 51
  destination, 10
  exotic, 43
  North American, 51
  as presented to tourist, 140
  See also indigenous people
current affairs, 49. See also crime; danger; drugs; narco

danger, 20, 67, 146, 158
  exoticization of, 66
  and gendered dimension of travel writing, 138
  and novelty, 194
  peril and violence, 136
  Semprún, Alfredo, 141
  touristic, 144
  See also cocaine tourism; crime; drugs
"De adioses y perdidas" (García Jambrina), 105

de Certeau, Michel, The Practice of Everyday Life, 57
de las Casas Samuel Ruiz Garcia, Cristobal, 148, 179
Del Atlántico al Pacífico (Gómez-Lucena), 45–46, 178–86
  anti-mythologizing, 184
  and historical figures, 183–84
  intertextual premise of, 97
  and Naufragios, 193
  quotidian detail, 173–74
  representation of violence, 185
  and tourism exigencies and indignities, 179
  written record in, 185
  See also Gómez-Lucena, Eloisa
desire, 22, 178
destinations
  branding, 40–41
  dangerous, 144
  images, 43–4, 66, 71
  impact of travel on, 10
  Mexico and America, 187
development, 57, 170, 172
diary, 93
  Fermin Heredero's, 161–62
  style of travel writing, 104, 153–54, 179
  travel, 196
Díaz Yanes, Agustín, Sólo quiero caminar, 49–50
Dickens, David, and Andrea Fontana, "Time and Postmodernism," 191–92
difference, 35
  cultural, 42–43, 171–73
  ethnic and racial, 58
  European portrayal of, 7
  "literary ghetto of," 141
  postcolonial, 55
  production of local, 35
  See also encounters; exoticism; otherness
discourses
  colonialisms, 163–64
  of development, 10
  historical, 2
  imperialist, 134

discourses (*continued*)
   journalistic, 141
   national identity, 59
   reproduction of, 11
   of transatlantic mobility, 187
discursive
   contagion, 10–11
   interventions, 5
   space, 1
   systems of meaning, 55
   See also discourses
displacements
   of indigenous peoples, 165–66
   and modern world, 144
   of water and people, 171
   Yaqui, 169–70
   See also indigenous people; Mourelo, Suso
Distrito Federal, 44
dominance, 102, 172, 190, 202n7
dominant, 9
   culture, 177
   discursive systems, 54
   images in travel, 152
   modes of representation, 13
domination, 78, 172, 177, 193
   colonial, 195
   global systems of, 65, 178
   histories of, 162
   scientific, 161
   vocabulary and instruments of, 108
   See also Solano, Francisco
Donde mueren los dioses (Mourelo), 20, 153–54, 165–78, 193
   critique of capitalism, 176
   and historicism, 175
   intertextuality, 165–66, 169, 173, 193
   justifications of dominance, 172
   See also ethnography; intertextuality; Mourelo, Suso; Rulfo, Juan
drugs, 47–48, 50–51, 66
   abuse of, 171
   flows of, 35
   traffickers, 207n44
   See also cocaine tourism; crime; danger; narco; *narcotráfico*

Duquesa Rosa, 31
Dussel, Enrique, 67

Eagleton, Terry, *Criticism and Ideology*, 74
economy
   class alignment, 74
   cultural difference, 171–73
   gaze and, 176
   system, 3
   touristic, 158
   See also under travel
"economy of signs," Urry, John, 137
ecotourism, 10, 163, 172
education, 52, 53
Ejército Zapatista de Liberación Nacional (EZLN), 148–49
elites. *See* leisure mobility
"emblematic places," 136
embodied selves, 35
emigration, 29. *See also* immigration; migrants
empire, 7, 32, 64
Empire Wilderness, An (Kaplan), 53, 124
empiricism, 58
encounters, 64, 75
   alternative modes of, 77
   bridging, 177–78
   contingency of, 194
   cross-cultural, 11
   cultural consequences of, 9
   defining conditions of, 191
   with difference, 20
   disruptive politics of, 15
   ethics of, 4, 6, 17
   Europeans and Mayans, 84
   historicized, 169
   and mobility, 24, 69
   narrating, 19, 82
   processes of, 16
   tourist, 85, 146, 173
   transatlantic, 63
   writing, 26
   See also first encounters; Solano, Francisco
escritura de viaje desde la perspectiva latinoamericana, La (Cantú), 9

espejo enterrado, El (Fuentes), 78
ethics, 4, 6, 17
ethnic difference, 58
ethnography
 style, 153
 traditional, 165
 voice, 169
ethnotourism, 155, 158, 162, 172
Eurocentrism, 7, 62
 power of, 9
 written record, 184–85
Euromonitor, "Tourism Flows Inbound – Mexico," 45
Euromonitor, "Tourism Flows Outbound – Spain," 38
European Union, 7, 32–34, 39, 53, 62
Exile and Cultural Hegemony (Faber), 30, 61. See also Faber, Sebastiaan
exiles, 1–2
 integration of, 61
 post-Civil War Republicans, 29–30
 transnational trajectories, 188
 La verdadera historia de la muerte de Francisco Franco (Aub), 167
 See also *Exile and Cultural Hegemony* (Faber); immigration; Mourelo, Suso; Perea, Héctor
exoticism, 7, 20, 26, 117, 137, 139
 alternative, 48
 conventions of travel writing, 195
 cultures, 43, 141–42
 and danger, 66, 151
 European hunger for, 67
 lure of, 65
 packaged, 44
 performance of, 35
 postcolonial, 136
exploitation of resources, 162, 166
Exporting Paradise (Clancy), 43–44

Faber, Sebastiaan
 Exile and Cultural Hegemony, 61, 214n20
 exiled Republicans, 30
Fabian, Johannes, *Time and the Other*, 205n11

Fehimović, Dunja, and Rebecca Ogden, *Branding Latin America* (2018), 200n6
first encounters, 26, 36, 64, 75, 177. See also encounters
flows, 18, 49. See also globalization
flu pandemic, 48, 51
Forneas Fernández, Maria Celia, "Periodismo o literatura de viajes?," 26, 143
Fox, Vicente, 48–49
Fradera, Josep, *The Imperial Nation*, 15
Franco, Francisco, 17, 26, 31, 52, 79–80. See also Republican exiles; Spanish Civil War
freedom, 74. See also mobilities
"From Wandering Pariah to Union Organiser" (Scurrah), 76
Fuentes, Carlos, *El espejo enterrado*, 78
fuereñez, 68
Fürsich, Elfriede, and Anandam P. Kavoori
 "*liminoid* situation," 139
 "Mapping a Critical Framework for the Study of Travel Journalism," 13, 143–44
 travel journalism, 140
future, 53, 64–65

Gabriela anda por el mundo (Mistral), 23
gachupines, 186
Gálvez, Bernardo de, 180
Gaos, José, 60–61
García Canclini, Néstor, *Hybrid Cultures*, 9
gaze
 directionality of, 175, 186
 external, 65, 66–67
 interplay of economics and, 176
 tourist, 112, 158, 175
 See also cosmopolitan gaze; exoticism; *Pedro Páramo ya no vive aquí* (Nadal)
gender, 82, 138
genocide, 141
genre, 5, 11–13, 27–28, 51, 65, 152, 199n3, 200n8, 205n32
 double reversal of, 139

genre (*continued*)
   features of, 4
   historical role of travel writing, 136–37, 196–97
   hybridity of, 63, 64
   journalistic discourse vs. literature, 130, 141–42
   slippage, 143
   See also Semprún, Alfredo; travel writing
geographical imagination, 71
geographies, 75, 184
Geography of Hard Times, A (Pérez Mejía), 58, 62, 202n3
geopolitical turmoil, 138
Glantz, Margo, *Viajes en México*, 203n18
global, 36, 65–67
global capitalism, 2–3, 35, 56, 59, 82, 126, 128–29, 135, 154–55, 161, 168, 188–89
   historical roots of, 186
   violences of, 176
   See also capitalism; *Donde mueren los dioses* (Mourelo)
"global consciousness," 35
global imaginaries, 50–51
globalization, 29, 50, 67, 144, 200n9, 201n11
   age of, 87
   ascendancy of, 103
   changing stories, 17–18
   concepts of mobility and, 34–35
   effects of, 9, 13, 93, 102, 112, 114
   forces of, 109
   history of, 82
   of information, 8–9
   modernism and, 55
   narratives of, 80
   postcolonial, 29
   as progress, 80
   See also Beverley, John; Lindsay, Claire
"Globalization, Sacred Principles, and Modernity" (Alasuutari), 11, 49
Global Politics of Contemporary Travel Writing (Lisle), 160, 204n3
   cosmopolitan gaze, 25, 41
global tourism, 24, 36–53

Gómez-Barris, Macarena, 159, 162
Gómez-Lucena, Eloisa, 154
   and Cabeza de Vaca, 178–86
   characteristics of journey, 175
   critiques of nationalism, 193
   Del Atlántico al Pacífico, 31–32, 174
   historical thinking of, 174, 179
Graham, Helen, "Coming to Terms with the Past," 52. *See also* memory
Grosfoguel, Ramón, *Sujetos coloniales*, 24
Guelke, Leonard, and Jeanne Kay Guelke, "Imperial Eyes on South Africa," 8

Harvey, Sally, "Alejo Carpentier," 30, 53
hegemony, 83
   Anglo-American, 2
   economic and military, 14
   hemispheric, 49
Heredero Salinero, Fermín, 153
   Chiapas, 147
   decentering authority, 193
   poetics of place, 164
   possibilities of resistance, 165
Hispanic transatlantic, 187
hispanidad, 7, 51, 145
Hispanism, 39. *See also* pan-Hispanism
Hispanoamérica, 60
Historia Patria (Boyd), 52
historical
   consciousness, 191–92
   contingencies, 53
   culpability, 58, 186
   discourses, 79–80
   imagination, 4–5, 79
   narratives, 35–36, 53
   stories, 80
   thinking, 74, 166
historiography, 178
   as framework for travel, 180
   limitations of, 182
   as orientation, 185
history
   conceptualization of, 178
   imagined, 1
   interpretation of in Spain, 81

history (continued)
  pre-Columbian, 58
  presence of, 62
  Spanish, 52
Holland, Patrick, and Graham Huggan, *Tourists with Typewriters*, 25, 27, 74, 124, 142
Hosts and Guests (Smith), 200n11
Huggan, Graham, 59–60
  naturalization of genocide, 141
  Postcolonial Exotic, The, 35, 136
  See also Holland, Patrick, and Graham Huggan
Hughes, John, *The Idea of Home*, 82
human geography, 75
human-made, 175–76
Hybrid Cultures (García Canclin), 9
hypermythologized sites, 68–69. *See also* mythmaking

Iberoamérica, 60
idea de América, La (Abellán), 62–64, 67, 68
Idea of Home, The (Hughes), 82, 91
ideas
  of America, 58–59, 63–64
  of Europe, 7, 34
  management of, 41
  of Mexico, 1, 34, 36, 46, 53–72
  of place, 112
  popular, 35
  volatility of, 146
identity
  American construction of, 30
  contingency of, 137
  performance of, 55
  shaping sense of, 179
images
  cultural, 34
  management, 189
  outside representations, 63
  and power, 35
  for Spaniards, 51–52
imagination, 4–5, 36, 71
Imagined Communities (Anderson), 42. *See also* Benjamin, Walter
immigration, 33. *See also* emigration; exiles; migrants; migration

immobilization, 146. *See also* mobilities
Imperial Eyes (Pratt), 7, 8–9. *See also* Pratt, Mary Louise
"Imperial Eyes on South Africa" (Guelke and Guelke), 8
imperialism, 29
  discourse, 134
  nostalgia, 140
Imperial Nation, The (Fradera), 15
impermanence, 142, 193
"Impossible Task?, An" (Pitman), 26, 47, 65, 89, 204n29, 205n32
  "colonialist mentality," 199n1
  representations of Mexico, 69–71
  See also permanence
independence, 46–47
indigenist narratives, 30, 58
indigenous people
  and agency, 56
  of Chiapas, 109–10
  communities, 147
  cultures, 165, 173–74
  and gaze, 175
  history, 43–44, 64
  and interventions, 172
  languages, 181
  See also Gómez-Lucena, Eloisa; Mourelo, Suso; Spanish-Mexican encounters; *specific tribes*
indios, 148
individualized reflections, 10
industrialized travel, 43
industry, 18, 24, 39
inequalities, 1, 10, 65, 198
inequities, 144
Infernal Paradise, 56–57
information, 8–9
interconnectedness, 178, 188
interculturality, 54
internationalism, 67
international media, 46, 48
internet, 38–39
interpretive schema, 191–92
intertextuality, 99, 112, 193
  focus, 95
  framing device, 173
  and historical thinking, 165–66
  and memory, 194

INDEX   237

intertextuality *(continued)*
  negotiation, 65
  references, 19, 21, 35, 51, 70, 74, 169, 189
  See also *Del Atlántico al Pacífico* (Gómez-Lucena); Jordá, Eduardo; Mourelo, Suso
Inventing America (Rabasa), 56–57
Iturriaga de la Fuente, José, *Anecdotario de viajeros extranjeros en México*, 203n818

Jameson, Frederick, 191
Jordá, Eduardo
  autobiographical focus of, 73
  La ciudad perdida, 97–112, 104, 105, 109, 110, 111, 208n45, 208n59
  embedded in past, 111
  experience of Mexico, 192
  and intertext, 112
  Los lugares que no cambian, 19, 97–112
  Mono aullador, 104–5
  Oaxaca, 110
  Palma de Mallorca, 105
  Pregúntale a la noche, 111
  Trayectos, 112
journalism, 138–41
  decentering, 193
  as modernist text, 140
  privilege, 143
  problematics of, 73
  Reverte, Javier, 73, 106–7
  travel, 137
  truth value of discourse, 141
  vs. travel writing, 139–40
"Journalism and Travel Writing" (Mee), 142. *See also* Mee, Catherine
journalistic travel writing, 144

Kaelber, Lutz, "Place and Pilgrimage, Real and Imagined," 111–12
Khatibi, Abdelkebir, 11
Klor de Alva, Jorge, 9

labor, 166, 176
"Lagging Behind" (Phillips), 27, 152
landscape, 170, 171
languages
  American, 173

languages *(continued)*
  colonialist, 177
  and identity, 145
Latin America
  names for, 60–61
  redefinitions of, 59
  relations with Spain, 2
  postcolonial difference, 55
  travel writing, 65
  as understood from within, 54
Latin Americans, 67–68
latinidad, 51–52
latino tropes, 50–51
Lawrence, D. H., 110
Lawrence, Karen, 74
Legacy of Christopher Columbus in the Americas, The (Bartosik-Vélez), 179
leisure mobility, 6, 136
  and currency, 172
  meanings of, 188
Ley de Extranjería, 33
Lindsay, Claire
  Contemporary Travel Writing of Latin America, 65–67
  fuereñez, 69
  globalization, 144
  "literary ghetto of 'difference,'" 141
  travel writing, 137
Lisle, Debbie
  Contemporary Travel Writing of Latin America (Lindsay), 160, 204n23
  cosmopolitan gaze, 25, 41
literary, 35, 111
  context, 77
  precursors, 189
  tourism, 167, 172
literature, 136, 141
Litvak, Lily, *El ajedrez de estrellas*, 200n12
Local Histories / Global Designs (Mignolo), 7, 9, 11, 54, 58, 63–64, 67
lo mexicano, 36, 44
Lowry, Malcolm, 110
Luengo, Jorge, and Pol Damau, "Writing Spanish History in the Global Age," 202n5
Lugares que no cambian (Jordá), 19, 97–112. *See also* Jordá, Eduardo

MacCannell, Dean, 200n11
macro-processes, 35
madre patria, 59
"Mapping a Critical Framework for the Study of Travel Journalism" (Fürisch and Kavoori), 13, 140, 143-44. *See also* Fürsich, Elfriede, and Anandam P. Kavoori
Martí Olivella, José, 39
McCarthy, Cormac, *Blood Meridian*, 124
McLurg Law of newsworthiness, 138
media, 149
Medina Sidonia, Duquesa de, 31
Mee, Catherine, 139-40
  "Journalism and Travel Writing," 142
memoir, 77, 111
"Memorias y buenas intenciones" (Menéndez), 104-5, 207n33. *See also* Jordá, Eduardo
memory, 73-112
  evocation of, 194
  and Spanish history, 52, 73
  See also Jordá, Eduardo; Menéndez, Fernando
Menéndez, Fernando, "Memorias y buenas intenciones," 104-5, 207n33
Mercille, Julien, "Media-Entertainment Industry and the 'War on Drugs' in Mexico, The" 49
Merrill, Dennis, *Negotiating Paradise*, 43-44, 146-47, 195
Mesoamerica, 3
mestizo, 9
metaphor, 10-11, 78. *See also* Youngs, Tim
metropolis, 8
Mexican nationalism, 67
Mexicanness, 34, 47, 65, 71
  discourses of, 187
  and empire, 53
  mythologies of, 63
  myths of, 58
  representation of, 82-83
  travelers' perceptions of, 55
  tropes of, 57
Mexican Revolution, 189-90
Mexicans, 61, 63

Mexican spaces, 189
Mexican travel writers, 69
Mexican Travel Writing (Pitman), 47, 70-71. *See also* Pitman, Thea
Mexico, 30, 47
  and cultural tourism, 44
  as destination, 25-36
  images of, 56-57
  independence, 47
  and mobility, 34-35
  place-image of, 41
  postnational identity, 69
  significance in Spain, 24, 29, 189
  See also exoticism; ideas: of Mexico
Mexico City, 44
Mignolo, Walter, 199n2
  Local Histories / Global Designs, 7, 9, 11, 54, 58, 63-64, 67
migrants, 33, 39
migration, 9, 33
  permanence of, 61
  post-Spanish Civil War Republican, 4
  pro-Mexico view of, 60
  Spain to Mexico, 52, 60-61
  transnational trajectories, 188
  See also exiles; Spanish: travelers
mirror, 78
Mistral, Gabriela, *Gabriela anda por el mundo*, 23
mobilities, 5, 10, 24, 182
  changing concepts of, 29, 34-35
  coercive, 188
  conditions of, 75
  global, 33
  and immobilization, 146
  and Mexico, 34-35
  Spanish-Latin American, 49-50
  transnational, 35
  voluntary and involuntary, 6, 146
  See also encounters; leisure mobility
Mono aullador (Jordá), 104-5. *See also* Jordá, Eduardo
Monsiváis, Carlos, "Travelers in Mexico," 55-56
Montiel, Alfredo. See *Donde mueren los dioses* (Mourelo)

more-than-human world, 169–70
Morgan, Tony, "1992: Memories and Modernities," 15, 32–33
Mourelo, Suso, 154, 169, 173
   Cabeza de Vaca, 177–78
   cultural difference, 171–73
   Donde mueren los dioses, 20, 153–54, 165–78
   history as transnational, 174
   intertextuality, 193
   Tiempo de Hiroshima, 169–70
   and Yaquis, 166
   See also *Naufragios* (Cabeza de Vaca)
Mundo Maya, 44
Musgrove, Brian, "Travel and Unsettlement," 27, 98
music, 51
Muskogee, 181
myth. See *Del Atlántico al Pacífico* (Gómez-Lucena)
mythmaking, 63, 79–80, 149–50
   Anglo-American, 49
   cultural identity, 80
   historical, 52
   of Latin American places, 65
   narrative character, 42–43
   and Republican exiles, 30
myths, 56–58
   authenticity, 56
   and landscape, 170
   of Mexico, 58
   multiple, 57
   and travel experience, 174
   See also ideas: of Mexico; mythmaking

Nadal, Paco, 172, 176
   authentic travel experience, 174
   Owen, Albert Kimsey, 175
   Pedro Páramo ya no vive aquí, 167–68
NAFTA, 68, 205n3
Nahuatl, 181
naming, 179
narco
   narratives, 204n29
   subcultures, 150
   violence, 47–48

narcoterror, 65–66
narcotráfico, 128. See also crime; drugs; narcoterror
narration, 166
   evolving, 178
   and journalistic discourse, 141
   relational, 170
narrative exchange, 2
narrative modes, 69, 188
   in *Bajo las nubes de México* (Solano), 174
narratives, 62
   of badlands travel, 10
   cross-cultural, 197
   of encounters, 4
   indigenist, 30
   Mexicans' about America, 63
   touristic, 23–72
   of transatlantic travel, 189
   of transformation, 191
narrator, 192
nation, 40, 42
national, 29, 188
national identity
   character, 42–43, 58
   destabilization of, 79
   and language, 145
   Mexican, 53, 64
   Mexican independence, 47
   Spanish discourses, 59
national image, 51
nationalism, 79–80, 190, 193–94. See also Franco, Francisco
nation-building, 29
nation-state, 40
natural disasters, 47
natural world, 147, 196–97
nature, 58–59, 164
Naufragios (Cabeza de Vaca), 31, 173, 177–79
   and *Del Atlántico al Pacífico*, 193
   Gómez-Lucena on, 178–79
   Mourelo on, 177
   See also Barthes, Roland; *Del Atlantica al Pacifico* (Gomez-Lucena)
Negative Horizons (Virilio), 5
Negotiating Paradise (Merrill), 43–44, 146–47, 195

neocolonialism
   and capitalism, 165–66
   hierarchies, 55–56
   and indigenous people, 174
   writing, 130
newsworthiness, 138. *See also* journalism
niche tourism, 44–46, 58, 77, 191
   heritage and cultural, 38
   and tourist infrastructure, 46
"1992: Memories and Modernities" (Morgan), 15, 32–33
Non-Places (Agué), 113
North America, 51, 68, 116
North American Free Trade Agreement (NAFTA), 68, 205n3
nostalgia, 76, 106, 140
   cultural, 142
   imperialist, 39, 140
   inbuilt, 196
   literary, 111, 113
   touristic, 142
   See also Mee, Catherine; Reverte, Javier
novelty, 20

Oaxaca
   in *Bajo las nubes de México* (Solano), 84
Jordá, Eduardo, 110
"Observaciones acerca de ciertas imágenes de la América Latina que se formaron los españoles a lo largo del siglo XX" (Siebenmann), 59–60
Occidentalism, 58
off-the-beaten-path travel, 10
Olins, Wally, "Branding the Nation," 42, 46
Organ Pipe (Bassett), 210n17
Orientalism. *See* otherness; Said, Edward
origin, 30–31, 187
otherness
   construction of, 7
   encounters with, 81
   exotic, 36, 140
   indigenous alterity, 44
   mutual determination of, 8
   remote, 141
   writing of, 188

otherness (*continued*)
   See also difference; encounters
outside gaze, 65
Owen, Albert Kimsey, 174–75
Oyarzún, Luis, 62

palimpsest, 56–57
Palma de Mallorca, 105
pan-Hispanism, 47, 51–52
Papadopolous, Nico, and Louise Heslop, "Country Equity and Country Branding," 41–42
para-literary, 4
Paz, Octavio, 9
Paz Soldán, Edmundo, 124
Pedro Páramo ya no vive aquí (Nadal), 167–68, 174. See also *Bajo las nubes de México* (Solano); *Donde mueren los dioses* (Mourelo)
Peñate Rivero, Julio, "Camino del viaje hacia la literatura," 5, 114, 123, 125, 130–31, 188, 202n3, 202n4, 203n8
Perea, Héctor
   post–Spanish Civil War Republican exiles, 29–30
   La rueda del tiempo, 61
Pérez-Reverte, Arturo, *La reina del sur*, 49
Pérez Villalón, Fernando, "Variaciones sobre el viaje," 62
performance, 35, 55, 134
Periodismo de viajes (Belenguer Jané), 137. *See also* Forneas Fernández, Maria Celia
"¿Periodismo o literatura de viajes?" (Forneas Fernández), 20
periphery, 8
permanence
   false, 134, 182
   illusion of, 193
   of migration, 61
   and mobilities, 188
   obscuring invention, 179
   of relocation, 77
Phillips, John, "Lagging Behind," 27–28, 152

photography, 132
physical location, 188
Pitman, Thea
   "An Impossible Task?," 89, 199n1, 204n29, 205n32
   Mexican Travel Writing, 47, 70–71
place, 168
   branding of, 34, 168, 187
   idea of, 112, 146, 155
   image of 8, 17
   mutability of, 180
   negotiation, 40
   poetics of, 164
   possibilities of, 35
   sacrality of, 111–12
   specificity of, 188
   volatility of ideas of, 146
   See also Price, Patricia; Selby, Jennifer; sense of place
"Place and Pilgrimage, Real and Imagined" (Kaelber), 111–12
place-images
   Chiapas (Heredero Salinero), 154–65
   cosmopolitan gaze, 57
   literary, 35
   management, 45–46
   pace of changes in, 49
   preexisting, 42
   production of, 192
   relation to tourism, 41
   transformation of, 155
   and travelers, 45–46, 175
"Place in Context" (Adams, Hoelscher, and Till), 23, 35, 75, 112–35
places
   histories of, 4
   names, 179, 182
   permanence of, 134, 177–78
   sense of, 189
"Politics of Pilgrimage, The" (Selby) 112
popular culture, 49, 50–51
popular imagination, 189
portrayals of Mexico. *See* ideas: of Mexico; representations: of Mexico; stereotypes

postcolonial
   difference, 55
   discourses of, 59
   elites, 54
   globalization, 29
   present, 76–98
   Spain, 17
   strategies, 65
   See also Solano, Francisco
Postcolonial Exotic, The (Huggan), 136. See also *Tourists with Typewriters* (Holland and Huggan)
post-Franco. *See* exiles; Franco, Francisco; Reverte, Javier; Spanish Civil War
postglobalization, 41, 49, 56
power, 195
   conceptualization of, 178
   and modern imaginary, 1
   and movement, 2, 35
   See also soft power
Practice of Everyday Life, The (de Certeau), 57
Pratt, Mary Louise, 57, 86, 134, 200n8
   Imperial Eyes, 7, 8–9
Precarious Life (Butler), 11
Pregúntale a la noche (Jordá), 111. *See also* Jordá, Eduardo
Price, Patricia, *Dry Place*, 8, 116, 118, 133–34
primitive, the, 56, 64. *See also* exoticism; otherness
Puerto Escondido, *La aventura de viajar* (Reverte), 108
Puerto Rico, 145

Quijano, Aníbal, and Immanuel Wallerstein, "Americanity as a Concept," 3

Rabasa, José, *Inventing America*, 56–57
racial difference, 58. *See also* difference; otherness
Rama, Ángel, 54
Rarámuri, 96, 173–76, 181. See also *Bajo las nubes de México* (Solano); indigenous people

reception, 6–7
recreation and suffering, 43
Reding, Sofía, *El buen salvaje y el caníbal*, 56
refugees, 60–61. *See also* asylum seekers; exiles; immigration; Spanish Civil War
reina del sur, La (Pérez-Reverte), 28
remote other, 141
representations
   El crimen del padre Amaro, 50
   cultural, 35, 187
   determination of, 8
   histories of, 111
   of Mexico, 46, 49
   questions of, 193
   struggle over, 7
Republican exiles, 2, 29–30. *See also* Franco, Francisco; Spanish Civil War
resistance
   vs. homogenization, 35
   possibilities of, 165
   sustaining, 176–77
   See also Mourelo, Suso
Reverte, Javier
   La aventura de viajar, 105–8
   information flows, 139
   journalism, 106–7
   La reina del sur, 28
Reyes, Alfonso, 64
"Rise of the Cocaine Tourist, The" (Baker), 48
Rodríguez Ducallín, Emira Josefina, et al., "Imagen turística de los países latinoamericanos en el mercado español," 42
Romero Flores, Colombo, 172
Roussel-Zuazu, Chantal, *La literatura de viaje española del siglo XIX*, 201n12, 202n3
routes, 173
Rubiés, Joan-Pau, 3, 199n3
Rulfo, Juan, 167–68, 173. See also *Donde mueren los dioses* (Mourelo)
rumor de la frontera, El (Armada and Arranz), 19, 66, 114–35, 117, 126, 134, 147, 152, 192–94. *See also* indigenous people

Said, Edward, 7, 57
scholars, 11, 40
Scurrah, Martin, "From Wandering Pariah to Union Organiser," 76
security, 47–48
Selby, Jennifer, "The Politics of Pilgrimage," 112. *See also* Urry, John
self, 177
self-determination, 176–77
self-reflection, 167. *See also* mirror
Seminole, 181
Semprún, Alfredo, 28, 107, 115, 137, 194
   characters, 143
   Chiapas, 146
   danger, 138
   displacement, 144
   "emblematic places," 136
   external focus, 192–93
   journalism, 138–39, 140, 141
   Viajes desaconsejables, 20, 66, 135–53
sense of place, 53–54, 58, 189. *See also* place
Siebenmann, Gustav, "Observaciones acerca de ciertas imágenes de la América Latina," 59–60
silence, 31
sistema-mundo. See Grosfoguel, Ramón; Quijano, Aníbal and Immanuel Wallerstein
sixteenth century, 4, 7, 67, 180, 183–85
Smith, Paul Julian, 40
Smith, Valene, *Hosts and Guests*, 200n11
social justice, 48
soft power, 3, 14, 34, 39, 47, 190, 195
Solano, Francisco, 77–97, 176, 194–95
   Bajo las nubes de México, 19, 206n20
   "fall of hegemony," 83
   and Gómez-Lucena, 175
   history, 192
   Mexicanness, 82–83
   national identity, 79
   Oaxaca, 84
   othering frameworks, 83–84
   sense of home, 82–83
   Tambores de ejecución, 79
Spain, 2, 4
   critical stances on, 190–91
   cultural wealth of, 29, 32–33

Spain (*continued*)
  democratic, 2
  and Europe, 26, 32–34
  European travel writing, 29
  history of, 26, 58
  as homeland, 36
  Latin America and, 2, 33, 39, 59
  and Mexico, 38, 60–61
  as origin, 25–36, 30, 35–36, 73, 111
  postcolonial, 17
  traveling affluent, 29
  See also exoticism; Mexico; otherness
Spanish
  empire, 29
  imagination, 36, 177
  travelers, 36–38
  travel writers, 4, 61
  tropes of superiority, 39–40
  See also Spain; Spanish Civil War
Spanish Civil War, 29, 79–80, 189–90
  reframing, 80–81
  refugees from, 60–61
  Republican exiles from, 2
  Solano, Francisco, 79
  See also Boyd, Carolyn P.; exiles; Mourelo, Suso; Republican exiles
"Spanish Colón-ialista Narrative, The" (Chabram-Dernersesian), 32–33, 109, 177–78
Spanish economic policy, 3
Spanish language, 33, 49, 102, 145
Spanish literary tradition, 3, 136
Spanish-Mexican encounters, 1, 12, 17–18, 22, 60, 187
Spanishness, 36, 71, 79–80
Spurr, David, *The Rhetoric of Empire*, 7–8
stereotypes, 42, 49. *See also* tropes
storytelling, 1, 149–50, 178. *See also* narratives; travel writing
strategies, 65, 71
subaltern, 54, 151–52
Subalternity and Representation (Beverley), 40, 54–55
subgenre, 98–99, 151
subjectivity, 7, 178
Sujetos coloniales (Grosfoguel)
superiority, 39–40

Tambores de ejecución (Solano), 79
Tarahumara. *See* Rarámuri
temporal bridging, 177–78
testimony, 32, 67
Tiempo de Hiroshima (Mourelo), 169–70. *See also* Mourelo, Suso
"Time and Postmodernism" (Dickens and Fontana), 191–92
Todorov, Tzvetan, *The Conquest of America*, 3, 9
tourism, 35, 41, 45–49, 51, 179, 187–89
  cocaine, 49
  development of, 3, 65–66
  discourse of, 136
  and displacement, 165–66
  heritage and cultural, 44
  impact of, 10
  as industrial product, 18, 24, 35, 38–39
  international promotion of, 45
  literary, 167, 172
  See also danger; touristic
"Tourism as Consciousness of Struggle" (Chang and Holt), 140
Tourism Encounter, The (Babb), 146
tourist gaze, 40, 112. *See also* Urry, John
Tourist Gaze, The (Urry), 40, 137, 200n11. *See also* Urry, John
tourist/host encounters, 85, 177
touristic, 1
  consumption, 173, 185
  crime, 48
  danger, 144 (*see also* crime)
  desires, 22, 158
  experience, 76, 182, 183
  gaze, 158, 175
  indistinguishability, 94
  multiproduct, 44
  narratives, 23–72, 157
  spectacle, 18
  See also current affairs; drugs; exoticism
"touristic emancipation," 87, *See also* Solano, Francisco
Tourists with Typewriters (Holland and Huggans), 25, 27, 74, 142
transatlantic
  convergence, 40, 178
  encounters, 63

transatlantic (*continued*)
  mobility, 187
  traffic, 39–40, 50, 51
  travel, 1, 189
  See also Virilio, Paul
trans-disciplinary studies, 10
transformative events, 148
transnational
  cultural space, 51
  cultural studies, 5–6
  historicism, 175
  interconnectedness, 40, 49–50
  mobilities, 35, 68
  trajectories, 188
transparency, 192
transterrados, 60–61
travel, 28–29, 71
  and domination, 65
  economy of, 35–36, 53
  impact, 10
  industrialized, 43, 188–89
  internet engagement with, 38–39
  and Latin Americans, 62
  North American, 45, 48, 121
  and Spanish literature, 136
  voluntary, 191
  See also leisure mobility
"Travel and Unsettlement" (Musgrove), 5
travelers
  as complicit, 71–72
  orientations, 175
  and place-negotiation, 40
  Spanish, 37
"Travelers in Mexico" (Monsiváis), 55–56
travel industry, 39, 43
traveling self, 37
traveling subject, 10–11, 168
travel journalism, 137, 140. *See also* journalism; Lindsay, Claire; Youngs, Tim
travel narratives
  current affairs, 49
  disrupting, 41
  and first encounters, 75–76
  gendered, 138
  and histories, 195

travel narratives (*continued*)
  intertextual, 50–51
  as interventions, 187
  as stories, 177
  See also Mexicanness; transatlantic
travel writing, 3, 17–18, 76, 156
  as middlebrow, 37, 107
  parameters of, 76–77
  self-referential, 5
"Travel Writing as a Genre" (Rubiés), 3
Trayectos (Jordá), 111. *See also* Jordá, Eduardo
tropes, 55
  colonial, 64
  in global imaginaries, 50–51
  of human against nature, 151
  of Mexicanness, 57
  of Spanish superiority, 39–40
  See also images; stereotypes
Turner, John Kenneth, *Barbarous Mexico*, 166, 173
twenty-first century, 187–88
2666 (Bolaño), 124

Unceta Satrustegui, Maria, "La escritura actual de los textos de viaje," 56
Urry, John, *The Tourist Gaze*, 40, 112, 137, 200n11
Usos de lo cubano en la transnación española (Álvarez), 39

"Variaciones sobre el viaje" (Pérez Villalón), 62
verdadera historia de la muerte de Francisco Franco, La (Aub), 167
Viajes desaconsejables (Semprún), 66, 135–53
  as destabilizing, 152
  global audience, 141–42
  migration, 146
  See also Semprún, Alfredo
violence, 47–48
  memory of, 147
  and other, 141
  of profit, 176
  representation of, 185
  in *2666*, 126

Virilio, Paul, *Negative Horizons*, 97
voices, 166

Walsh, Catherine, "Interculturalidad crítica y pedagogía de-colonial," 54
War of Dreams, The (Augé), 113–14, 196
"Where Are We Going?" (Youngs), 10. *See also* Youngs, Tim
Witness and the Other World, The (Campbell), 200n8
writers, 4, 28
writing
 encounters, 26, 77
 idealization of, 55
 of otherness, 188
 and social inequality, 54
 written record, 185

Yaqui, 165, 165–78
 cultural patrimony, 172
 displacement, 169–70
 inclusion of, 166
 See also drugs; indigenous people; Mourelo, Suso
Year of Spain (1992), 32
Youngs, Tim, 29–30
 "Where Are We Going?," 10, 116
Y tu mamá también (Cuarón), 49–50

Zapatistas, 148
 Chiapas, 146
 demonstrations, 47
 uprising, 146–47, 155
 zones, 149
Zavala, Oswaldo, "Imagining the US-Mexico Drug War," 204n29

www.ingramcontent.com/pod-product-compliance
Lightning Source LLC
Chambersburg PA
CBHW030538230426
43665CB00010B/948